THE SOCIAL COSTS OF
PRIVATE ENTERPRISE

THE SOCIAL COSTS OF PRIVATE ENTERPRISE

K. WILLIAM KAPP

SCHOCKEN BOOKS • NEW YORK

TO MY WIFE

First SCHOCKEN PAPERBACK edition 1971

Copyright © 1950, 1971 by K. William Kapp
Library of Congress Catalog Card No. 79-144788
Manufactured in the United States of America

CONTENTS

CONTENTS

INTRODUCTION TO THE 1971 EDITION

WHEN *The Social Costs of Private Enterprise* was originally published, it aimed at a critique of the theory and practice of business enterprise. The book intended to expose the existence of costs not accounted for in entrepreneurial expenses and to show that conventional economic theory failed to take adequate if any account of those social costs that confront us today in the form of a serious deterioration of man's natural and social environment. My central thesis was and has remained that the maximization of net income by micro-economic units is likely to reduce—particularly under conditions of rapid and uncontrolled technological change—the net income (or utility) of other economic units (both producers and consumers), and that the conventional measurements of the performance and "growth" of the economy in terms of national income indicators are inadequate and hence misleading. They leave out of account important social costs of production borne by third persons and future generations. In fact, in their present form, national income indices not only fail to subtract these social costs, but include money spent to repair the damages caused by productive activities of the past and present. Under these circumstances, conventional economic theory has a tendency to conceal rather than to elucidate the sequence of events in the actual world of affairs: its definition of and search for levels of equilibrium under static conditions and its measurement of the growth of the economy do not constitute an adequate theoretical representation of the economy. Nor are they relevant for the formulation of general criteria of rational choice or for the evaluation of the investment and the production patterns in the market economy; nor do they secure the maintenance of a reasonable relationship between economic growth and an environment compatible with requirements for human health, well-being, and survival.

These long-neglected problems and hard facts have been cited by critics and dissenters from the mainstream of economic thought for more than a century. They are finally attracting world-wide attention, after having been allowed to reach the point of an environmental and ecological crisis in many countries. I am convinced today, as I was when this book was written, that the disruption of man's environment and the social costs resulting from productive activities are among the most fundamental and long-term issues mankind has ever faced. Their implications may well turn out to be as far-reaching as some of the problems raised by nineteenth-century social reformers and socialist critics who concentrated their attention on exploitation, poverty, and economic instability. Ultimately the disruption of man's environment may reveal itself as our most crucial problem, exceeded in overall significance only by the urgent necessity of guaranteeing human survival in an age of nuclear weapons. Just as the new techniques of warfare call for new international institutions, the phenomena of environmental disruption and social costs as well as the urgency of devising effective means of control call for a radical change of the present institutionalized system of investment and decision-making by private firms and public agencies with regard to the choice of investment and production patterns.

Before turning to the practical implications of social costs and environmental disruption, the author may be permitted to offer some comments to those readers whose attention is drawn to the subject by the current discussion of the environmental crisis. The extraordinary intellectual, political, and legislative activities [1] cur-

---

[1] We mention only a few of the many national and international activities that have dealt with specific aspects of environmental disruption and social costs: The UNESCO Conference on the Utilization and Conservation of the Biosphere, Paris 1968; The Colloque Internationale contre les Pollutions organized by the International Association for World Law, Royan 1970; The

rently under way in an effort to come to terms with our environmental crisis are, of course, a belated recognition of the social costs incurred in the course of an unprecedented expansion of production and population during the last three decades. These activities may create the impression that we are well on the way to successfully coping with the problems of environmental disruption. Actually, there are several reasons to doubt this.

The success of any program of environmental control depends ultimately on a correct analysis of the manner in which social costs are incurred, on the adequate assignment of responsibilities for them, as well as on the effectiveness of the practical and institutional measures adopted to overcome them, and finally on the adequacy of the funds appropriated. A superficial and hence incorrect analysis is likely to lead to ineffective measures of control, and even a correct program will see its chances of success jeopardized by the allocation of inadequate funds and the lack of appropriate institutional arrangements.

One word of caution: The increasing use of the terms "environment" and "ecology" in recent discussions of social costs is to be welcomed, provided these terms are interpreted in a sense suffi-

---

International Symposium on Environmental Disruption in the Modern World: A Challenge to Social Scientists, Tokyo 1970, sponsored by International Social Science Council, Paris. In addition there will be the Intergovernmental (East-West) Conference on the Protection and Improvement of the Environment in Prague (1971) and the U.N. Conference on Environment in Stockholm (1972). Among the legislative steps there are the Clean Air Act (1963) and the Clean Water Act (1965) in the United States. Japan and other countries have installed monitoring services designed to measure the degree of air and water pollution in critical areas, and the city of Tokyo can even boast to have introduced the first daily air pollution forecast service. Individuals, citizen groups, and governmental agencies have endeavored to mobilize the traditional legal and administrative machinery, with varying degrees of success, in an effort to seek redress for specific damages suffered and to protect property rights negatively affected. Lawyers are raising the question whether and how the common law and the substantive content of constitutional provisions could be used or extended to establish a fundamental right to a clean environment. Cf. David Sive, "The Environment: Is it Protected by the Bill of Rights?," *Civil Liberties,* August 1970.

ciently broad to include not only the impairment of the physical environment but the impairment beyond certain definable threshold levels of the aggregate of all external conditions and influences affecting the life and development of human beings, human behavior, and hence society. Only in this way will it be possible to counteract the widespread but false impression that we are confronted only with a problem of ecology in the narrower physical sense of the word. Even if we succeeded in purifying the air and water in and around large urban agglomerates, we would still not have come to terms with the important social costs that arise from the impairment of the human factor. Twenty or thirty years ago, it was still correct to say that the social costs of air and water pollution had attracted less attention than the impairment of the human factor, which had found recognition by workmen's compensation acts and social insurance schemes. Today the situation seems to be reversed. The current emphasis on ecology and environment may lead to a neglect of some of the much older, direct human costs of production and economic growth which find their expression in death and disabling injuries from industrial accidents and chronic occupational diseases, as well as technological unemployment, poverty, and physical and mental burdens caused by rapid structural changes and uncontrolled economic growth. Neither the existing industrial safety legislation nor "safety on the job" campaigns nor workmen's compensation for accidents have been able to prevent the officially recorded rate of industrial accidents from rising by 23 per cent between 1958 and 1967. Unofficial estimates place the current number of annual accidents at 4 million in the United States (exclusive of 500,000 cases of workers disabled by occupational diseases). As one lawyer in a compensation case of silicosis is reported to have put it: "With a maximum liability of only $12,500 plus medical and funeral expenses it has been so inexpensive to disable or kill a man . . . that it has not been worthwhile to clean up." [2] Work-

[2] *Newsweek,* August, 17, 1970, p. 45.

men's compensation acts and social security legislation are notoriously insufficient, and are progressively made more inadequate by built-in secular inflationary pressures. Added to this must be the distribution of sickness, disability, and unemployment and the continued social stratification in general, which particularly affect the more vulnerable racial minority groups, seasonal workers, and "guest-workers" in the most economically advanced countries. The market mechanism is apparently unable to eliminate these arbitrary and discriminatory conditions. On the contrary, it seems to re-create and perpetuate them. In addition, there are the adjustments forced upon specific groups of the working population by structural changes, particularly in periods of rapid technological advances. Among the victims have been above all farmers and retailers, who have been forced to abandon their activities and residences without adequate—or even any—compensation and who have reached threshold levels of psychological frustration and despair in some countries. Even more significant, although less noticed and less explored, are those human costs of modern competitive production and consumption that find their expression in the pathology of everyday life in all affluent societies. The symptoms of this psychic and psychosomatic pathology are all around us—they are reflected in functional disturbances of various sorts, from psychic strain and stress to premature neuro-circulatory diseases, arteriosclerosis, fatigue, and insomnia, as well as neurosis in general. These symptoms have become part of our social environment; they play a manifest role in the increasing social disorganization, irrationality, and violence of contemporary life. To dismiss these phenomena as "noneconomic" because they occur outside the market complex is possible but neither ingenious nor tenable in view of the fact that, apart from their obviously human aspect, they have a price for both the individual and society.

The analysis of social costs raises important problems of definition and measurement that cannot be discussed within the present context.[3] It should be emphasized that the statistical data and estimates used in this book to illustrate the magnitude of the social costs are not only out of date but inadequate. They should be understood in terms of what they were intended to do—to illustrate the nature and kind of losses and to show the reader that even these far-from-satisfactory estimates are of such a magnitude as to make it imperative to bring them into the open. Even today our statistical data are inadequate; there is as yet no agency that gathers and publishes data on social costs in any systematic way. For this reason it would be highly desirable to collect sets of data that would make it possible to measure or estimate in both real and monetary terms the social costs and losses arising in a profit-oriented system of investment and production. Such data could then be used to correct and reconstruct the inadequate and misleading system of national accounts which is currently used to measure the performance and growth of the economy. But quite apart from the availability of reliable estimates of social costs, it is safe to say that the disruption of the environment and the resultant social costs have a tendency to increase both absolutely and relatively as production and consumption and hence factor input and residual waste increase, and as these wastes are emitted or dumped into the environment without adequate prior treatment and prior assessment of the consequences.[4]

The principal pollutants of the atmosphere in the United States have been estimated to reach 125 million tons per year, consisting primarily of carbon monoxide (52 per cent), oxides of sulphur (18 per cent), and hydrocarbons (12 per cent). The major sources of these pollutants are transportation (59.9 per cent), manufacturing (18.7 per cent), and generation of elec-

[3] They have been dealt with in some detail in two articles by the author: "Social Costs and Social Benefits—A Contribution to Normative Economics," in *Verdhandlungen auf der Arbeitstagung des Vereins für Sozialpolitik,* E. v. Beckerath *et al.,* eds. (Berlin: Gesellschaft für Wirtschafts- und Sozialwissenschaften, 1963), pp. 183–210; and "On the Nature and Significance of Social Costs," *Kyklos,* XXII (1969), 334–47.

[4] Cf. K. William Kapp, "Environmental Disruption: General Issues and Methodological Problems," *Social Science Information,* IX, No. 4, 15–32.

tricity (12.5 per cent).[5] In addition there are emissions of solid wastes (refuse), food wastes (garbage), and rubbish which are estimated to reach a volume of 320 million tons a year.

Current estimates of the amounts that would have to be spent during the remainder of the century in order to provide for moderately clean air and water and the disposal of accumulating waste products place these costs at $275 billion.[6] Government estimates place the annual property damage caused by air pollution alone at $11 billion, exclusive of the decline in real estate values in affected neighborhoods. None of these data makes allowance for the fact that some of the pollutants represent potentially valuable and recoverable resources, such as the sulphur contained in the harmful sulphur dioxide emitted into the atmosphere.

The Social Costs of Private Enterprise undertakes to diagnose the causes that tend to give rise to the disruption of our physical and social environment. It views the causal chain within the context of the organizing principles of a system of business enterprise in which investments take place for and in accordance with their expected net revenues. The author holds the view that the institutionalized system of decision-making in a system of business enterprise has a built-in tendency to disregard those negative effects on the environment that are "external" to the decision-making unit. Even if an individual firm intended (and would be in a financial position, as many oligopolists obviously are) to avoid the negative effects of its applied technology, it can do so only by raising its costs; that is, by deliberately reducing its profit margin and its profit-earning capacity. Hence, a system of decision-making operating in accordance with the principle of investment for profit cannot be expected to proceed in any way other than by trying to reduce its costs whenever possible and by ignoring those losses that can be shifted to third persons or to society at large.

[5] Committee on Pollution, *Waste Management and Control* (Washington, D.C.: National Academy of Sciences, 1966), Publication 1400, p. 11.
[6] James J. Hanke and Harold D. Kube, "Industry Action to Combat Pollution," *Harvard Business Review*, Sept.–Oct. 1966, pp. 49–50 and *passim*.

Predictably, this critical view, which runs counter to the presuppositions and biases of conventional economic analysis, has not met with general approval. Thus, various alternative explanations for the occurrence of social costs have been advanced. These have one thing in common: to exonerate the principle of investment for profits from any causal connection with environmental disruption. Some economists fall back upon Marshall's concept of externalities or speak generally of "market failure" when they are faced with the problem of social costs. Others identify technological and industrial change as factors responsible for social costs. More recently, the growth and increasing density of the population as well as natural factors such as climate and topography are held responsible or co-responsible. Finally, by showing that public utilities, public enterprises, governmental agencies, and even planned economies have not been immune to environmental disruption, the current discussion of our environmental crisis (with some notable exceptions) conveys the impression that environmental disruption and social costs are simply an inevitable concomitant of industrial civilizations in general, and are independent of economic institutions and the principle of investment for profits which guides the process of allocation and hence determines the investment and production pattern. In this way, the critical implications of the theory of social costs are in danger of being neutralized and rendered innocuous. It cannot be emphasized too strongly that these attempts reflect the continued vitality of old biases and preconceptions in economic analysis, which in turn support ineffective policies of control and protection of the environment against the devastations caused by uncontrolled productive activities and economic growth.

The process of causation that gives rise to social costs is indeed a complex one. While stressing the institutional factor, *The Social Costs of Private Enterprise* did not ignore the interplay of physical, technical, and climatic factors and the cumulative and self-reinforcing character of the causal process. Nor did we argue that social costs do not occur in pre-capitalist societies or could not occur under alternative forms of social organizations. It was clearly pointed out that the growth of population and the increasing density of settlement could not but upset the earlier ecological balance. The reader will find repeated references throughout the book to this complex and cumulative interaction of a great variety of physical, technical, climatic, and demographic factors. Nor did the author deny that public utilities, public enterprises, and public agencies are contributing to the destruction of the environment and are responsible for social costs. But the reader will also find the following passage which is indicative of the manner in which the author dealt and would still deal with the assignment of responsibility for the outcome: "If the farmer fails to [adapt his methods of cultivation to the natural environment] and if rapid erosion sets in as a result of a combination of natural factors and farm practices, it is obviously the latter which must be considered as the cause of the devastation of the land and not the rainfall or the steepness of the slope" (p. 132). This reasoning also applies *pari passu* to all factors such as climate, topology, population, technology, etc., which in combination tend to contribute to air and water pollution as well as to other forms of environmental disruption and social costs.

The process of production—i.e., the choice of factor inputs and the determination of what is to be produced according to the principle of investment for profit—proceeds without an adequate prior assessment of the actual costs and consequences, including a host of "side-effects" which from the narrow and hence false perspective of the individual firm are regarded as "external" costs or benefits. This micro-economic method of assessing costs and consequences of investment decisions from the point of view of the individual firm has always been the crux of the matter. It is this method that accounts for the serious social costs that have been incurred in the past as well as for the continued failure to subject the production and allocation processes to an assessment of their total consequences—both costs and benefits. The lack of such an assessment and control of investments (choice of factor inputs) and production (choice of outputs) with regard to their possible social costs and benefits implies not only an inefficient use of resources, but makes it possible for some to obtain income by causing damage to others—a fact that for equity reasons alone would seem to call for far-reaching changes in the manner in which investment (i.e., allocation and production) decisions are to be made.

There is no doubt that municipalities and public authorities may also contribute to the disruption of the environment. Even socialist planning agencies may act in a similar way under certain conditions. Does this refute our central thesis? If municipalities and public or planning authorities set the stage for an impairment of the environment—when they attract industries in order to increase their tax income regardless of possible negative effects —they sacrifice the quality of the environment for revenues by choice; that is, their action is similar to that of a private firm operating in accordance with the principle of investment for profit. Both try to maintain an artificial, purely formal short-run financial solvency by ignoring social costs. Some of the current attempts to render public decision-making more "rational" in terms of market costs and returns carry the danger that this disregard of some or all of the negative effects of decisions may become even more general and typical. Instead of reducing the incidence of social costs, such attempts are likely to increase them.

Before turning to some practical conclusions, it will be useful to present a general outline of the causal chain that gives rise to environmental disruption and social costs. Human action—both individual and public decisions—takes place within and has repercussions on our natural (and social) environment. This environment is itself a complex composite of structures, each of which is subject to specific regularities or organizing principles. If these regularities are not known or deliberately ignored at the time when the allocation and production decisions are made, the consequences of the decision will differ from what was originally aimed at. Furthermore, the interaction of the socio-economic with the physical and biological spheres is much more complex and much less explored than the operation of any of the various systems which the conventional academic disciplines have isolated for separate study. If we want to understand the causal process, it is evident that its analysis cannot be carried on successfully in terms of one or the other of the compartmentalized social, physical, and biological disciplines. Neither social nor natural scientists, nor engineers, nor public health experts—trained in their limited disciplines and familiar only with their narrow concepts and theories—are able to focus attention on the whole relevant pattern of interaction. It is true that we still lack a theory and/or science capable of elucidating the mode and outcome of the complex interaction of several systems. Hence, our knowledge of the causes and extent of environmental disruption is incomplete and will probably continue to remain incomplete for the foreseeable future. In other words, we will have to act on the basis of imperfect knowledge, as we have done in the past and may have to do, though to a lesser extent, in the future.

However, we do know that the process of causation is complex and circular and, as such, has a tendency to become cumulative unless deliberate action is taken to arrest or redirect it. For instance, air and water pollution are not merely the result of, and are not proportionate to, the volume of production and the emission of residual waste products. They are also governed by the interaction of a whole series of variables which may react upon one another. Thus, waste products of various kinds react not only upon each other but also upon other elements in the environment, and in this way give rise to additional toxological effects on plant, animal, and human life, with delayed but cumulative consequences on human health. The actual rate of air and water pollution is at any given time governed by such intervening environmental variables as wind velocities and direction, topography, temperature inversions, stream flows, and water temperatures. In addition, there are points beyond which any further discharges of pollutants cause not constant but disproportionate changes and damages.[7] To this must be added the fact that there are interdependencies between different kinds of environmental disruption and social costs. Thus the magnitude of air pollution in and around large cities stands in circular and cumulative relation to the breakdown of the suburban transport system, which induces people to use their automobiles over congested traffic lanes while the transport system first deteriorates and finally goes bankrupt.

These complex circular interdependencies with their cumulative effects may also serve to illustrate the important fact that both the impairment *and* the quality of the environment (and of society) must be understood as aggregates. For the effect in terms of damage to human health, vitality, and actual experienced discomfort caused by any particular type of environmental disruption is always a function of the combined effects of all sources of disruption, which may include, in addition to air and water pollution, factors such as excessive noise; urban concentration; long hours spent in travel to and from work in metropolitan areas under chaotic traffic conditions; inadequate, congested transport facilities with high accident and death rates; and inadequate time for leisure and recreation.

This general pattern of causation must be kept in mind in approaching the urgent task of elaborating general principles for the control and minimization of social costs. Viewed from the perspective of conventional economic theory, it may appear sufficient to aim at internalizing the social costs into the cost accounts of the individual firm. By holding the individual firm responsible for the total costs caused by its productive activities (including its production of specific goods, as, for instance, automobiles), it

---

[7] "Up to a certain level of concentration, disposal of wastes, disfigurement of the landscape, and congestions are, at worst, local irritations. Air and water and earth room can absorb a lot without great damage. Beyond that point, real trouble ensues. Differences of degrees of frequency and concentration create differences in kind." H. Jarrett, ed., *Environmental Quality In a Growing Economy* (Baltimore: Johns Hopkins Press, 1966), pp. ix–x.

might be assumed that the social costs will be minimized and the disruption of the environment be avoided or at least kept under control. This principle of internalization of social costs guides some proposals designed to prevent these costs by such indirect methods of control as the levying of fines on producers who pollute, of penalties according to the volume of effluence, or of offering incentives (e.g., tax reductions or subsidies) to producers in order to induce them not to pollute. In the light of the accumulated evidence of the last twenty years and in view of the circular and cumulative character of the pattern of causation discussed above, there is reason to question the adequacy of these indirect methods of controls. Such methods may be helpful in specific cases, but as a general rule they are of doubtful value and effectiveness. They seem to be unreliable both as to their efficacy and efficiency; they leave the decision of control to individual units, they are slow to take effect and difficult to administer, and hence their results are uncertain. Moreover, a fine or incentive of a given amount will affect different producers in varying degrees, depending on their financial resources, their profit expectations, and their fiscal liabilities in terms of tax rates and tax brackets. While they may be effective in one case, they may be totally ineffective in another.

The whole appraisal of what is to be done in terms of market costs and market returns suffers from one additional inherent weakness: the fact that the information and valuations provided by actual market systems in terms of entrepreneurial outlays and returns do not possess the "objective" relevance and validity which economic theory tends to attribute to or claim for them. Prices of factor input and of final products in actual markets are the result of a host of "distortions" resulting from the very interdependencies that give rise to social costs, as well as from existing inequalities in income distribution and prevailing conditions of unequal market power. For this reason particularly, it is important to insist that the issue of environmental control must not be sidetracked by the argument that its costs will be prohibitive or may not be warranted in terms of the monetary benefits obtainable therefrom. Nor must we permit ourselves to be intimidated into inaction by questions of who pays and whether all the necessary information has been fully assembled.

In view of the circular and cumulative pattern of causation and the far-reaching interdependencies that give rise to social costs, it appears to us that the progressive deterioration of the environment (both natural and social) calls for more fundamental steps and measures than those hitherto envisaged. In fact, the phenomena of environmental disruption and social costs compel modern industrial societies and the social sciences to face the question of whether the principle of investment for profits is not in need of some fundamental amendments. What is put in doubt by the phenomena of social costs is the entire complex of decision-making, including particularly the choice of technology and factor inputs as well as the determination of output patterns based only on a comparison of market costs and returns from the perspective of the micro-economic unit. Indeed, what is needed is an evaluation of the total costs and total benefits of investments (including those related to research and development) from a broader and more comprehensive macro-economic perspective than that which has guided the system of business enterprise since it freed itself from the medieval and mercantilist controls. What is called for is not a return to these earlier controls but an assessment of the implications of alternative technologies for the maintenance of human life, evaluated by objective standards of human health and well-being. This is the problem of social minima, not only in terms of individually and socially tolerable levels of concentration of pollutants, but in terms of necessary and desirable conditions for life, including, for instance, settlement and production densities in specific localities. In other words, instead of a search for *remedies,* an effective approach to the solution of the environmental crisis calls for prior assessment and control of the "input mix" and output pattern with a view to preventing social costs and the impairment of the environment before they occur. So far no comprehensive assessment and sub-sequent control of the techniques and the design of production have ever been carried out, except perhaps in the food and pharmaceutical industries and in the use of atomic energy. In this context the burden of proof that a new technology, a new product, a new process, and a particular input (and output) pattern are safe would have to rest in principle upon the producer and not upon the damaged person or society. Institutionalized agencies would have the function and responsibility to anticipate, appraise, and judge beforehand the hazards and benefits of alternative tech-nologies, techniques, and locations. On the basis of such an assessment it would be possible to direct investments with respect to both permissible choice of factor inputs and the location of specific industries, in accordance with criteria that take account of the full range of the costs and consequences of new techniques for the individual and society as well as the world community. We cannot enter here into a more detailed discussion either of the methods of evaluating costs and benefits or of the institutional implications of such a program. Suffice it to say that the latter would indeed be far-reaching and radical. To control technological change, to select the factor input and output patterns, to plan investments accordingly, and to determine the location and con-centration of production implies a radically new form of decision-making and planning by institutions responsible to the com-munity and society. It calls for a replacement of the present micro-economic point of view by a macro-economic perspective in evaluating the optimal use of resources in terms of social objec-tives and consequences. The absolute necessity of taking account of social costs and environmental disruption rather than any other factor will compel the industrial society to replace the individual allocation and investment decision, the private choice of tech-nology, and the selection of the site of production by new forms of social economic planning more responsive to human needs and social requirements than the traditional micro-economic calculus employed by independent economic units.

This brings us finally to the related question of the broader implications of social costs and environmental disruption for economic science and of the relevance of conventional economic theory as a framework for the analysis of the rationality of production in contemporary industrial societies. We believe that an adequate treatment of the problems raised by social costs and environmental disruption would require a radical change of the nature and scope of economic theory. Our emphasis on the need for prior assessment of the consequences of new technologies and new factor inputs may serve to make this clear. Of course, it may be argued that rational action and decision-making have always called for deliberate forethought about the consequences of human action, including its possible side-effects. In this sense it may be felt that our emphasis on the need for such an assessment is nothing fundamentally new and can easily be assimilated into the traditional ends-means dichotomy and the analysis of rational choices as practiced by modern economic theory. Such, however, is not the case. For let us consider for a moment the full meaning of what we hold to be the key to rational choice and action in the light of the problems raised by social costs and environmental disruption. A pre-investment appraisal of the consequences of different technologies and alternative allocation patterns goes beyond any merely instrumental evaluation of the fitness and efficiency of "given" means to "given" ends. Such an assessment would indeed give rise to a dynamic and thus more relevant concept of rationality than that which conventional static economic theory has used until now. For the prior assessment not only provides the information required for the choice of alternative technologies and techniques (including the location patterns) but also for the evaluation of alternative goals. In fact, only by a deliberate pre-assignment of the consequences of alternative technologies and techniques available for the attainment of public and private goals (including their possible side-effects) can we hope to secure the information necessary to appraise and revise our public goals and private objectives. In short, assessment of alternative technologies and allocation patterns is the prerequisite of a deliberate choice among alternative objectives. Ultimately, only an appraisal of our goals and a prognosis of the consequences can give us an idea of the full range of the choices before us. But this is merely another way of saying that both means and ends are brought within the purview of scientific analysis, and that the traditional distinction of "given" means and "given" (postulated) ends cannot offer an adequate framework for the analysis of rational action. Rational action is much more than the adaptation of given technologies to given goals; it must be understood as a continuous process of adjusting ends to means and means to ends in the light of their fullest possible range of consequences. This dynamic notation of rationality is in open contrast not only to the ends-means dichotomy which serves as a basis for the systematization of economic science, but also to the way in which the micro-economic firm pursues its goal of profit maximization. Here the end is indeed "given" and never questioned, with the result that, so long as a particular line of action appears profitable (or more profitable than any alternative), evaluated by private cost-benefit calculation, it will be continued or preferred. Hence, even the oligopolistic business unit does not consider the full range of choices offered by modern technology. This is illustrated, for instance, by the fact that, instead of developing a new engine and a new type of automobile designed to minimize the pollution of the atmosphere and to increase the safety of the driver, automobile manufacturers have devoted the major part of their "Research and Development" expenditures to purposes they consider more profitable in terms of their micro-economic calculations of net returns. This has meant frequent restyling, a multiplication of brands and body frames, new gadgets, and built-in obsolescence—all in an effort to increase sales rather than introduce improved means of transportation which reduce air pollution and offer greater safety.

This frustration of science and technology, to which I have devoted a separate chapter, will probably be overcome only if we are prepared to shift all basic research—and particularly those fields related to the prevention and control of environmental disruption by new technology—to research agencies operating under public auspices. For instance, instead of developing a "better" commercial pesticide, it may be safer to have public agencies and experiment stations turn their attention to the development of new plant varieties with greater inbred resistance to insects and pests.

As far as the adequacy of conventional economic theory for the elucidation of social costs and environmental disruption is concerned, the last twenty years have brought no new departures. Despite considerable changes and refinements, neither micro- nor macro-economic analysis seems to have evolved in a manner as to make them more relevant for the theoretical treatment of the phenomena of social costs. Both micro- and macro-economics fall back upon the formal concepts of "externalities" [8] and of cost-benefit analysis, but the fact of the matter is that the theoretical presuppositions and logical framework of pure economics from which these concepts are derived are too narrow and too static to be useful for the study and interpretation of the cumulative processes that give rise to environmental disruption and social costs.

The mainstream of economic analysis still avoids placing man, with his actual needs and requirements, in the center of its theoretical considerations. It has continued to consider only market prices and effective demand, irrespective of whether the latter is manipulated by sales promotion and advertising, as a basis for the evaluation of the rationality of the allocation process. In fact, conventional economic theory refuses to distinguish between less important and more important human needs; as long as it continues to do so, and does not make man the measure of all things,

---

[8] *The Social Costs of Private Enterprise* also made use of the Marshallian concept of externalities. For a more recent discussion of the inadequacy of the concept, see K. William Kapp, "On the Nature and Significance of Social Costs," *Kyklos*, XXII (1969), 334–47, and "Environmental Disruption and Social Costs: A Challenge to Economic Theory," *Kyklos*, XXIII (1970), 833–48.

it will be unable to evolve and widen its scope. Our models have become more abstract, more mathematical and quantitative, and their relevance for the elucidation and treatment of the impairment of man's social and natural environment and the quality of society has decreased rather than increased. The reformulation of basic concepts, the broadening of investigation in order to include the substantive human needs and social minima—in short, the "humanization" of economic analysis called for by the phenomena of social costs—remain on the agenda for the future.

Indeed, the need for a "humanization" of economics is becoming more urgent by virtue of the fact that a number of new sources of social costs and environmental disruption not specifically dealt with in this book have made their appearance. Here we shall list only the following: the potential and actual dangers (e.g., in terms of gene damage and mutation) resulting from a contamination of man's environment by radioactivity and heat generated by nuclear reactors; the potential and actual damages caused by certain pesticides; the harmful effects on human health by any prolonged, repeated, and severe exposure to high-intensity noise from industrial sources and air traffic; increased stress due to overcrowding and urban living conditions; the growing environmental disruption caused by the disposal of solid waste and garbage (particularly of the non-degradable type), which according to some estimates may double in volume every ten years in such cities as New York and Tokyo; the rising volume of marine pollution due to underwater production and large-scale ocean transportation of petroleum (with such serious dangers as blowouts of wells, ruptures of pipelines, collision and wreckage of tankers, as well as the polluting effects of dredging operations for tin, diamonds, oyster shell, sand, and gravel); and finally the progressive absorption of free space and open landscapes, together with the increasing physical decay and aesthetic deterioration of our urban and rural environment by apparently remunerative but unnecessary advertisements of all sorts.

In view of the magnitude and the character of the threats and the values at stake, social costs and environmental disruption may be considered the principal contradiction within the system of business enterprise. By making it necessary for modern industrial society increasingly to replace the individual investment decision —including the choice of technology and site, and indeed of the whole allocation and output pattern—by public assessment and measures of control, social costs and environmental disruption may well become the principal driving forces of institutional change in the foreseeable future.

K. William Kapp

Institut für Sozialwissenschaften
University of Basel, Switzerland
August 1970

PREFACE

THE MAIN PURPOSE of this book is to present a detailed study of the manner in which private enterprise under conditions of unregulated competition tends to give rise to social costs which are not accounted for in entrepreneurial outlays but instead are shifted to and borne by third persons and the community as a whole. Thus, the present study deals at the same time with a specific technical economic question and with broad issues of social philosophy and economic knowledge. The technical question involved is whether our concept of costs is not incomplete and apparently in need of correction. The broader issues of social philosophy and economic knowledge which the analysis of the social costs of production raise become clear only if we view the phenomenon of social costs within the framework of the basic premises of classical political economy and of the proposition still found in neoclassical economic thought that perfect competition tends to maximize output and the want-satisfying power of available scarce resources. To present a brief outline of this framework is the purpose of the first chapter. The second and third chapters are designed to provide a general introduction to the detailed analysis of social costs by describing the general meaning of social costs and examining the contributions of those economists who have questioned the validity of the main trend of neoclassical economic thought, and in this context have dealt with the phenomenon of social losses and social waste. The threads of these theoretical arguments are then brought together in the concluding chapters, which are designed to summarize the results of the detailed analysis of social costs contained in the main part of the book and to draw a number of theoretical and methodological inferences from them.

The basic idea of the present study was first advanced in a highly tentative manner in the author's attempt to deal with the problem of economic calculation in connection with his analysis of the economic relations between a foreign trade monopoly and private exporters and importers.[1] His interest in the problem of social costs was further stimulated by J. M. Clark's contributions to "Social Economics" as well as by the results of the unique and still largely neglected research carried out under the auspices of the National Resources Planning Board. Professors J. M. Clark and Robert Lynd read an earlier draft of the introductory and concluding chapters and have offered critical comments, which are gratefully acknowledged.

The contribution which my wife has made to this book is too comprehensive to be explained fully. She rendered indispensable aid in connection with the research work; she has prepared preliminary drafts for certain sections; and she has borne many of the numerous burdens involved in the final completion of the study. I also wish to mention with warmest thanks that Dr. Joseph Finnegan has helped with the editorial work on parts of the manuscript.

The untiring coöperation of Mr. Mulford Martin, Librarian of the School of Commerce, Accounts and Finance of New York University, and his staff greatly facilitated the collection of material. I am further indebted for information and material dealing with specific phases of the study to the following agencies and institutions: The Bureau of Labor Statistics of the U. S. Department of Labor, the Bureau of Mines of the U. S. Department of the Interior and the United Mine Workers of America for various data on work injuries; the Mellon Institute of Industrial Research at the University of Pittsburgh, the Air Hygiene Foundation of America in Pittsburgh, the Office of the Mayor of the City of Saint Louis, the New York Chamber of Commerce, the Smoke Prevention Association in Chicago, the U. S. Public Health Service and the Advisory Committee on Atmospheric Pollution at Birmingham University (Great Britain) for material related to the chapter on air pollution; the Bureau of Mines for data on the disposal of oil-field brines in connection with the chapter on water pollution; the library of the

---

[1] *Planwirtschaft und Aussenhandel* (Geneva: Georg et Cie, S.A., Librairie de l'Université, 1936).

League of Nations in Geneva (Switzerland) for information on the question of pollution of the sea by oil; the Fish and Wildlife Service of the U. S. Department of the Interior for data on the depletion of animal resources; the National Resources Planning Board, the Atlantic Refining Company, the Independent Petroleum Association of America and the Bureau of Mines for data dealing with the depletion of energy resources; the Soil Conservation Service of the U. S. Department of Agriculture, the Agricultural Extension Service of Ohio State University, the Oklahoma Agricultural Experiment Station, Stillwater, Oklahoma, the Illinois Farmers Institute, Springfield, Illinois, and the Forest Service of the U. S. Department of Agriculture for material on soil depletion, erosion and deforestation; the Tennessee Valley Authority and the Interstate Commerce Commission for information concerning diseconomies in transportation; the U. S. Department of State and the Office of Scientific Research and Development for material dealing with scientific research and atomic energy.

I wish to thank the following publishers for permission to quote from their publications: A. & C. Black, Ltd., London; The Brookings Institution, Washington, D. C.; Columbia University Press, New York; The Commonwealth Fund, New York; Comstock Publishing Company, Ithaca, New York; E. P. Dutton & Co., Inc., New York; Harper & Brothers, New York; D. C. Heath and Company, Boston; International Publishers, New York; Richard D. Irwin, Inc., Chicago; Little, Brown & Company, Boston; Longmans, Green & Co., Inc., New York; Macmillan & Co., Ltd., London; The Macmillan Company, New York; McGraw-Hill Book Company, Inc., New York; W. W. Norton & Company, Inc., New York; Oxford University Press, London; Oxford University Press, Inc., New York; Pitman Publishing Corporation, New York; Rinehart & Company, Inc., New York; The Ronald Press Company, New York; Routledge and Kegan Paul Ltd., London; Charles Scribner's Sons, New York; Staples Press Limited, London; The Twentieth Century Fund, New York; The University of Chicago Press, Chicago; The University of Minnesota Press, Minneapolis; The Viking Press, Inc., New York;

John Wiley & Sons, Inc., New York. Detailed references to publisher, author, title, and year of publications appear in the text.

I also wish to acknowledge gratefully a grant-in-aid which I received from the Institute of Social Research at Columbia University from November 1943 to May 1944. In this connection I wish to record my gratitude to Dr. F. Pollock, Associate Director of the Institute of Social Research, who read the entire manuscript and made many valuable suggestions related to specific phases of the study. The technical completion of the final draft of the manuscript was greatly facilitated by a grant from the Research Committee of Wesleyan University. I am also indebted to the Harvard University Press for many valuable suggestions concerning both the substance and the form of the manuscript.

I have made a deliberate attempt to keep the discussion as free as possible from all technical terminology in order to make the book readable for a wider circle than the limited group of professional economists.

K. W. K.

ROCKFALL, CONNECTICUT
OCTOBER 1948

THE SOCIAL COSTS OF
PRIVATE ENTERPRISE

"Systems, scientific and philosophic, come and go. Each method of limited understanding is at length exhausted. In its prime each system is a triumphant success; in its decay it is an obstructive nuisance."

"No science can be more secure than the unconscious metaphysics which tacitly it presupposes."

"Without adventure civilization is in full decay."

A. N. WHITEHEAD

1

SOCIAL COSTS AND ECONOMIC SCIENCE

THE COMMON CHARACTERISTIC of all Western knowledge appears to be the fact that it is "only in part factually given, and always involves in addition a hypothesis 'proposed a priori.'"[1] It is the hypothetical character of the premises concerning the nature of man and the world he lives in, which accounts for the lack of finality of our knowledge and its diversity if compared over long periods of time. New empirical data contrary to old premises repeatedly have made necessary far-reaching reconstructions in all our systems of knowledge. The history of economic thought since the Middle Ages is no exception in this respect.

This is not to say that old preconceptions die out quickly or are easily abandoned after their further usefulness and validity have been disproven by factual evidence to the contrary. The observation of empirical "facts" in opposition to accepted premises often gives rise to refinements of traditional theory, as in the famous case of the epicycles which enabled Ptolemy and his medieval followers to maintain the geocentric conception of the universe in the face of certain "irregularities" in the courses of the planets. In other instances, especially in the social sciences where the extreme difficulty of experimentally proving or disproving a given theory accounts for a much higher rate of survival of old doctrines, systems of thought based

---

[1] F. S. C. Northrop, *The Meeting of East and West* (New York: copyright 1946 by The Macmillan Company and used with their permission), p. 295.

upon hypotheses "proposed a priori" manage to survive because the former have so defined and redefined their basic concepts and the scope of their investigations that all empirical facts which seem to refute the conclusions deduced from the basic assumptions are either attributable to minor disturbances or else fall outside the "proper" subject matter of the science. In still other cases new empirical facts merely lead to a preoccupation with new lines of factual research and nobody bothers to formally disprove old and outworn preconceptions. Nevertheless, scientific reconstruction ultimately depends upon new theoretical premises which can be established on a firm theoretical basis only if one comprehends fully the meaning and significance of the old ones. Such reconstruction is overdue in the case of economic thought where the basic classical propositions, derived from the philosophical premises of the eighteenth century, concerning the beneficial character of perfect competition have been preserved with but little qualification by some of the most prominent representatives of neoclassical thought. A brief outline of some of the philosophical preconceptions upon which the classical propositions of political economy rest, will not merely help us to appreciate the specific contribution of Adam Smith and his predecessors and successors but will, at the same time, enable us to set the stage for a better understanding of the broader issues of social philosophy and economic knowledge which the study of social costs raises.

It is impossible to appreciate the unique theoretical contributions of classical political economy to social thought without having a clear conception of the general climate of opinion (and the corresponding philosophical preconceptions) of the eighteenth century. Classical political economy arose at a time of widespread revolt against all forms of medieval and mercantilist governmental regulations of economic life. Moreover, the philosophical outlook of Adam Smith and his predecessors was shaped by the revolution in science, which not only had swept away the pre-Copernican world view but which had also led to impressive new insights and practical results in physics, chemistry and biology. The new social and political sciences which developed during the eighteenth century were inspired by a peculiar mixture of a political creed which opposed most forms of governmental planning and the new scientific conceptions concerning the nature of the universe which were associated with the names of Galileo and Newton. Like the latter, the philosophers and political scientists of the eighteenth and early nineteenth centuries were convinced of the existence of a natural order of the universe. In fact, they believed that not only nature but society, and with it the production and distribution of wealth, were subject to natural laws which it was the task of the political economist to discover and which it was possible to reduce to certain fundamental principles. Just as the natural sciences had succeeded earlier in formulating the laws of celestial mechanics and the basic principles of chemistry, physics and biology, the political thinkers of the eighteenth century hoped to formulate the natural laws of political and social affairs. Neither Sir William Petty[2] nor Richard Cantillon[3] nor the Physiocrats[4] nor Adam Smith[5] had any doubts about the existence of a natural order in economic affairs. In harmony with the prevailing antimercantilistic aspirations of the rising bourgeosie, the founders of the new system of political economy visualized the "natural" economic order as a "system of natural liberty" not requiring conscious regulation by government authorities.

[2] Petty criticizes the limitation of usury by referring to "the vanity and fruitlessness of making Civil Positive Laws against the Laws of Nature." See "A Treatise of Taxes and Contributions" in C. H. Hull (ed.), *The Economic Writings of Sir William Petty* (Cambridge, 1899), p. 48.

[3] Cantillon was one of the first who conceived and analyzed various phases of the market mechanism, the automatic operation of which he described in detail. See H. Higgs (ed.), *Essai sur la nature du commerce en général* (London: Macmillan and Co., 1931), esp. pp. 23 ff., and p. 53.

[4] The close connection of the Physiocrats and the concept of natural law has often been commented upon and is made explicit by both Quesnay and Mercier. See Mercier de la Rivière, *L'Ordre naturel et essentiel des sociétés politiques* (Paris, 1767; reprinted, Paris, 1910) and F. Quesnay, *Le Droit Naturel* (Paris, 1765). For a recent translation, see K. W. and L. L. Kapp (ed.), *Readings in Economics* (New York: Barnes and Noble, 1949), pp. 97–102.

[5] The philosophical preconceptions of Adam Smith need no further elaboration. See W. Hasbach, *Untersuchungen über Adam Smith und die Entwicklung der politischen Ökonomie* (Leipzig, 1891), and *Die allgemeinen philosophischen Grundlagen der von François Quesnay und Adam Smith begründeten politischen Ökonomie* (Leipzig, 1890); cf. also J. Bonar, *Philosophy and Political Economy* (London, 1893).

Like all previous conceptions of natural law (in the sense of natural order), the system of natural liberty was conceived, from the very outset, as the ideal order which tended to maximize the welfare of society as a whole. It was the task of political economy to correlate such specific features of the economic process as prices, costs, profits, wages, rent, and capital with one another within a coherent system as an exemplification of the natural and beneficial order of economic life. This approach, which has marked the scientific methods of one generation of economists after another, found its culmination in the work of A. Marshall, who, like Böhm-Bawerk, succeeded in synthesizing the multitude of detailed economic phenomena within "a whole Copernican system, by which all the elements of the economic universe are kept in their places by mutual counterpoise and interaction." [6]

It is not difficult to show that the classical approach to the study of economic life has had far-reaching consequences for the subsequent development of economic science. In the first place, economics has been preoccupied, from the very beginning, with a search for an assumed orderliness in economic life or, as J. M. Clark puts it, with "a search for levels of equilibrium." [7] Second, it was inevitable that economists, in their search for natural orderliness in economic life, began to see both reality as a whole and specific phenomena in a light which tended to confirm their philosophical preconceptions. Indeed, "the details of economic life [were] construed for purposes of general theory, in terms of their subservience to the aims imputed to the collective life process." [8] Basic concepts such as wealth, production, utility, costs, returns, etc., were formulated in such a manner as to make them integral parts of the general scheme of thinking. In addition, economists concentrated their attention on those phenomena which could be shown to serve the purpose which they imputed to the economic process. In fact, "those features of detail which will

[6] J. M. Keynes, *Essays in Biography* (London: Macmillan and Co., 1933), p. 223.

[7] J. M. Clark, "Economics and Modern Psychology," *Preface to Social Economics* (New York: Rinehart and Company, Inc., 1936), p. 93.

[8] T. Veblen, "Industrial and Pecuniary Employments," *The Place of Science in Modern Civilization and Other Essays* (New York: The Viking Press, Inc., 1919), p. 282.

bear construction as links in the process whereby the collective welfare is furthered, are magnified and brought into the foreground." [9] In contrast, other phenomena which could not be shown to be integral parts of the system of natural liberty because they upset rather than furthered its assumed orderliness were presented as untypical exceptions or minor disturbances. In other words, the philosophical presuppositions of classical economics determined the selection of the phenomena to be studied by economic science, the scope of which was thus more and more adapted to its original (normative) aim of demonstrating both the existence and the superiority of the system of natural liberty over alternative forms of economic organization.

Furthermore, under the influence of the rationalistic presuppositions of the eighteenth century, theoretical economic analysis, especially value theory, confined itself more and more to the study of market phenomena. In fact, political economy became "economics," which was said to be concerned only with those ends (and means) whose importance could be measured in terms of exchange values. That is to say, those ends and means which could not be expressed in terms of market prices came to be regarded as "noneconomic" and as such outside the proper scope of economic analysis. Thus, only rational behavior was said to be relevant for purposes of economic analysis. In other words, nonrational behavior was assumed to be either nonexistent or at least of no importance in connection with the analysis of the conditions of equilibrium in an essentially stationary economy which required study only at a given point of time (instead of a dynamic, irregularly expanding economy which would call for analysis of the processes of adjustment extending over different points of time). Merely another aspect of this procedure which tended to eliminate the dynamic and less congenial factors of reality from economic analysis is the theoretical economist's preoccupation with money costs and returns and his tacit assumption that entrepreneurial outlays and private returns constitute a theoretically adequate measure of the costs and benefits of productive activities.

The dominant neoclassical system of thought is no exception in

[9] Veblen, *loc. cit.*

this respect. On the contrary, it has continued and completed the demonstration that the natural law operates for the good of mankind in the economic life of nations and the world;[10] its subjectivism permitted the most systematic application of rationalistic conceptions of human behavior to economic analysis and prepared the way for a new classicism designed to demonstrate, on the basis of the mechanics of private interests, that social justice is possible without socialism. More specifically, the new classicism, which views the market situation as the outcome of forces set into motion by the action of rational individuals, was dominated from the very outset by the desire to demonstrate that "free competition procures the maximum of utility," [11] and that under static conditions labor receives what it produces.[12]

It is true some of the most prominent representatives of neoclassical thought have qualified the normative identification of the position of competitive equilibrium with one of maximum aggregate satisfaction. Thus, Alfred Marshall took exception to the doctrine on the ground, first, that it assumes that equal sums of money measure equal utilities to all concerned, which clearly they do not under conditions of inequalities in the distribution of income and wealth. In the second place, Marshall pointed out that the doctrine of maximum satisfaction ignores conditions of increasing returns which make it possible to increase production beyond the equilibrium point without injuring the producer, since decreasing costs would make it possible for prices to fall and thereby to increase the consumers' surplus.

---

[10] For evidence of the continued role of natural law concepts in neoclassical thought, cf. E. Böhm-Bawerk, *The Positive Theory of Capital* (New York: G. E. Stechert and Co., 1930), p. 78; J. B. Clark, *Theory of Distribution* (New York: The Macmillan Company, 1938), pp. 175 and 180.

[11] M. E. L. Walras, *Études d'économie politique appliquée,* ed. Leduc (1936), p. 466, quoted from W. Stark, *The History of Economics* (New York: Oxford University Press, 1944), p. 56.

[12] J. B. Clark, *Theory of Distribution,* p. 180; cf. also the significant title and content of one of J. B. Clark's addresses: *Social Justice without Socialism* (Boston, 1914). On the whole subject, with particular reference to the role which religious conceptions of social justice played in the development of neoclassical economic thought in America, see J. R. Everett, *Religion in Economics* (New York: King's Crown Press, 1946).

In this case, therefore, Marshall held that the free play of demand and supply does not produce a maximum of aggregate satisfaction and suggested that "the direct expense of a bounty sufficient to call forth a greatly increased supply at a much lower price would be much less than the consequent increase of consumers' surplus."[13]

Similarly, Knut Wicksell was careful to point out that the doctrine of maximum gain under free exchange cannot in strict theory be defended, partly because of individual differences in the capacity of enjoying "the good things of life" as well as social differences and unequal distribution of income. "Thus, for example, the fixing by society, or by a union of workers, of a maximum working day would, within certain limits (which may sometimes be very narrow), be of distinct advantage to the workers and consequently to the most numerous class of society."[14]

By far the most general qualification of the doctrine of maximum satisfaction and indeed of the entire system of neoclassical equilibrium analysis is that of P. H. Wicksteed. After insisting that the differential (marginal) method makes it more important than ever for economists to keep in touch with the wider ethical, social and sociological problems and explanations, Wicksteed makes it explicit that the economic machine is constructed and moved by individuals for individual ends; that its social effects are incidental; that the collective wealth of the community has ceased to be of much direct significance to us; that the market does not tell us in any fruitful sense what are the "national," "social," or "collective" wants, or means of satisfaction, of a community; that the categories under which we usually discuss these things conceal rather than reveal their meaning; that production is a means only, and derives its whole significance from its relation to "consumption"; that to recognize this will be to humanize economics; and that "the more we analyse the life of society the less we can rest upon the 'economic harmonies'; and the better we understand the true function of the 'market,' in its

[13] A. Marshall, *Principles of Economics* (London: Macmillan and Co., ed. 8, 1930), p. 472. Used with the permission of The Macmillan Company.

[14] K. Wicksell, *Lectures on Political Economy* (New York: The Macmillan Co., 1934), p. 77.

widest sense, the more fully shall we realise that it never has been left to itself, and the more deeply shall we feel that it never must be. Economics must be the handmaid of sociology." [15]

In the light of these qualifications and strictures by some of the most prominent representatives of neoclassical thought, it is pertinent to raise the question as to what has been done since "to humanize economics" and to broaden the scope of its theoretical analysis. Neoclassical economists will point to the emergence of a body of "welfare economics" as evidence of the fact that value theory has moved beyond the stage reached at the time of Wicksell and Wicksteed and that many of the social costs mentioned in the present study have found recognition at least in this separate branch of economic analysis. In a sense, this is correct, and there can be no doubt that Pigou's *Economics of Welfare* represents, as will be shown later, one of the most important attempts to assimilate the phenomena of social costs to economic analysis. And yet the fact that this analysis of social costs is carried on not within the main body of value and price theory but as a separate system of so-called welfare economics indicates how much the phenomenon of social costs is still regarded as the exception rather than the rule.

In any event, as far as the basic philosophy of neoclassical theory is concerned there is as yet little evidence that social costs (and social returns) have found the full recognition which they deserve. The implicit identification of entrepreneurial costs and returns with total costs and total benefits has continued to govern the methodological approaches of one generation of economists after another. Perhaps this is inevitable. After all, most economic theory reflects the historically given social conditions and patterns of behavior at any given time; it endeavors to give more or less systematic expression to a particular way of solving the economic problems of the time. In this sense economic theory merely "describes" what is happening in the economy. Neither social costs nor social returns enter

---

[15] P. H. Wicksteed, "The Scope and Method of Political Economy in the Light of the 'Marginal' Theory of Value and Distribution," *Economic Journal*, XXIV (1914), 11–12.

into the cost-price calculations of the private firm unless special provisions to this effect are made by law and by the systematic application of the principles of social insurance, as in the case of workmen's compensation acts. Fundamentally, therefore, the treatment of social costs as a minor and exceptional disturbance rather than as a characteristic phenomenon of the market economy reflects merely the very imperfect way in which these costs are taken into consideration in the present system of economic calculation of costs and returns.

In the light of these facts it is not even surprising that the doctrine of maximum satisfaction, and particularly the traditional identification of competitive equilibrium with the optimum solution of the economic problem, far from having been abandoned, still play an important role in contemporary writings.[16] Marshall's and later Wicksell's and Wicksteed's qualifications, which were directed against certain optimistic formulations of the doctrine advanced by Walras and Pareto, have led merely to a refinement of the general proposition that competitive equilibrium is a position of maximum satisfaction so that it is now carefully related to the usual assumptions of static equilibrium analysis. However, if in its present form the doctrine is unassailable, it is also meaningless and irrelevant for any realistic appraisal of the performance of the competitive market economy. For if the existing distribution of resources and income is taken for granted, if entrepreneurial (money) costs and returns (measured in terms of exchange values) are assumed to be not only accurate measures of outlays and benefits but are regarded in fact as the only relevant cost and return elements, and if the volume of commodities to be exchanged is assumed to be fixed—that is to say, if the whole process of competitive price adjustment is viewed as essentially stationary, thereby eliminating any cumulative changes of supply and demand and price over different points of time—then competition and rational behavior on the part of both consumers and producers, based upon a constant comparison and final equaliza-

---

[16] Whoever is inclined to doubt the validity of this statement needs only to consult a number of representative treatments of price theory, particularly those parts dealing with the comparison of price and output adjustments under conditions of (static) competition, with those of monopoly.

tion of marginal costs and marginal gain, may indeed be said to tend toward a state of economic equilibrium which is both theoretically determinate and superior to any other conceivable state of affairs (conceivable, that is, under those conditions). However, the formal correctness of the deductions does not make them more relevant for an interpretation of capitalist reality. Indeed, as Schumpeter points out, "in appraising the performance of competitive enterprise, the question whether it would or would not tend to maximize production in a perfectly equilibrated stationary condition of the economic process is . . . almost, though not quite, irrelevant . . . [and] the theorem [of maximum satisfaction of wants] is readily seen to boil down to the triviality that, whatever the data and in particular the institutional arrangements of a society may be, human action, as far as it is rational, will always try to make the best of any given situation. In fact, it boils down to a definition of rational action and can hence be paralleled by analogous theorems for, say, a socialist society." [17]

In the light of this brief survey of the evolution of classical economic analysis, the phenomenon of social costs assumes a much broader significance than that of a specific technical question related to private cost accounting. Indeed, a detailed analysis of social costs opens the way for the demonstration that the social performance of the free market economy would still fall short of the economic op-

[17] J. A. Schumpeter, *Capitalism, Socialism and Democracy* (New York: Harper and Bros., 1942), p. 77 n. In fact, as Sidgwick pointed out earlier, practically the whole system of theoretical conclusions of modern economic science could be deduced from the assumption of rational economic conduct. "Thus, it may be argued first that from the universality of the desire for wealth, from the superior opportunities that each individual has, as compared with any other person, of learning what conduces best to the satisfaction of his wants, and from the keener concern he has for such satisfaction, any sane adult may be expected to discover and aim at his own economic interests better than government will do this for him. Then, this being granted, it may be argued, secondly, that consumers in general . . . seeking each his own interest intelligently, will cause an effectual demand for different kinds of products and services, in proportion to their utility to society; while producers, generally seeking each his own interest intelligently, will be led to supply this demand in the most economic way, each one training himself or being trained by his parents for the best rewarded, and therefore, most useful services for which he is adapted." See H. Sidgwick, *The Principles of Political Economy* (London, 1901), p. 29.

timum even if it should be possible to achieve an approximation to perfect competition and to counteract the cumulative and self-sustaining tendencies toward general disequilibrium in modern capitalism which have preoccupied economists in recent years. For the fact that private entrepreneurs are able to shift part of the total costs of production to other persons, or to the community as a whole, points to one of the most important limitations of the present scope of neoclassical value theory, which, because it is confined to exchange value, has so far been incapable of assimilating to its reasoning and to its conceptual system many of the costs (and returns) which cannot easily be expressed in dollars and cents.

However, the demonstration that private enterprise tends to shift part of the costs of production to third persons and to the community as a whole constitutes only one of the reasons why the original presumption against governmental regulation and the bias against planning which still pervades much of neoclassical value theory must be abandoned. There are two further reasons why, in our estimation, the unplanned market economy fails to achieve the maximization of the want-satisfying power of scarce resources: (1) obstacles to rational behavior of consumers and entrepreneurs as well as outright nonrational behavior patterns in modern industrial society; (2) the existence of social returns which diffuse themselves throughout society and, since they cannot be sold in markets and cannot be appraised in terms of dollars and cents, are largely neglected by private enterprise. The first of these factors has been analyzed by the author in some detail.[18] The much more important analysis of social returns and the related subjects of public investments which likewise seem to break out of the framework of traditional neoclassical economic analysis has to be reserved to a separate study. The present work must thus be understood as part of a larger inquiry, the purpose of which is twofold: to measure the performance of the economy by yardsticks which transcend those of the market, and to prepare the ground for a broadening of the scope of economic analysis so as to

[18] K. W. Kapp, "Rational Human Conduct and Modern Industrial Society," *The Southern Economic Journal*, X (1943), 136–150.

include those omitted aspects of reality which many economists have been inclined to dismiss or neglect as "noneconomic." Such a new science of economics will have to be based upon the recognition that we are able to obtain a valid picture of a situation and a real understanding of reality only if we view them as a whole, i.e., in their totality. Only by overcoming the present departmentalization of our knowledge in the social sciences or, more specifically, by accepting the fact that the "economic" and the "noneconomic" are intrinsically interrelated and must be studied together, will we be able to lay the foundation for a new science of economics which will be "political economy" in an even more comprehensive sense than the term was ever understood by the classical economists and their predecessors. But this raises broader issues which transcend the scope of the present investigation. Suffice it to repeat that the main emphasis of our study rests upon the demonstration that entrepreneurial outlays fail to reflect important social costs of production and, therefore, are no adequate measure of total costs. As a first step in this demonstration it is important to discuss briefly the meaning and the general nature of social costs.

2

THE NATURE AND SIGNIFICANCE
OF SOCIAL COSTS

THE TERM SOCIAL COSTS refers to a wide variety of cost elements. In fact, for the purposes of our investigation the term covers all direct and indirect losses suffered by third persons or the general public as a result of private economic activities. These social losses may be reflected in damages to human health; they may find their expression in the destruction or deterioration of property values and the premature depletion of natural wealth; they may also be evidenced in an impairment of less tangible values. As an instrument of analysis the concept carries no quantitative connotation; it will serve its purpose if it helps to trace and to reveal a substantial proportion of the social losses of production for which neither law nor custom has as yet established an adequate responsibility of the individual producer.

Social losses may arise in different ways. Some clearly have their origin in individual industries and can be traced to particular productive processes and business practices. Other social costs arise in the operation of the competitive system within a given framework of generally accepted institutions and government policies. This institutional origin of some social costs raises a number of interesting and important issues, which will be taken up in the various chapters devoted to their analysis.

In some cases, the social costs of production are felt immediately; in other instances the ill effects of private production remain hidden for considerable periods of time, so that the injured persons do not become immediately aware of their losses. Furthermore, certain social losses affect only a limited group, whereas others may be felt by all members of society. Indeed, the actual damages caused by private productive activities may be distributed over so many persons that any one of them may individually sustain only a relatively small loss. Although aware of his losses, the individual may not consider it worthwhile to take defensive action against the particular industrial concern responsible for his losses. In short, the term social costs refers to all those harmful consequences and damages which third persons or the community sustain as a result of the productive process, and for which private entrepreneurs are not easily held accountable.

This concept of social costs is comprehensive enough to include even certain "social opportunity costs," that is, those social cost elements which take the form of wastes or inefficiencies of various kinds. As will be seen later, the elimination of these wastes and inefficiencies represents an opportunity for genuine economies; it is doubtful whether a private-enterprise economy can avail itself of these economies without a radical change in its basic structure.

It would be easy to show that an increasing proportion of public policy in a liberal democratic state is devoted to the prevention and repair of various social losses caused by private producers. In the absence of these preventive measures private business would continue to shift part of the costs of production to society. Fundamentally, the adoption of such preventive measures and the need for remedial action may be considered as the most convincing evidence for the occurrence of social costs in the competitive market economy. However, as far as economic theory is concerned, this recognition of the phenomenon of social costs has been confined mostly to A. C. Pigou's welfare economics and several critics of formal equilibrium theory. As pointed out before, the main body of neoclassical value theory has continued to regard such losses as accidental and exceptional cases or as minor disturbances. At best, social losses are considered as "external" costs falling outside the scope of economics proper.

To dismiss the entire problem of social costs in this manner is, however, to beg the question. For whether or not these costs are "external" in character and fall outside the scope of economics can be decided only after their general nature, their significance and their probable magnitude have been thoroughly explored. Similarly, to dismiss the problem of social costs on the grounds that measures are constantly being taken not only by governments but also by private organizations with a view to minimizing or remedying their negative effects, is to miss the most important issue, namely, the question of the extent to which such interference with the economic process is justified and economically worthwhile. This question, too, can be answered only after an attempt has been made to apprehend the nature and possible magnitude of the social costs of production. In any event, the existence of preventive regulations and private restrictions in some spheres of economic life has as yet not led to the elimination of social costs. Indeed, in many instances closer analysis of existing legislation reveals that present measures and private restraints do not prevent the occurrence of social losses and that there are still many cases of social costs which have found either no or only inadequate recognition.

It may be argued, and it has indeed been asserted, that social costs are implicit in the competitive structure of contemporary society and are merely the by-product of any process of rapid economic change and growth. As such, social costs are sometimes regarded as the short-run price paid for a high level of long-run efficiency and social performance of the economic system. There would be no basic quarrel with any of these formulations[1] if it were not often implied in them that the social losses are justified by the change and that not much is to be gained from a detailed analysis of social costs. However, whether progress and growth are worth their price can be determined only after we have a complete knowledge of the *total* costs involved. And whether one prefers to look upon social costs as the price to be paid for economic growth or—what is essentially the same thing—as the (short-run) inefficiency of (long-run) efficiency

[1] See, however, our discussion *infra* pp. 157–159.

in no way affects the importance of knowing the full price paid for either. In fact, to trace and measure the social costs incident upon change and long-run efficiency would be entirely within the spirit of economic rationality, with the development of which the rise of capitalism is often credited. A measuring rod which is shorter than standard can lead to correct measurement only by accident and nothing is more irrational than an incorrect standard and an incomplete system of cost accounting.

The above thesis may be extended to include the proposition that the growing recognition given in recent years to the phenomenon of social costs reflects merely a shift in the balance of power from those groups in society responsible for initiating economic change to those who bore the brunt of the social losses in the past and who now are using their growing political and economic power in an effort to protect themselves against the undesirable consequences of progress. This broader thesis raises a number of issues which are of the greatest significance. The political history of the last 150 years can be fully understood only as a revolt of large masses of people (including business) against the shifting of part of the social costs of production to third persons or to society. And it is also obvious that the steady increase of protective social legislation, the enforcement of minimum standards of health and efficiency, the prohibition of destructive practices in many fields of production, or even the efforts of farmers, businessmen and labor to peg the prices of their products by means of oligopolistic restraints of trade, reflect at least in part a gradual shift of the balance of power away from those producers and innovators who were formerly able to transfer part of the costs of production to the community. Viewed in this fashion, however, the struggle for a more equal distribution of social costs or their prevention and the shift in the balance of power are nothing but an integral part of the general expansion of democracy which has marked the history of the last 150 years.

Of course, this is not to say that the means used as protective measures against the shifting of some of the costs of rapid economic change have always halted at the point of social optimum (whatever definition we care to give to this important concept). Pressure groups and vested interests have doubtless been able to distort and abuse the legitimate struggle for a more equal distribution of social costs to the detriment of society. Most certainly, not every oligopolistic restraint of trade can be interpreted merely as a measure designed to remedy the wastes of unregulated competition. In many instances these restraints are techniques of plundering the consumer and as such must themselves be regarded as the sources of important social costs. And yet, after everything has been said about the misuse of power by vested interests, the fact remains that, on the whole, the increased emphasis on the elimination of and protection against social losses and the shift in the balance of power referred to above are direct results of an expansion of democracy in the sense of popular control over economic institutions and policy.

However, the whole argument according to which social costs are merely the price of economic progress and rapid growth reaches its most explicit formulation in the assertions of those who believe that the drive for elimination or more equal distribution of social costs and the insistence on planned change are in reality moves to end all change and growth.[2] In this form the argument requires the most careful and detailed analysis. In its most plausible formulation it runs somewhat as follows: Unlike all previous forms of social organization, in which vested interests were able to block new methods of production and economic change through regulations of all sorts, capitalism has been marked by a maximum of opportunities for new social groups and ideas to invade and destroy established patterns of "doing business." This, together with the spirit of economic rationality which permeates the whole culture of the competitive market economy, has enabled the capitalist form of economic organization to promote and assimilate technical progress in the most rapid fashion, and it is therefore no accident that the history of capitalism has been associated with the most pronounced scientific progress and

[2] "However unconsciously, the present movement to plan change and growth is in many of its forms really a movement to end change and growth." Cf. D. M. Wright, *The Economics of Disturbance* (New York: copyright 1946 by David McCord Wright; used with the permission of The Macmillan Company), pp. 91–92.

economic growth on record. It is true that this rapid expansion, together with certain other intrinsic peculiarities of the competitive economy—primarily the discontinuous nature of the production of durable capital and the periodic overexpansion of productive facilities resulting from the combined effort of many independent producers to fill gaps and changes in demand—have resulted in substantial social losses and have made capitalism a highly unstable form of economic organization. The further consequence has been a growing hostility to competition and the emergence of an anti-capitalist climate of opinion, coupled with an intense quest for greater security by large masses of people who have to bear the brunt of the social losses occasioned by rapid change. It is these groups, interested in preserving the status quo, who, with the aid of political democracy, have gained in political influence as against those who stand to gain most by, and who therefore favor, technical progress. If this process continues under capitalism the whole movement of change and growth may come to an end. The same outcome is in prospect for democratic planned societies, because here, too, pressure groups with a vested interest in the maintenance of the status quo would be able to use their political influence in an effort to perpetuate existing methods of doing business, to the detriment of society as a whole. So far the thesis.

What bearing has this proposition on the problem of social costs? In the first place, even if the pessimistic outlook outlined above were sound, the end of progress and change would be the outgrowth of democracy. For obviously, it would be the democratic element in the political structure of either society which, by subjecting economic affairs to popular control, would enable the majority interested in the status quo to arrest progress and change altogether. That is merely another way of saying (still assuming that the main line of the above argument is correct) that rapid change, whether under competitive capitalism or in a planned society, depends upon the survival of undemocratic elements in the political structure which make it possible for a small group of people interested in change to impose upon the great majority of the population the burden of social costs, instability and personal insecurity.[3] If it were really true that democracy and rapid economic growth are alternatives the question obviously remains whether we consider the preservation of democracy or rapid change as the supreme value. And it would be legitimate to raise the further question whether the lament about the imminent end of all change and growth said to result from the quest for security and protection against social costs does not reflect, however unconsciously, a movement away from social and political democracy.

But is the argument sound? Is it really correct that the choice is between democracy and progress? Must we assume that the whole movement in favor of protection against social costs can only end in a complete stoppage of all change? Is there no compromise possible between economic growth and protection against the social costs caused thereby? Is mankind living in the atomic age actually confronted with the dilemma outlined above? There are several reasons that support our more optimistic outlook.

First, it is reasonable to assume that the opposition by vested interests to progress and growth would decline considerably if the total costs of such change were more rationally allocated than in the past and if full compensation were made for the social losses suffered. In fact, the opposition to change and long-run growth is, at least in part, also due to the general economic instability to which the competitive process, for reasons other than progress and change, gives rise. Since this instability can be materially reduced by measures of anticyclical economic control, it is reasonable to assume that the opposition to change would decline with the achievement of a higher degree of over-all economic stability. Furthermore, with a more complete system of social accounting and the decline of opposition to change, the cleavage between those who cling to the status quo and those who expect to gain from change ought to be amenable to the typical processes of democratic bargaining and compro-

[3] The histories of both early capitalism in England and the rapid economic change of Soviet Russia could be cited as empirical examples of social regimes to illustrate this thesis.

mise. Finally, and most important of all, the general world situation and the coexistence of capitalist competitive and socialist planned regimes makes it quite impossible for either to arrest the pace of technological progress and change. Whatever may be the hazards of living in the atomic age with the world divided into two rival blocks, technological stagnation is not likely to be one of them.

There are, however, some philosophical considerations which make the study of social costs a matter of concern for the social scientist. It is these considerations which, more than any other single factor, have motivated the present investigation. An economic system which shifts part of the costs of production to third persons, and a body of doctrine which disregards these social costs, are in opposition to one of the most fundamental tenets of our professed humanistic ideals: respect for the human personality. Instead of being treated in his own right the individual becomes a mere instrument in the interest of long-run progress or whatever other "cause" if we fail to consider the human costs of production. This neglect of the individual needs to be remedied not only at the level of social legislation but also at that of economic theory, and it is within this broader context that the analysis and elimination of social costs offers a challenge to the economist.

Turning now to the practical problem of eliminating or repairing social losses caused by private production, or to the reduction of social costs to a minimum by making private producers as fully accountable for them as possible, it will not suffice to indicate merely the general nature of the harmful consequences and possible damages which third persons or the public in general might suffer as a result of productive activities; what is required for these purposes of policy making is some kind of quantitative measurement of the social costs of production. As a first step toward such a quantitative determination of the possible magnitude of the social costs of production, the general discussion of specific cases of social losses in the subsequent chapters is followed, as far as possible, by brief summaries of factual evidence of social losses and short résumés of available estimates of their relative magnitude expressed in monetary terms. These estimates are based largely on data published by various private and public agencies during the last 30 years. If some of the estimates appear to be out of date, for example in comparison with current series of prices and production, it is well to remember that data on social costs are found only occasionally in publications dealing with particular phases of industrial production; they are neither gathered nor kept up to date as systematically as are other statistical series.

In presenting these quantitative estimates of social losses it is not intended to convey an accurate measure of the social costs of production during any particular year, but rather to convince the reader of the importance and possible magnitude of social losses in comparable monetary terms and to point the way toward further factual research. The ultimate authority and responsibility for these quantitative estimates rests, moreover, with the original authors and sources from which they are quoted. If the available figures seem to indicate that the social costs of production are substantial, it is important to emphasize again that they represent, at best, only an incomplete picture of such costs inasmuch as so far no systematic study of social costs has been made with a view to ascertaining their full magnitude for any particular industry. Moreover, even if the available monetary estimates of social losses were complete, they would still have to be considered as fragmentary, because some of the social losses are intangible in character and have to be evaluated in other than monetary terms.

In the light of these considerations it becomes evident that the final determination of the magnitude of social costs of production is ultimately a matter of social evaluation; i.e. the magnitude of the social costs depends upon the importance which organized society attributes to both the tangible and the intangible values involved. Such social evaluations do not, however, pose an entirely *new* problem. For the formulation of public policy nearly always requires a general evaluation of "means" and "ends" whose relative importance can only be estimated, since a substantial proportion of all "costs" and "returns" of economic policies are "political" and intangible in character. Of course, this is not to say that the problem of policy formulation on the basis of general estimates of possible costs and returns has been fully explored and offers no further theoretical difficulties. Quite on the contrary, the issues raised by the concept of "social value" and "social evaluation" belong to the most important unsolved problems of economic science. Without presuming to offer a definite solution, the concluding part of the present study merely hints at the general direction in which a solution of these problems might be found.

Meanwhile it will be sufficient to realize that social evaluation in the sense of a social estimate of the magnitude of social costs lies outside the realm of scientific inquiry. The individual economist has no way of determining "scientifically" the "social values" of the damages and losses caused by private production. To evaluate these social losses in terms of his own standards and preferences would mean the introduction of highly subjective value judgments into economic analysis and would make the conclusions derived therefrom equally subjective, arbitrary and unscientific.[4] Economic science and the individual economist cannot do more than reveal the causal relationship between various productive processes and business practices on the one hand, and social losses and damages on the other. It is likewise within the province of scientific inquiry to present factual evidence of social losses and damages and to advance various estimates of the possible magnitude of the more tangible losses in monetary terms. Any final evaluation of the magnitude of social costs, however, can only be postulated, and subsequent theoretical and practical conclusions are dependent upon such postulates. Before it is possible to formulate even the most tentative premises as to the relative magnitude of social costs of production, it is necessary to understand the manner in which they arise in modern in-

---

[4] Needless to say, this danger of introducing subjective value judgments into economic analysis and thereby setting the cause for normative and unscientific conclusions is not avoided by simply disregarding all social costs. For, to do so and to leave social losses out of account on the ground that they are "external" and "noneconomic" in character would be equivalent to attributing no or "zero" value to all social damages, which is no less arbitrary and subjective a judgment than any positive or negative evaluation of social costs.

dustrial society. To provide a general background for the development of this understanding is the main purpose of the following discussion.

No attempt has been made to organize the discussion in accordance with the relative significance of the social costs; on the contrary, some of the most important social costs of production are discussed in the last chapters of our study. The analysis starts rather with those cases in which it is relatively easy to establish responsibility and to trace causal relationships between private production and social losses. This applies, for example, to the impairment of the human factor of production by occupational accidents and diseases. Thereafter, more complex cases of social costs are taken up, such as the damages resulting from water and air pollution, as well as the losses arising in the competitive exploitation of various kinds of natural resources. Finally, the social costs of technological progress and unemployment are studied. The concluding chapters deal with special cases of social costs, namely, the social losses caused by monopoly, social costs in distribution and transportation, and the social losses arising as a result of the frustration of science. These social losses differ from other social costs inasmuch as they do not necessarily involve a shift of costs to third persons but rather tend to be reflected in reduced efficiency of the operation of the economic system as a whole.

In order to trace as fully as possible the social costs involved in such phenomena as air and water pollution and the depletion of natural wealth, it was necessary to deal with certain technological and legal aspects of production which normally lie outside the field of economic analysis. The discussion of these aspects of modern economic life may sometimes appear somewhat lengthy and technical. Yet the author feels that a complete understanding of the social costs of production can be obtained only on the basis of such an analysis.

Most of the factual evidence of social costs presented in the following chapters pertains to economic life in the United States. This emphasis on social costs in the American economy may give rise to the impression that they are a typical American phenomenon. Such is, however, not the case. Social costs are a common phenomenon in competitive economies; what should, perhaps, be emphasized is the fact that American capitalism provides a particularly clear illustration of the operation of the capitalistic process, because it remained relatively free of governmental control throughout the nineteenth century and up to the Great Depression of the thirties.

We wish to make it clear that in tracing the social costs of private enterprise we are not implying that regulation and economic planning would necessarily eliminate these costs. Nor are we comparing unregulated private enterprise with a system of economic planning. Whether or not a system of economic planning would avoid the social costs of production depends upon whether the planners wish to avoid or neglect them. In the last analysis this is probably a matter of the political structure of the planned economy; that is to say, whether or not the social costs of production will be avoided under alternative forms of organization depends upon whether or not the content of the economic plan as an essentially political act of decision making is subject to review at the polls. The fact that our thesis does not rest upon a comparison of private enterprise and economic planning and that we do *not* argue that social costs are implicit in the structure of the liberal democratic state makes it unnecessary, within the context of this study, to enter into an examination of the political and economic problems of alternative forms of social organization. The questions raised by the current debate on the "road to serfdom" are important enough, but they have only a very indirect bearing on the problems here under discussion. Nor will an attempt be made to describe specific techniques and policies which would have to be adopted to eliminate social costs. To do so would transcend the scope of the present study, which is confined, as was pointed out before, to the tracing of a maximum number of cases of social costs under conditions of competitive economic life.

Before turning to this detailed analysis of social costs it will be worthwhile to review briefly the contributions of those economists who have questioned the validity of the main trend of reasoning of classical and neoclassical economics and in this context have dealt with the phenomenon of social costs.

3

EARLIER DISCUSSIONS OF SOCIAL COSTS

EVER SINCE the human mind conceived the idea that production and distribution are fundamentally self-regulating processes capable of achieving the optimum solution of the economic problem without positive direction by public authority, individual economists as well as entire schools of doctrine have questioned the general validity of such an optimistic interpretation. In dissenting from the tenets of the classical school the critics made extensive references to what can be considered as social costs in the broad sense in which the term will be used here. Indeed, confronted with the mass of factual evidence unearthed by the critics, one wonders why the older optimistic preconceptions of a natural regularity and orderliness of the competitive process were not abandoned long ago and replaced by premises postulating instead basic tendencies toward disorder and waste which could have served as a basis either for a far-reaching critique of the existing order or for a new system of theoretical conclusions in favor of economic planning.

There seem to be three reasons why the critics did not carry their discussion to this conclusion. First, most critics shared the basic presuppositions of their time, which made them unable to reject the rationalistic and optimistic notion of a "natural" order in social and economic affairs. Second, old preconceptions die slowly, especially if they reflect deep-seated political creeds and ideologies. And third, it is much easier to build a system of theoretical generalizations upon the notion of natural law and rational economic conduct than it is to build a system of liberal economic thought upon the conception of a tendency toward disorder and waste in economic affairs. It is thus not surprising that the factual evidence unearthed by the critics in contradiction to the basic presuppositions of classical and neo-classical economic thought has as yet not led to the elaboration of a new and equally systematic body of doctrine.

For reasons of exposition it will be helpful to survey earlier discussions of social costs under the following headings: (1) The Classical Economists, (2) The Historicists, (3) The Socialists, (4) Pigou's *Economics of Welfare,* (5) Veblen and His Followers, (6) The Theory of Monopolistic and Oligopolistic Competition, (7) Dynamic Sequence Analysis.

Without attempting a comprehensive survey of the specific contributions of each of these critics and schools, and, indeed, without intending to provide an exhaustive analysis of their major doctrines, we shall be satisfied with bringing to light the role which social costs have played in the general trends of thought of particular authors or schools. In many instances it was found unnecessary to prove our point by detailed quotations. Only when the matter under discussion required some elaboration or was set forth particularly well by an individual author, was it considered necessary and worth while to quote verbatim.

1. The Classical Economists

It may seem paradoxical to start this discussion with the classical economists, and it would doubtless be an extension of the argument to assert that the founders of political economy were champions of the doctrine of social costs. And yet some of the classical economists were much too competent philosophers not to qualify the doctrine of the invisible hand which their writings initiated. Even and particularly Adam Smith was fully aware of the fact that the market mechanism could be relied upon to secure the optimum solution of the economic problem only if at least three conditions were fulfilled: first, that there would be free competition; second, that the free competitors were restrained in their action by "sympathy" and "moral sentiments"; and third, that in addition to defense and the administration of justice, the government erects and maintains certain "public institutions" and "public works" which "though they may be in the highest degree advantageous to a great society, are, however, of such a nature, that the profit could never repay the expence to any individual or small number of individuals, and which it, therefore, cannot be expected that any individual or small number of individuals should erect or maintain."[1]

It is true that Adam Smith took it for granted that the prerequisites of free competition would be fulfilled, and it is not difficult to understand why, at his time, he felt it unnecessary to inquire further whether this assumption would always be fulfilled in the future. In 1776, i.e., prior to the series of technological advances usually referred to as the Industrial Revolution, and the concentration of great sums of capital in joint-stock companies, it would have been impossible to foresee that the time might come when production and distribution would no longer be carried on by a multitude of small-scale businessmen actively competing with each other. It is well known that despite this "immature" state of the economy at his time, Adam Smith made some very shrewd observations concerning the natural propensity of "masters" to combine with each other to the disadvantage of the workingman and the consumer in general.

Smith's reliance on moral sentiments as prerequisites of any workable system of competition has often been lost sight of and even denied by later generations of economists who preferred to popularize Smith's reference to the invisible hand as evidence of his glorification of selfishness. Nothing could be further from the truth. It is unthinkable that a moral philosopher of the stature of Adam Smith, who published *The Theory of Moral Sentiments* in 1759, would have abandoned his conceptions of the moral laws governing human behavior in 1776 when he published *The Wealth of Nations,* without making such a change of view explicit. It is, therefore, imperative that *The Wealth of Nations* be read in conjunction with

[1] Adam Smith, *The Wealth of Nations* (New York: Modern Library, 1937), p. 681.

the earlier *Theory of Moral Sentiments* in order to understand that Smith presupposes the existence of a natural moral law as a result of which the prudent man was believed to be anxious to improve himself only in fair ways, i.e., without doing injustice to others. We cannot blame Adam Smith for not having had a more modern understanding of human nature and of the fact that in the struggle for commercial survival it is often the most unscrupulous who sets the standard for moral restraint.

Finally, Smith's elaborate discussion of "public works" (in Book V of *The Wealth of Nations*) makes it abundantly clear that the founder of British classical political economy was fully aware of the fact that the investment of the nation's resources could not be determined exclusively by the competitive calculus if the optimum solution of the economic problem were to be achieved. There is a close connection between Smith's treatment of "public works" and later theories of "public wealth," "productive forces," "inappropriable utilities" and "public investments" which are associated respectively with the names of Lord Lauderdale, Friedrich List, J. B. Clark and J. M. Keynes. It would be possible to see in all these theories, and particularly in Adam Smith's insistence that "the duty of the sovereign" includes the erection and maintenance of certain public works, evidence of the recognition of social costs, inasmuch as serious social losses would arise if these works were left to private enterprise. However, this may be stretching Adam Smith's recognition of the existence of social costs a little too far; in any event, it is much more satisfactory to regard his theory of "public works" as an early specimen of the classical realization of the social returns of public investments which we have reserved to a later study. Nevertheless, even though it cannot well be said that Adam Smith included the doctrine of social costs in his system of thought, he must at least be regarded as one of the economists who was not unaware of the theoretical and practical limitations of the system of competition.

There were other members of the classical school whose writings reveal an awareness of some of the disequilibrating tendencies of private enterprise and of specific aspects of social costs. For example, T. R. Malthus's analysis of the rapid accumulation of capital as a possibly disturbing element in the progress of wealth may well be regarded as an early example of an approach to economic analysis which questions the self-equilibrating tendency of the market economy and points to the social losses occasioned by prolonged unemployment, which will be examined in detail in Chapter 11. It is well known that there is a certain connection between Malthus's views, which were shared and in part even anticipated by Sismondi, and those of J. A. Hobson and J. M. Keynes.

Even David Ricardo, whose great analytical ability was never matched by his philosophical and methodological insights, finally revised his earlier optimistic contention of the impossibility of lasting displacement of labor by the introduction of machinery; he admitted that the advantages of technological progress, if introduced suddenly and to a considerable extent, are paid for by the losses borne by the working population.

2. The Historicists

But it remained for the Historicists among the economists of the nineteenth century to deliver the first systematic blow against the basic preconceptions of classical political economy. From Auguste Comte to Gustav Schmoller, the members of this school were united in their denial of the thesis that the principle of self-interests is able to promote the social welfare and that there was no need for government planning and regulation of the economic process. In their insistence upon the need for viewing social and economic reality as a whole and for giving economic theory greater empirical content by means of detailed case studies, the Historical School led the way in tracing in detail many of the evils of competition, such as extreme inequalities in the distribution of wealth and income, social insecurity and destitution of old and sick people, depressed areas and industries, which, in their opinion, demanded far-reaching social and economic reforms by means of social legislation very much along the lines of the American New Deal. In fact, the Historical School anticipated many of the ideas which were expressed later by other economists and are now pretty generally accepted, at least as far as practical social policy is concerned. It would, therefore, lead to unnecessary repetition to trace in greater detail its individual contributions to the theory of social costs.

3. The Socialists

What distinguishes the socialists and especially Marxian socialists from the classical school is not a difference in method and preconception, but the fact that they arrive, on the basis of the same central doctrine (the labor theory of value), at conclusions diametrically opposed to those of the classical school. Instead of harmony of interest, Marx demonstrates the existence of exploitation and inevitable conflict between labor and capital. Instead of automatic equilibrium between consumption and production, Marx deduces crises and ultimate breakdown of the capitalist order. Basically, the socialist theory of surplus value, according to which the price of labor (wages) tends to fall typically short of the laborer's contribution (in terms of value) to the total product, implies a concept of social costs. This was clearly seen and stated by one of the earliest proponents of the theory of surplus value, namely Simonde de Sismondi. Without even formally accepting the labor theory of value, in fact in a chapter which bears the general title "How the Returns of the Entrepreneur are derived from Capital," Sismondi points out that their dependence and their general state of poverty often forces workers to accept any kind of work under the most unsatisfactory conditions and at the lowest possible wages. "The returns of the entrepreneur sometimes represent nothing but the spoliation of the worker; the former makes his money not because his business yields returns far in excess of the costs of production but because he does not pay the total cost of his enterprise; he fails to give an adequate compensation to the worker. Such an industry is a social evil." [2]

Sismondi also seems to have been the first economist to have set forth in a systematic way other aspects of social costs, especially

[2] Translated from J. C. L. Simonde de Sismondi, *Nouveaux Principes d'économie politique* (Paris, ed. 2, 1827), vol. I, p. 92.

those arising in connection with technological improvements.[3] Without denying the existence of equilibrating tendencies of the market, Sismondi makes it clear that the attainment of a new equilibrium, for instance, after technological innovations, is usually achieved only at the price of extraordinary human costs and capital losses. "Let us beware of this dangerous theory of equilibrium which is supposed to reëstablish itself automatically . . . It is true a certain equilibrium is reëstablished in the long run, but only after a frightful amount of suffering. It is a fact that capital is withdrawn from a particular industry only as a result of bankruptcy of the owner, and workers give up their occupations only when they die; indeed, laborers who find it easy to shift to other occupations and move to other places must be regarded as exceptions and not the rule." [4]

As a result of this immobility of fixed capital and labor, technological changes have, according to Sismondi, the effect of destroying the value of old investments—a fact that exposes manufacturing industries to violent shocks. As far as the losses of labor are concerned, Sismondi points out that "the immediate effect of machinery is to throw some of the workers out of employment, to increase the competition of others and so to lower the wages of all. This results in diminished consumption and a slackening of demand. Far from being always beneficial, machinery produces useful results only when its introduction is preceded by an increased revenue, and consequently by the possibility of giving new work to those displaced." [5]

Countless official and private investigations into the conditions of the working class during the Industrial Revolution, especially in England, have confirmed Sismondi's thesis. These studies provide a detailed picture of the social costs caused during the transition period following the introduction of the machine method of pro-

[3] Concerning the question of Sismondi's priority over and relation to Ricardo and Malthus, see G. Sotiroff, *Ricardo und Sismondi* (Zurich, New York: Europa Verlag, 1945), pp. 41–47.

[4] Translated from Sismondi, *Nouveaux Principes,* vol. II, p. 220.

[5] Quoted from C. Gide and C. Rist, *A History of Economic Doctrines from the Time of the Physiocrats to the Present Day* (New York: D. C. Heath and Company), p. 180.

duction; they have remained to the present day classical examples of a discussion of social costs due to the impairment of the health and efficiency of the working population.

In a more fundamental sense, the social cost of technological change may be regarded as a special case of the costs of transition in general, which remain largely unaccounted for in entrepreneurial cost calculations. Marx dealt with these social costs of transition in his discussion of the effects of the abolition of the corn laws in England, in his *Address on Free Trade* in 1848. Quoting with approval Ricardo's statement that the importation of cheaper corn will lead to lower wages,[6] Marx continues: "And do not believe, gentlemen, that it is a matter of indifference to the worker whether he receives only four francs on account of corn being cheaper, when he had been receiving five francs before."[7] And to those economists who argue that the decline of wages and the keener competition among workers are temporary sufferings during the transition period, Marx replies that "these temporary evils have implied for the majority the transition from life to death, and for the rest a transition from a better to a worse condition."[8] In fact, "under this free trade the whole severity of the economic laws will fall upon the workers"[9] and "all the destructive phenomena which unlimited competition gives rise to within one country are reproduced in more gigantic proportions in the world market."[10] In short, according to Marx "the free trade system hastens the social revolution. It is in this revolutionary sense alone, gentlemen, that I vote in favour of free trade."[11]

[6] "If, instead of growing our own corn . . . we discover a new market from which we can supply ourselves with these commodities at a cheaper price, wages will fall and profits rise." D. Ricardo, *The Principles of Political Economy and Taxation* (New York: E. P. Dutton and Co., Inc.; Everyman's Library, 1937), p. 80.

[7] K. Marx, "Address on the Question of Free Trade," reprinted in *The Poverty of Philosophy* (New York: International Publishers), p. 199.

[8] *Ibid.*, p. 204.

[9] *Ibid.*, p. 206.

[10] *Ibid.*, p. 207.

[11] *Ibid.*, p. 208.

Similarly, other socialists have spoken of social costs implicit in the competitive structure of society. Thus, Robert Owen, in a critical appraisal of the effects of the new methods of production, in 1821 writes: "The steam engine and spinning machines, with the endless mechanical inventions to which they have given rise, have, however, inflicted evils on society, which now greatly overbalance the benefits which are derived from them." [12] Similarly, Charles Kingsley, an early Christian Socialist with a conservative outlook, has a notion of social costs of private enterprise when he complains about "the slavery, starvation, waste of life, year-long imprisonment in dungeons narrower and fouler than those of the Inquisition, which goes on among thousands of free English clothes-makers at this day." [13]

Friedrich Engels, who conducted an early investigation into the "human costs" of the Industrial Revolution in England, called attention to another kind of social costs, the full magnitude of which was brought to light only in the twentieth century, namely, the damage caused by air pollution. In London, Engels speculates, "two hundred fifty thousand fires crowded upon an area three to four miles square, consume an enormous amount of oxygen which is replaced with difficulty because the method of building cities in itself impedes ventilation. The carbonic acid gas, engendered by respiration and fire, remains in the streets by reason of its specific gravity and the chief air current passes over the roofs of the city. The lungs of the inhabitants fail to receive the due supply of oxygen and the consequence is mental and physical lassitude and low vitality." [14]

Charles Fourier discussed certain social costs of agricultural production without, however, analyzing them systematically. Comparing the effects of modern forestry with conditions prevailing in more primitive times, Fourier is led to the conclusion that "we fall far below

[12] R. Owen, *Report to the County of Lanarck* (Glasgow, 1821), reprinted in *Introduction to Contemporary Civilization in the West* (New York: Columbia University Press, 1946), vol. II, pp. 407–8.

[13] C. Kingsley, "Cheap Clothes and Nasty," reprinted in *Alton Locke* (London, 1911), p. xlvii.

[14] F. Engels, *The Condition of the Working Class in England in 1844* (New York, 1887), p. 64.

the savages . . . For we do not like them confine ouselves to leaving them [the forests] uncultivated and in their primitive state; we bring the axe and destruction, and the result is landslides, the denuding of mountain-sides, and the deterioration of the climate. This evil, by destroying the springs and multiplying storms, is in two ways the cause of disorder in the water system. Our rivers, constantly alternating from one extreme to the other, from sudden swellings to protracted droughts, are able to support only a very small quantity of fish, which people take care to destroy at their birth, reducing their number to a tenth of that which they ought to produce. Thus, we are complete savages in the management of water and forests." [15]

An early systematic treatment of social costs in agriculture is contained in Justus von Liebig's celebrated treatise entitled *"Die Chemie in ihrer Anwendung auf Agricultur und Physiologie,"* which influenced parts of Marx' analysis of capitalist agriculture. In an introductory section Liebig discusses the history and effects of soil depletion since the earliest days of recorded history, and ends his historical survey with the following warning: "If we do not succeed in making the farmer better aware of the conditions under which he produces and in giving him the means necessary for the increase of his output, wars, emigration, famines and epidemics will of necessity create the conditions of a new equilibrium which will undermine the welfare of everyone and finally lead to the ruin of agriculture." [16] It remained for Karl Marx to formulate, obviously on the basis of Liebig's inductive researches, the statement that ". . . all progress in capitalistic agriculture is a progress in the art, not only of robbing the laborer, but of robbing the soil; all progress in increasing the fertility of the soil for a given time is a progress towards ruining the lasting sources of that fertility. The more a country starts its development on the foundation of modern industry, like the United States, for example, the more rapid is this process of

---

[15] *Selections from the Works of Fourier* (London, 1901), p. 109.

[16] Translated from Justus von Liebig, *Die Chemie in ihrer Anwendung auf Agricultur und Physiologie,* Erster Teil, "Der Chemische Prozess der Ernährung der Vegetalien" (Brunswick, ed. 7, 1862), p. 155.

destruction. Capitalist production, therefore, develops technology, and the combining together of various processes into a social whole, only by sapping the original sources of all wealth—the soil and the laborer." [17]

From these earlier treatments of social costs by socialist writers a direct road leads to the analysis of social losses by later social reformers and particularly to the Fabian Socialists in Great Britain. The works of J. A. Hobson and the two Webbs were devoted in large measure to the tracing of social costs in the industrial sphere. Because these contributions are well known and will be referred to later and, moreover, because they have influenced contemporary thought and practice far beyond the narrower circle of Fabian Socialists, it will be sufficient merely to list some of the more representative works.[18]

Among contemporary socialist writers, Oskar Lange has paid considerable attention to social costs and makes the possibility of taking into account all the costs of production one of the features which distinguish a socialist economy from a private-enterprise economy. "The . . . feature which distinguishes a socialist economy from one based on private enterprise is the *comprehensiveness* of the items entering into the price system . . . Into the cost account of the private entrepreneur only those items enter for which he has to pay a price, while such items as the maintenance of the unemployed created when he discharges workers, the provision for the victims of occupational diseases and industrial accidents, etc., do not enter, or, as Professor J. M. Clark has shown, are diverted into social overhead costs." [19]

[17] Karl Marx, *Capital* (Chicago, 1906), vol. I, pp. 555–6; for a further elaboration of Marx's views on the exploitation of natural resources (*"Naturelemente"*) and the fact that the latter enter into the productive process without entering into private cost calculations, see vol. III, pp. 938, 944–6.

[18] For J. A. Hobson, see *Work and Wealth—A Human Valuation* (New York, 1916). For the Fabian Socialists, see Sidney and Beatrice Webb, *The Decay of Capitalist Civilization* (London, 1923), chap. v, and H. D. Dickinson, "The Failure of Economic Individualism," in *Studies in Capital and Investment* (London: Victor Gollancz, 1935).

[19] Oskar Lange and F. M. Taylor, *On the Economic Theory of Socialism* (Minneapolis: The University of Minnesota Press, 1938), pp. 103–4.

4. *Pigou's* Economics of Welfare

Among the neoclassical economists it is primarily A. C. Pigou who, in addition to Marshall's occasional references to social losses, has paid considerable attention to social costs. In fact, subsequent to his *Economics of Welfare,* which constitutes his first attempt to integrate the phenomenon of social costs into the conceptual system of neoclassical equilibrium economics, Pigou has broadened his approach and now speaks of general disharmonies and wastes arising in production and distribution, and those connected with industrial fluctuations. Under these headings he deals with such matters as losses sustained by outsiders as a result of private production, the inability of private entrepreneurs to estimate future demand, the misallocation of resources by monopolies, the social costs of technical improvements, the costs of advertising, the tendency to discounting future needs in favor of present wants, the social losses entailed by extreme inequalities of income, especially those resulting from unequal wage bargains between employers and unorganized labor, and the neglect of social returns. In all these instances, Pigou surmises that we may be confronted with evidences of "the bankruptcy of capitalism" and a "prima facie case for extending the range of public ownership and public operation to industries in which they have not yet been invoked." [20] At the same time, Pigou rejects the socialist thesis that public ownership and central planning offer the only safe guarantee for the elimination of social costs and the optimum allocation of scarce resources. The main reason which, according to Pigou, speaks against the socialist thesis is the difficulty of obtaining the necessary data required for the calculation and measurement of the relative costs and benefits of alternative methods of adjustment.

Pigou's theoretical approach to the problem of social costs will be understood best in the light of the following summary of the central thesis concerning the divergence of social and private costs. The

[20] A. C. Pigou, *Socialism versus Capitalism* (London: Macmillan and Co., 1947), pp. 43 and 45; used with the permission of The Macmillan Company. See also *Economics in Practice* (London: Macmillan and Co., 1935), Lecture 5.

analysis is based upon a comparison of the "marginal social product" with the "marginal private net product." The marginal social product includes the "total net product of physical things or objective services due to the marginal increment of resources in any given use or place, no matter to whom any part of this product may accrue." [21] Since the investment of additional resources may throw costs "upon people not directly concerned through, say, uncompensated damage done to surrounding woods by sparks from railway engines," [22] the marginal net social product of a given unit of investment may diverge and, indeed, be considerably smaller than the marginal private net product. The latter is defined as "that part of the total net product of physical things or objective services due to the marginal increment of resources in any given use or place which accrues in the first instance—i.e., prior to sale—to the person responsible for investing resources there." [23]

The distinction between private net product and social net product enables Pigou to trace a number of cases in which the private product is greater than the social product, that is to say, where private productive activities tend to give rise to social losses of various kinds. Pigou lists as examples of such a divergence of private and social product the overrunning of a neighbor's land by rabbits originating from game preserves; the destruction of the amenities and lighting of neighboring sites by the construction of a factory in residential districts; the wearing out of the surfaces of roads by motor cars; the increase in expenditures for police and prisons made necessary by the production and sale of intoxicants; the costs of diplomatic maneuvers, military preparedness and actual war caused by foreign investments; the negative effects of woman labor in factories; the costs of competitive advertising; the costs of bargaining, including deception as to the physical nature of commodities offered for sale and the future yield of securities; and various negative effects of

[21] A. C. Pigou, *The Economics of Welfare* (London: Macmillan and Co., ed. 4, 1932), p. 134; used with the permission of The Macmillan Company.

[22] *Ibid.*, p. 134.

[23] *Ibid.*, pp. 134–5.

monopolistic practices. Pigou speaks even of the money value of the marginal social net product in the sense of what the social product, and hence the social losses, are worth in the market, although he makes it clear later that many of the social losses caused by private productive activities cannot "be readily brought into relation with the measuring rod of money." [24]

This attempt to discuss the phenomena of social costs within the terminological and conceptual system of traditional equilibrium economics is characteristic of Pigou's approach to social costs. Fundamentally, it reflects a belief that the so-called "disservices" caused by private productive activities can be remedied within the framework of the unplanned market economy. And it is consistent with this premise that the greater part of Pigou's work is devoted to a discussion of governmental measures (taxes, prohibitions, social legislation) designed to bring about the closest possible identity between (marginal) social and private product of individual economic activities in order to maximize the "national dividend" and through it total welfare.

More recent formulations of the theory of welfare economics have considerably restricted its scope, with the result that the phenomena of social costs and social returns no longer play the central role in the conceptual system of the new welfare economics that they did in Pigou's *Economics of Welfare*. This is due primarily to the fact that the "new" welfare economics conceives of the welfare of the community in terms of the sum total of the utilities of individuals, and tries not only to dispense with all quantitative comparisons of utilities but also with any social evaluation of the utilities of individuals. Thus, the new standard definition of welfare has been formulated as follows: "Instead of attempting to give 'content' to the idea of welfare directly, we define a welfare indicator which increases and decreases with welfare—welfare is that which varies with this indicator. The indicator is defined as follows: *welfare increases (decreases) whenever one or more individuals become more (less) sat-*

[24] *Ibid.*, p. 183.

isfied without any other individuals becoming less (more) satisfied." [25] If one individual or group of individuals is injured by a particular measure, its effect on the welfare of the community ("total welfare") is said to be ascertainable by the "compensation principle," under which injured groups are compensated by "bounties" paid out of taxes levied upon persons benefited by the change. Hence *"welfare will be increased, decreased or left unchanged by a given economic reorganization depending upon whether the algebraic sum of all compensating taxes and bounties is positive, negative or zero."* [26]

It is impossible within the scope of this study to attempt an exhaustive appraisal of these new departures in neoclassical welfare economics.[27] Suffice it to say that it is difficult to see how the so-called compensation principle could ever be made to encompass the phenomena of social costs (and social returns). Above all, there seems to be no indication that the system of bounties and taxes envisaged can be made to yield theoretically defensible estimates of social costs and social gains. For example, by what operation is it to be ascertained whether individuals find themselves equally (or more or less) satisfied after they have paid the tax and are freed, for instance, from the effects of air and water pollution, as compared with the state of affairs before they paid the tax and suffered from the consequences of polluted air and water? In fact, if the compensation principle lacks practical applicability, the whole concept of "welfare" as the sum total of the utilities of individuals once more becomes ambiguous, and we are compelled finally to conceive of the welfare of the community in terms of interpersonal comparisons of utility and to include the social evaluation of social costs and social gains within the realm of scientific discussion. Indeed, the facts that the new welfare economics operates with a welfare concept defined as the sum total of the utilities of individuals, and that difficulties in

[25] M. W. Reder, *Studies in the Theory of Welfare Economics* (New York: Columbia University Press, 1947), pp. 14–15.

[26] *Ibid.,* p. 17.

[27] For a critical evaluation of these new developments, see G. J. Stigler, "The New Welfare Economics," *American Economic Review,* XXXIII (June 1943), pp. 355–359.

the way of accurate and quantitative interpersonal comparisons of utilities are believed to make the latter so completely immeasurable that simply no social action can be based upon such comparisons, seem to indicate rather that the new welfare economics despairs of any possibility of including social costs (and social returns) within the realm of economic analysis.

5. Veblen and His Followers

Veblen's critique of the basic preconceptions of economic science has already been noticed. Against the teleological imputation of rationality into the economic process which, he felt, was characteristic of all subjective theories of marginal utility, Veblen sets forth as the central aim of economic science the theoretical analysis of economic change and long-run development. In the course of the elaboration of such a theory of economic dynamics outside the realm of marginal utility economics, Veblen, and notably his followers, have analyzed a wide variety of social costs which arise primarily in connection with technical progress, depressions and monopolistic practices. A detailed survey of these contributions to the theory of social costs is neither practical at this point nor necessary, in view of the fact that they will be discussed in the individual chapters concerned with the social costs of technical progress, unemployment and monopoly.

6. The Theory of Monopolistic and Oligopolistic Competition

The theory of monopolistic and oligopolistic competition which, like Pigou's *Economics of Welfare,* stays within the terminological and conceptual framework of marginal analysis, is regarded by many merely as an extension of neoclassical equilibrium economics. In some respects this is doubtless correct. The new theory of monopolistic competition has made us aware of what perfect and pure competition (as a theoretical concept) really implies. It reflects and reinforces the widespread belief that contemporary conditions are far removed from the "ideal" of perfect and pure competition, and, by providing a seemingly unanswerable theoretical indictment of the social wastes of monopolistic practices, it has lent vigorous theoretical support, however unwittingly, to the perennial fight for a return to the golden age of perfect competition. In reality, however, the new theory represents a break in the continuity of the whole classical and neoclassical tradition. Instead of the intellectual model of perfect competition, with a determinate state of equilibrium toward which the forces of supply and demand tend to gravitate, the new theory considers perfect competition merely as a limiting case and emphasizes the ubiquity of monopolistic elements in most actual situations of selling (and buying). Outside of agriculture and certain markets for industrial materials, most firms sell nonhomogeneous goods in distinct markets and hence are able to exercise a considerable influence over supply and therefore over price. Product differentiation and the ability to control supply invite sales promotional efforts. Moreover, if there are only a few sellers in the market, each being of decisive importance to the other (oligopoly), competition may take the forms of "cutthroat competition" and economic warfare, the outcome of which is uncertain and hence theoretically indeterminate and not subject to generalization. In fact, by showing that the theory of perfect and pure competition does not fit the case of most actual selling situations and that the classical conception of "beneficial" competition as a restraint on the pursuit of private gain is not a realistic conception, the new theory may be said to call for a far-reaching reversal of the classical and neoclassical stand on social control. For if "an essential part of free enterprise is the attempt of every businessman to build up his own monopoly," [28] and if "the typical outcome of private enterprise is not pure competition, but monopolistic competition," [29] which eventually tends to degenerate into economic warfare and cutthroat competition, "pure competition may no longer be regarded as in any sense an 'ideal' for purposes of welfare economics." [30]

More specifically, the new theory must be credited with a clear-cut

[28] E. H. Chamberlin, *The Theory of Monopolistic Competition* (Cambridge: Harvard University Press, ed. 6, 1948), p. 213.

[29] *Ibid.*, p. 213.

[30] *Ibid.*, p. 214.

condemnation of the social evils of monopoly which may be summarized as follows. Under conditions of monopolistic competition the equilibrium price is shown to be invariably higher than the one indicated under conditions of perfect and pure competition. With higher prices, output and sales will be lower; hence demand will be diverted to goods less urgently desired, and unused capacity and unemployment are the result. Under conditions of monopolistic competition and oligopoly there is said to be no or little pressure to pass lower costs or higher than average profits on to the consumer or worker; nor is there any pressure to eliminate wastes and apply cost-reducing innovations. While these conclusions are perhaps not altogether new, the new theory nevertheless brings into clear focus the social wastes of market situations in which monopolistic elements are present. It is needless to add that all these conclusions seem to point to a need for some form of social control over competition.

Thus the new theory of monopolistic competition may be regarded as a departure from previous normative identifications of competition with the "ideal"; it represents a new approach to the theory of value in so far as it explores the middle ground left unexplained by both the theory of perfect competition and that of "perfect" monopoly. It is true that social costs as such play no role in it; in fact, the new theory of monopolistic competition never intended to provide theoretical models which would fit the case of costs not borne by the entrepreneur. The theory is of interest within the context of this survey of earlier discussion of social costs only in so far as it questions the ideal character of competition.

7. Dynamic Sequence Analysis

Finally, we ought to mention certain developments in dynamic theory which, although not directly concerned with the problem of social costs, have called renewed attention to the disequilibrating tendencies of the competitive market mechanism. By abandoning the preoccupation with stationary models and the analysis of a small segment of the economic system (partial analysis) in favor of a dynamic analysis of the total development over time (sequence analysis), dynamic theory has been able to show quite effectively how equilibrium conditions may be disrupted and to describe the repercussions of such disruptions. Dynamic theory has thus led to results which to a certain extent confirm earlier doubts of the critics of the whole equilibrium concept.

Of course, it cannot be denied that the market mechanism is able, often through extraordinarily costly and lengthy adjustment processes, to reduce disproportions and general discrepancies which may have arisen. But the outcome of these processes is not always determinate and predictable. In fact, "once equilibrium has been destroyed by some disturbance, the process of establishing a new one is not so sure and prompt and economical as the old theory of perfect competition made it out to be; and [there exists] the possibility that the very struggle for adjustment might lead such a system farther away from instead of nearer to a new equilibrium. This will happen in most cases unless the disturbance is small. In many cases, lagged adjustment is sufficient to produce this result." [31]

There are many well-known examples of this tendency away from equilibrium. We need only refer to the cumulative and self-sustaining tendencies of contraction and expansion of income, production and profits during the depression and expansion phase of the business cycle. Other cases in point are the tendency of prices to rise or fall in accordance with speculative expectations and behavior; the tendency of producers acting in response to price rises and without accurate information of what their competitors do to overexpand production, thereby rendering false their own cost and price expectations; the "acceleration" of the demand for and production of producers' goods resulting from a relatively small change in the rate of increase or decrease of the demand for consumers goods, and finally the irregular shape of the supply curve of labor, reflecting the possibility that a fall of wages may be accompanied by a greater offer of labor hours and hence to a further drop in wages.

Two concrete illustrations may suffice to indicate the wasteful consequences of these tendencies *away* from equilibrium. In the field of

[31] J. A. Schumpeter, *Capitalism, Socialism and Democracy,* p. 103.

agriculture, for example, a higher price of farm products may induce farmers to expand production in such a manner as to set the conditions of next year's slump. Or similarly, a fall in the price of farm products may induce farmers to work harder and even increase the area under cultivation in an effort to supplement their family income, with the subsequent result of causing a still further drop of their prices. During the Industrial Revolution, which opened the way for unskilled woman and child labor, the displacement of workers by machinery tended to depress wages and forced women and children into factories to supplement the family income. Thus, far from resulting in a decrease of the amount of labor offered, the drop of wages increased the supply, thereby contributing further to the tendency of wages to fall. It was this tendency of wages to fall which, together with a general scarcity of capital, gave relative validity to Ricardo's iron law of wages as well as Marx's later conception of the tendency of wages to fluctuate around the minimum subsistence level. Doubtless, the general principle which is revealed in this shape of the supply curve of labor holds true not merely in times of rapid economic change but also under "normal" conditions of depression, in the absence of protective labor legislation and collective bargaining. The matter has been sufficiently investigated to require no further analysis here.

The foregoing summary is anything but an exhaustive survey of the main contributions made to the exploration of social costs in contemporary economic society.[32] In particular, no attempt has been made to survey the results of the extremely fruitful researches by psychologists, sociologists and anthropologists into the relation be-

[32] Among the more important works not surveyed in the preceding discussion are Stuart Chase, *The Tragedy of Waste* (New York, 1925); S. von Ciriacy-Wantrup, "Land Conservation and Social Planning," *Plan Age* (April 1939), pp. 109–119; H. S. Davis, *The Industrial Study of Economic Progress* (Philadelphia: University of Pennsylvania Press, 1947); L. K. Frank, "The Principle of Disorder and Incongruity in Economic Affairs," *Political Science Quarterly*, XLVII (December 1932), 515–525; F. Lavington, "An Approach to the Theory of Business Risks," *Economic Journal*, XXXV (June 1925), 186–199; L. Mumford, *The Culture of Cities* (New York: Harcourt, Brace and Company, 1938); J. Putnam, *The Modern Case for Socialism* (Boston: Meador Publishing Company, 1946); M. W. Watkins, *Industrial Combination and Public Policy* (Boston, 1927), chap. vi.

tween contemporary culture and personal maladjustments. These researches, which regard personal maladjustments, whether they take the form of neuroses, mental disorders, delinquency or family disorganization, as human reactions to cultural disintegration and to a fundamentally sick society, provide a wealth of evidence of a kind of social costs which economists can hardly afford to neglect much longer. Among those who have pioneered in combining the insights of psychoanalysis with the results of modern sociology and anthropology are Franz Alexander, Erich Fromm, Karen Horney, Abram Kardiner and Harry Stack Sullivan.

4

THE SOCIAL COSTS RESULTING FROM THE
IMPAIRMENT OF THE HUMAN FACTOR
OF PRODUCTION

PERHAPS THE MOST generally recognized case of social costs of competition is the impairment of the physical and mental health of laborers in the course of the productive process. These so-called human costs of production have found widespread recognition in various kinds of protective labor legislation and social insurance, so that their inclusion in a study on social costs calls for special explanation. It might be argued, for example, that existing protective labor legislation tends either to prevent the occurrence of social losses or to translate these losses if they do occur into entrepreneurial outlays. Such reasoning neglects, however, a number of things. In the first place, it is a mistake to assume that the enactment of preventive social legislation is a guarantee of its effectiveness in the prevention of social losses. As a matter of fact, the present system of social and labor legislation represents, at best, only a first step toward the elimination of the phenomenon of social costs. There are numerous instances in which the impairment of the human factor continues to be borne by the injured worker and remains either partly or entirely unaccounted for in entrepreneurial outlays.

Moreover, the present study is concerned with the general thesis that entrepreneurial outlays do not measure the actual total costs of production; as previously pointed out, this thesis is not invalidated but rather confirmed by the existence of and need for protective legislation designed to prevent or minimize specific social losses caused by private production. Finally, even if the present system of protective labor legislation were successful in translating all human costs of production into entrepreneurial outlays, the impairment of the human factor would still offer the best starting point for our discussion because it represents a particularly simple and typical case of social costs. This will become clear especially in the light of the following general observations on the impairment of the human factor in modern industrial production and the subsequent brief studies of industrial accidents, occupational diseases and woman and child labor.

1. General Observations

In its economic implications, the impairment of the health and efficiency of human beings in the course of the productive process does not differ from the gradual deterioration of durable agents of production. In both cases a progressive reduction or even complete destruction of the economic usefulness of valuable factors of production is taking place. And yet, in the absence of a comprehensive system of social insurance, the market economy, operating as it does within a given framework of contractual obligations, tends to deal with these two cases of deterioration of valuable factors of production in an entirely different manner. Indeed, no owner of durable factors of production would be willing to make use of such agents, if some provision were not made to compensate him for the deterioration of his asset. Such provision is usually achieved by depreciation charges designed to furnish the funds required for the replacement of any given fixed agent of production or, in the terminology of accounting, "to maintain intact the value of the original capital investment." [1] In any event, by furnishing a convenient and more or less satisfactory method of accounting for that part of the costs of production which results from the use of durable agents of pro-

---

[1] R. B. Kester, *Advanced Accounting* (New York: The Ronald Press Co., 1933), p. 245.

duction, depreciation charges enable the individual producer to see to it that his total monetary outlays do not exceed the returns obtainable from the goods and services produced.

In sharp contrast with this treatment of durable agents of production is the manner in which the competitive process deals with the impairment of the human factor. This difference is largely due to the fact that laborers, as human beings, are not subject to private ownership rights. They are free persons whose services may be hired but who have to provide for their own livelihood. If these free laborers are affected adversely by the productive process, there is nobody—except perhaps the laborer himself—who has any interest in seeing to it that an adequate "depreciation charge" is made for the impairment of his physical and mental health. In fact, the entrepreneur, in his desire to reduce costs of production as far as possible, will generally be reluctant to consider the impairment of the physical and mental capacities of his laborers as part of the costs of his enterprise.[2] His unwillingness to do so will be the greater the easier he finds it to replace "worn-out" workers by new laborers. On the other hand, the laborer, because of his relatively weaker bargaining position, will find it difficult to have his claim to special financial compensation in case of hazardous occupations recognized by the entrepreneur, particularly in times of widespread unemployment. Under such conditions, therefore, it is unlikely that wages will include an adequate or even any compensation for the possible impairment of the worker's health in the productive process.

It might be argued that entrepreneurs, in their own interest, will tend to provide for healthy and safe working conditions because damages to the workers' health reduce their efficiency and, by the same token, increase the costs of production. However, this argument neglects two things. First, the private producer is under no obligation to keep inefficient laborers, but may simply hire new workers whose efficiency has not yet been affected by unhealthy

---

[2] It is hardly necessary to point out that this is in contrast with the conditions prevailing under slavery systems and feudalism, where the producer is likely to consider any impairment of the human factor by the productive process as a depreciation of the capital value of his property and thus as part of the costs of production.

working conditions. Second, the introduction of safety and health-protecting devices, though ultimately contributing to a higher labor efficiency and lower costs, will necessarily add to the producer's present costs and thus affect adversely his competitive position. Or, it might simply be more profitable to operate the plant without safety devices—considering even adverse effects on labor efficiency—than to introduce such devices (still assuming their introduction to be worth while in terms of outlays and expected "returns" in the form of greater efficiency and good will). In this case, as well as in the probably much greater number of cases where the provision of healthier working conditions is directly unprofitable in terms of entrepreneurial outlays and returns, the deterioration and even destruction of the human factor are likely to become chronic features in competitive economies if not corrected by comprehensive social legislation.

The losses caused by such impairment of the human factor will be borne either by the injured worker or by the taxpayer in the form of greater public expenditures for medical care, hospitals and relief. The fact that these losses, in the absence of adequate social legislation, are not charged against the operating costs of private enterprise but are borne largely by the laborer or the community makes them typical social costs in the sense in which the term is used in this study. It is the purpose of the following paragraphs to trace these social costs more fully and to analyze their possible extent and magnitude.

2. Work Injuries

The impairment of the human factor by modern industrial processes is reflected, first of all, in the great number of work injuries occurring each year over a wide range of industries.

For all manufacturing groups (i.e., not including mining) the average number of disabling injuries for each million employee-hours worked is about 20 (with lumber, furniture, stone, clay and glass, food products, iron and steel, and paper products showing a much higher injury frequency rate.) The average number of days lost owing to these work injuries is about 75, a figure which measures the average severity rate of work injuries in American manufacturing industries (with rubber, chemicals, iron and steel, and lumber showing a considerably higher severity rate). (See Appendix I.)

In coal mining the number of workers killed annually is higher than 1000. Fatal and nonfatal injuries, either per million man-hours or per million tons of coal produced, show an underlying stability which may be said to be the measure of the "human costs" of production under present conditions of safety and accident prevention. (See Appendix II.)

It is true that the introduction of safety measures has led to a reduction of both injury frequency and injury severity rate in recent decades. However, these reductions seem to be confined to industries with large-scale methods of production. Thus, while many large firms have reduced their injury rates by more than 90 per cent of the former figure, "small firms as a class have shown relatively few gains." [3] If in the light of these facts we consider that the greater part of the working force in America is employed by smaller firms (employing 500 workers or less) it appears reasonable to conclude that a substantial proportion of the labor force has been "little touched by safety." [4] This general conclusion is supported by the results of a recent survey (1947) of the Bureau of Labor Statistics which shows that 70 per cent of all accidents occur in plants that are not reached by the organized safety movement. [5]

The foregoing figures are of interest not only because they show the magnitude of the accident problem in modern industrial society but also because they serve as an indication of what the situation

[3] *Safety Subjects*, U. S. Department of Labor, Bulletin No. 67 of the Division of Labor Standards (Washington: U. S. Government Printing Office, 1944), p. 3.

[4] In fact, the Division of Labor Standards of the Department of Labor estimated that at least 75 per cent of our labor force has been "little touched by safety." See *Safety Subjects*, p. 4.

[5] *Hearings before the Subcommittee of the Committee on Appropriations*, House of Representatives, Eightieth Congress, First Session on the Department of Labor-Federal Security Agency Appropriation Bill for 1948. Part 1 (Washington, 1947), p. 106.

might be in the absence of workmen's compensation acts in the United States. Indeed, under such conditions the frequency of accidents and occupational diseases would likely be higher because even large-scale employers would have no or relatively little incentive to introduce and maintain proper safety devices in their factories. It is, therefore, safe to conclude that in the absence of social legislation the total costs of work injuries would exceed substantially the present losses resulting therefrom. This does not mean, of course, that the present system of protective labor and social legislation has already exhausted all possibilities of economical accident prevention. On the contrary, according to estimates of the National Safety Council, an additional investment of $5,000,000 in accident prevention in and out of factories would result in 750,000 fewer injuries to workers, 92,000,000 more man-days of production and a saving of $750,000,-000 to our national economy, or a return of $125 for every dollar invested.[6] Similarly, the U. S. Health Service is reported as authority for estimates according to which "the prompt adoption throughout industry of already known medical and engineering controls would immediately reduce by 10 per cent the time lost due to sickness and accidents of an occupational character." [7]

For the purposes of this study it is convenient to distinguish three different kinds of cost items in connection with work injuries. There are first the direct outlays, reflected in costs of medical and hospital care. Second, there arise various indirect costs for the individual plant due to such factors as the loss of time of the injured worker and fellow workers who stop work, damage to equipment, interruption of plant operation, temporary idleness of machinery, spoilage and wastage of material, the lower efficiency of the inexperienced workers, and the selection and training of new laborers. In addition to these indirect costs, which are largely reflected in entrepreneurial expenses, there are the broader repercussions of work injuries on the injured worker and his family. Thus, industrial accidents may have

[6] *The New York Times,* April 24, 1942.

[7] National Resources Planning Board, *National Resources Development,* Report for 1943. Part I. Post-War Plan and Program (Washington: U. S. Government Printing Office, January, 1943), p. 63.

the effect of either partially or totally disabling the injured worker and of preventing him from earning any further income. His reduced earning power, in turn, may have serious consequences for the general economic and social status of his family, with all the subsequent effects on family life, health, and education of children, which usually accompany a lowering of the laborer's scale of living. Such a reduction of the earning capacity of the victims of industrial accidents means the loss of financial support for all those who have been dependent upon the disabled person. In one way or another, the financial support of these dependents may have to be provided out of public funds. Finally, there are the loss of life and the physical suffering incident upon work injuries for which there can be no compensation.

The costs of medical and hospital care, whether paid for directly, or indirectly in the form of insurance premiums to an insurance company, are entrepreneurial outlays and as such cannot be considered as social costs. The same is true of the costs caused by the loss of time and by damage to materials and equipment. These losses are also borne by the firm and as such are not social costs. However, it would be a mistake to believe that the entrepreneur has a clear conception of the nature and size of these costs of work injuries. Most indirect accident cost items are hidden and affect many or all productive processes. Moreover, in so far as compensation and medical costs are paid by an insurance company the entrepreneur is likely to consider these costs as solely the concern of the carrier. "He realizes that insurance premium rates are based on experience. However, since the experience of the individual small employer is so small a part of the total on which the rates are based and since a considerable part of his premium goes to overhead expenses and profit, it is very difficult for him to obtain a premium reduction even reasonably commensurate with his reduction in accidents. Private insurance companies generally find it impractical to give any form of merit rating to a risk whose premium averages less than about $500–$750 per year . . . The result is that the average small policy holder, unless he is threatened with the possibility of increased premiums or canceled coverage, has little direct financial incentive to reduce accidents. Ignorant of the 'indirect costs,' he feels that his premium covers practically the entire cost of injury, and that a reduction in costs is of concern only to the insurer." [8]

By far the greater part of the repercussions of work injuries on the injured worker and his family are not reflected in entrepreneurial outlays. Even if the injured worker receives compensation for the loss of income, he is usually entitled to only a fraction of his normal wage. Payments for permanent total or partial disability may, and in many cases do, fall short substantially of the actual loss of earning power occasioned by the disability. In case of death even the most liberal compensation usually fails to avert financial disaster for the worker's family. In addition, as will be pointed out below, several categories of workers (such as workers in small plants, domestic servants, farm workers, workers in nonhazardous employments, and those whose employers are free to choose not to be covered by compensation laws) are not protected by workmen's compensation acts and may have to bear the *full* effects of work injuries.

3. Occupational Diseases

Perhaps less dramatic but certainly not less destructive than industrial accidents are occupational diseases. It is a matter of common knowledge that workers in certain industries are exposed to and suffer from various typical diseases, which are followed sooner or later by extended or permanent incapacity for work. The following are the principal industrial health hazards primarily responsible for occupational diseases: abnormalities of temperature and humidity, compressed air, dampness, defective illumination, dust, infections, radiant energy (x-rays, radium and other radioactive substances), repeated motion, pressure, shock, etc., and poisons.[9] There are no less than 94 industrial poisons,[10] that is, "raw materials and

---

[8] *Safety Subjects,* p. 15.

[9] L. J. Dublin and R. J. Vane, *Occupation Hazards and Diagnostic Signs,* U. S. Department of Labor, Bureau of Statistics, Bulletin No. 582 (Washington: U. S. Government Printing Office, 1933), pp. 13–49.

[10] *Ibid.,* pp. 27–49.

products, by-products and waste products which in their extraction, manufacture and use in industrial processes, notwithstanding the exercises of ordinary precaution, may find entrance into the body in such quantities as to endanger, by their chemical action, the health of the workmen employed." [11] One of these industrial poisons, "lead, is in daily use in about 150 trades, causing 'painters' colic,' 'wrist drop,' or even death. Connected with dusty trades of all sorts, from silk weaving to quarrying, are found nonpoisonous dusts which by infiltration and mechanical irritation produce various occupational lung diseases. One of the most common of these is silicosis, a disease of the lungs, common among rock drillers, granite cutters and others who work over a period of years in an atmosphere loaded with fine silica dust . . . Anthrax . . . may infect tanners and makers of hair goods, while . . . 'miners' hookworm' menaces those who toil in warmth and moisture underground. Less easy to trace are the more obscure ailments which may arise in any industry, from insufficient or excessive lighting, from extremes of heat, cold, and humidity, or from work too heavy, too persistent, and too intense without adequate periods of rest." [12] More generally, it has been shown that the speed and monotony of modern industrial processes are liable to create serious disturbances in the human organism and frequently have injurious effects upon the workers' health.

J. A. Hobson was one of the first to stress these effects of modern production. He called attention to the fact that muscular and nervous overstrain often result in injurious fatigue, nervous disorder, greater susceptibility to industrial and nonindustrial diseases and accidents, and other physical and moral injuries which are the natural accompaniments of this overstrain. Hobson, likewise, stressed the ill effects resulting from irregular employment and "the related injury inflicted on the physique and morale of the worker by sandwiching periods of overexertion between intervals of idleness." [13]

As in the case of industrial accidents, the social losses of occupa-

[11] J. R. Commons and J. B. Andrews, *Principles of Labor Legislation* (New York: Harper and Brothers, 1936), p. 166.   [12] *Ibid.*, p. 166.
[13] J. A. Hobson, *Work and Wealth—A Human Valuation* (copyright 1914 by J. A. Hobson; used with the permission of The Macmillan Company), p. 80.

tional diseases are reflected in entrepreneurial outlays only to the extent that they reduce the efficiency of the laborer. When a loss of efficiency occurs, injuries find expression in higher labor costs and are passed on to the consumer in the price of the product. Similarly, if employers bear the costs of medical care and pay compensation either directly by meeting the claims of the injured workers or indirectly by paying premiums into an insurance fund, losses from occupational diseases are translated into direct costs of production.

However, neither reduced efficiency nor compensation payments constitute an adequate measure of the total losses caused by occupational diseases. Most compensation acts cover only a selected list of industries and occupations. In addition, there is always the possibility that employers will be able to avoid legal responsibility of paying compensation by replacing workers whose productivity is reduced as the result of occupational diseases. Furthermore, it must not be overlooked that it is difficult to determine "where and when an occupational disease was originally acquired, or whether a disease is occupational in origin or not, or the extent to which a latent disease is accelerated by conditions which might in themselves have independently but more slowly produced an occupational disease." [14] This difficulty not only causes serious problems in the technical administration of workmen's compensation acts but may give rise to a shift of some of the costs of production to the shoulders of injured workers and their dependents. This is especially true in the absence of a general system of health insurance which would at least offer sick benefits to the injured worker for diseases not covered by compensation acts. In these instances the injured worker or his family bear part of the ill consequences of occupational diseases.

4. Woman and Child Labor

Today there exists substantial agreement as to the general character of the social losses caused by the employment of women and children. Here again the social losses may be difficult to trace because

[14] W. F. Dodd, *Administration of Workmen's Compensation* (New York: The Commonwealth Fund, 1936), p. 772.

the ill consequences of woman and child labor affect not only the health of the woman or child worker but may undermine the state of health of the worker's family and the well-being of the young generation. Such social losses are likely to arise because "the distinctive physical characteristics of women make them more susceptible than men to certain industrial hazards. Noise and vibration probably have a more detrimental effect upon their nervous systems; long periods of standing or sitting have been demonstrated to be injurious to them and their offspring; overstrain is more likely to produce organic disturbances; and there is respectable medical opinion that women exhibit greater susceptibility to some industrial poisons than do men." [15] In view of these facts, it is not surprising to find that morbidity rates are substantially higher for working women than for nonworking women and that infant mortality among children born to working women is similarly higher than among women who do not work.[16]

The social losses resulting from the employment of children and young persons are equally significant. "When children leave school at an early age and seek gainful employment, their opportunity for normal physical development . . . is curtailed. Normal family life very often is disrupted. Frequently, thrown into environments that are conducive to harshness, crudity, roughness and disrespect for the privileges and immunities of others, child workers are likely to become juvenile delinquents and public charges." [17] In addition, the gainful employment of children usually implies a restriction of opportunities for education. As a result of limited educational opportunities, their mental faculties are not fully developed; adaptability to occupational conditions is reduced and general productivity in later years lessened. Moreover, child labor not only is responsible for raising the accident rates of the trades in which children work but also results in bad health of the children in later years because "un-

---

[15] From *The Economics of Labor*, vol. I, *Labor's Progress and Some Basic Labor Problems*, by H. A. Millis and R. E. Montgomery, copyright, 1938, p. 404. Courtesy of McGraw-Hill Book Company.

[16] *Ibid.*, p. 404.

[17] *Ibid.*, p. 417.

developed muscular and nervous systems are unable to resist the strain incident to many industrial occupations . . ." [18]

The employment of women and children is thus seen to give rise to social losses which go far beyond those sustained by the individual woman or child laborer. By disrupting family life and by preventing the full mental development of young persons, woman and child labor may have particularly far-reaching and detrimental effects upon society and future generations.

5. Evidence of Social Costs Resulting from the Impairment of the Human Factor

It is difficult to indicate with any degree of accuracy the possible magnitude of the social losses caused by the impairment of the human factor of production in modern industrial societies. Available statistical data on the number, frequency, and effects of industrial accidents and occupational diseases offer only a partial answer to the question as to the actual magnitude of the social costs resulting therefrom. Most of these data are intended to indicate the total number of injured persons, the number of man-hours lost, or the annual wage loss caused by work injuries. Such figures do not reveal the extent to which the total losses are shifted to and actually borne by the injured worker and his dependents.

And yet, it is significant to note that more than two million workers are being disabled by work injuries annually. Approximately 20,000 of these injuries represent fatalities and permanent total disabilities, whereas up to 100,000 persons are permanently partially disabled—the impairments varying from the loss or loss of use of both eyes, both hands or arms, or both legs or feet to the partial loss or loss of use of eyes, hands, and fingers, legs, etc. (see Appendix III). The annual loss of working time caused by temporary total disabilities only has been estimated at 32,000,000 man-days of working time.[19] This is a conservative figure which does not take into consideration the loss of productive capacity due to permanent disablements and

[18] *Ibid.*, p. 418.
[19] *Safety Subjects*, p. 1.

due to death caused by work injuries. The annual loss of productive capacity due to temporary total, permanent partial, and permanent total disabilities, as well as to fatal work injuries, has been estimated at approximately 250 million man-days in the United States.[20] This does not include output lost owing to interruptions of work and other related indirect consequences of work injuries.

The National Safety Council places the total monetary losses caused by work injuries at 2 to 2.6 billion dollars, of which 800 million dollars represent loss of wages, approximately 130 million dollars are medical expenses, 300 to 400 million dollars go for overhead cost of insurance, and 1300 million dollars represent indirect costs (see Appendix IV).

In order to calculate the social costs resulting from the impairment of the human factor in the course of private productive activities it is necessary to determine the extent to which existing schemes of social insurance and workmen's compensation fail to translate these losses into entrepreneurial outlays. In other words, it is necessary to calculate the ratio of the compensation received to the sum total of losses sustained.

While it is impossible, in the light of available figures and in view of the lack of uniformity of existing workmen's compensation acts, to arrive at an over-all proportion of losses compensated, it is feasible to calculate a ratio of wage losses compensated. To this effect, it is necessary first to have an idea of the relative inadequacy of existing workmen's compensation acts. The most important factors making for an inadequate compensation of losses due to work injuries are incomplete coverage of occupations, waiting periods, and insufficient indemnification scales. Despite the steadily expanding scope of workmen's compensation, the most recent measurement of coverage based upon 1940 census data indicate that only approximately 27.2 million employees or about 53 per cent of the nation's working force were covered by workmen's compensation acts. The proportion of eligible employees covered was 82 per cent in 1940. The most important cate-

[20] H. A. Millis and R. E. Montgomery, *The Economics of Labor*, vol. II, *Labor's Risk and Social Insurance*, p. 187.

gories of workers normally excluded are domestic and farm workers. Other persons not covered by workmen's compensation acts of certain states are workers engaged in nonhazardous employments and employees of small firms as well as casual workers and public employees. These figures represent the results of the most recent measurement of coverage.[21] Earlier studies placed the number of eligible employees not covered by compensation acts at 6.5 million "or 29.8 per cent of the total of employees . . . in the 45 compensation states."[22]

Furthermore, all compensation acts provide for waiting periods (ranging from 3 days to 2 weeks) before any compensation can be claimed. The declared purpose of such waiting periods is to bar temporary injuries and fraudulent claims. However, it has been estimated that "for the country as a whole . . . 44 per cent of temporary injuries are barred altogether . . . While another 45 per cent are compensated, but not for the waiting period."[23]

A third reason for the inadequacy of existing workmen's compensation acts is to be found in far-reaching limitations placed upon benefit and compensation payments which tend to make for a totally insufficient indemnification of the impaired worker. Thus, most laws place an arbitarary limit on the amount and duration of death benefits. Rates of compensation for dependents in case of fatal injuries vary from less than 50 per cent to 70 per cent (in only two states) of weekly earnings and, in most instances, are limited as to both duration and maximum total compensation, irrespective of working-life expectancy.[24] Similarly, compensation for permanent total disability falls far short of full indemnification for the total loss of earning power for the rest of the injured worker's life. Not only is the compensation substantially below past average earnings, but

[21] A. H. Reede, *Adequacy of Workmen's Compensation* (Cambridge: Harvard University Press, 1947), pp. 9–29, 56.

[22] C. Hookstadt, *Comparison of Workmen's Compensation Laws of the United States and Canada up to January 1, 1920,* U. S. Department of Labor, Bureau of Labor Statistics, Bulletin No. 275 (Washington: U. S. Government Printing Office, 1920), p. 36.

[23] A. H. Reede, *Adequacy of Workmen's Compensation,* p. 58.

[24] *Ibid.,* p. 92.

benefit scales also limit payments as to both maximum amount and maximum duration, which again bear no relation to working-life expectancy. Similar limitations apply to compensation benefits for permanent partial disabilities. The most important shortcomings are compensation at "less than 66⅔ per cent of past earnings, weekly maximums of less than $25, and period or amount limitations in serious cases shorter than working-life expectancy." [25] The existing scales of benefits for the overwhelming majority of industrial injuries, namely, cases resulting in temporary disabilities, are likewise severely limited and restrictive. As far as the scale of medical benefits is concerned, suffice it to mention that payments are usually limited as to maximum duration and maximum amounts (the two respective weighted averages being 63.0 days and $258.12 as of July 1940).[26] At the same time "the large industrial state of Pennsylvania retains an inflexible 60-day limit, and provides compensation in excess of $150 only for hospitalization. In Vermont . . . limits of two weeks and $50 are raised to thirty days and $100 in hospital cases." [27]

The foregoing highly condensed summary of an extremely heterogeneous system of provisions governing compensation payments for work injuries in the United States was necessary in order to make more intelligible the following observations concerning the probable magnitude of the social costs of work injuries expressed in terms of the proportion of the wage loss borne by the injured worker or his family. On the basis of an ingenious calculation of the working-life expectancy of gainfully employed workers and by using standard percentages of disability for the calculation of severity of different work injuries leading to partial disabilities such as the loss of one eye or the loss of a finger, A. H. Reede[28] was able to estimate the total wage loss of injured workers in Massachusetts in 1935 for fatal and permanent total and permanent partial disability cases. By comparing this figure with the compensation actually paid it was possible to calculate the proportion of the wage loss borne by the injured

[25] *Ibid.*, p. 169.
[26] *Ibid.*, p. 163.
[27] *Ibid.*, p. 172.
[28] *Ibid.*, pp. 187–192.

worker. The results of these calculations together with the corresponding figures of temporary disabilities are listed in Table 1.

TABLE 1

PROPORTION OF WAGE LOSS COMPENSATED IN MASSACHUSETTS[1]
(Policy Year 1935)

Extent of disability	Number of cases	Estimated wage loss[2]	Compensation paid or reserved[3]	Per cent compensated
Fatal..............	178	$ 4,085,000	$ 602,521	14.7
Permanent total.....	13	207,000	138,488	66.9
Major permanent....	443	3,219,000	1,090,304	33.9
Minor permanent...	724	760,000	297,876	39.2
Temporary.........	19,262	3,823,000	2,098,987	54.9
Total...........	20,620	$12,067,000	$4,180,469	35.0

[1] A. H. Reede, *Adequacy of Workmen's Compensation* (Cambridge: Harvard University Press, 1947), p. 212.

[2] From an analysis of individual case reports of serious and other open cases furnished by the Massachusetts Rating and Inspection Bureau, and for other cases estimated from reports filed with the Massachusetts Department of Industrial Accidents. In temporary cases, estimate is based on weekly wage and dates of injury and reëmployment, or termination of disability. In fatal or permanent total cases it is based on weekly wage, and on working-life expectancy. In partial disability cases working-life expectancy was multiplied by per cent of disability.

[3] As reported to the Massachusetts Rating and Inspection Bureau, except for adjustments where amendments changed the benefit scale during the policy year 1935.

In the light of these data it appears that the social costs of work injuries expressed in terms of the percentage of wage losses borne by the injured worker varies from 85.3 per cent in the case of fatal injuries to 33.1 per cent in the case of permanent total injuries. For all cases the proportion of wage losses absorbed by the injured worker would be 65 per cent. In short, considerably more than half of the total wage loss caused by work injuries is borne by the injured workers. These figures apply to Massachusetts. In other states, with even less adequate provisions for the compensation of injured workers, a still larger proportion of the total wage loss tends to be absorbed by the injured person and his family.

The foregoing calculations concerning the relative magnitude of the social costs of work injuries do not include losses sustained by injured workers and their families as a result of the failure of private insurance companies which carry the employers' insurance against liabilities arising from workmen's compensation acts. These private carriers "have frequently failed with heavy losses both to the insured employers and to the injured workers, their widows and dependents." [29] According to Dodd the failure of six stock companies before 1924 "involved compensation claims of substantial amount . . . and . . . three of these failures resulted in thousands of dollars of unpaid compensation claims." [30] In one of these cases "the legislature of California appropriated between $60,000 and $70,000 of public money to pay in full the larger claims of employees of that State. In other states either the employers or the injured employees had to bear the loss, depending on whether the compensation act made the employer liable in the event of the failure of the insurance company." [31] Writing during the Great Depression of the thirties, the Industrial Commissioner of the State of New York, speaks of "the appalling suffering that has been visited upon thousands of injured wage earners, their families and survivors by the failure of 18 stock companies which have been placed in liquidation by court order since June 1, 1927 . . . These 18 companies have a total workmen's compensation liability estimated at about $2,600,000. Approximately 6,500 claims for workmen's compensation are on file against these insolvent companies . . . In hundreds of instances, workers who have received awards have been unable to collect a penny of compensation, either from the insolvent insurance carriers or their own employers, who in many instances are financially unable to pay. As a result, these injured workers and their families have been forced upon private and public relief rolls." [32] While numerous similar examples of failure and estimates of losses might be quoted,[33] it would

[29] J. B. Andrews, *Progress of State Insurance Funds Under Workmen's Compensation*, U. S. Department of Labor, Division of Labor Standards, Bulletin No. 30 (Washington: U. S. Government Printing Office, 1939), p. 11.

[30] W. F. Dodd, *Administration of Workmen's Compensation*, p. 541.

[31] *Ibid.*, p. 541.

[32] E. F. Andrews, "Exclusive State Fund Needed for Compensation Insurance," *American Labor Legislation Review*, XXIII–XXIV (December 1934), pp. 165–166.

[33] For a further discussion of such examples, see W. F. Dodd, *op. cit.*, pp. 544–552.

still be impossible to present a complete picture of the total social losses resulting therefrom owing to the absence of any information regarding the total number of stock company failures and the results of their financial liquidation.

The social costs caused by occupational diseases are doubtless of considerable magnitude, although the great differences in the existing legal situation in various states make any precise calculation of the proportion of total losses borne by the affected worker or his dependents difficult if not impossible. The original workmen's compensation acts made no provision for the coverage of occupational diseases. And even at present, occupational diseases covered in one state may not be covered in others and many such diseases are still completely outside the scope of compensation acts. A similar lack of uniformity exists with respect to the coverage and treatment of the problem of aggravating existing diseases or illness only indirectly attributable to the occupation. A more thorough analysis of the conditions under which workers injured by occupational diseases go without compensation would require a highly technical discussion of certain legal and administrative problems inherent in the operation of workmen's compensation acts. Such an analysis lies, however, outside the scope of the present study.[34] Suffice it to say, therefore, that in so far as workmen's compensation acts cover occupational diseases at all, they apply in many cases only to a specified list of diseases and place maximum limits as to amount and duration of compensation payments. This inadequacy of present workmen's compensation acts is usually defended on the ground of incalculable and excessive costs. Needless to say, this amounts, particularly in the absence of a national health insurance system, to a shift of the losses caused by occupational diseases to the worker and his family.

The social losses caused by child labor are not subject to monetary calculations. Suffice it to say that although the regulation of the employment of young persons has made considerable progress in recent decades and tends to follow a well-defined pattern, existing laws still

[34] See, however, W. F. Dodd, op. cit., pp. 757–783, and A. H. Reede, op. cit., pp. 45–53.

vary widely "in the standards of conditions which they set up for the employment of boys and girls. They are also extremely uneven in the occupations to which they apply. Some provisions extend to all gainful employment. Many, however, apply only to specified establishments or occupations, or exempt certain types of employment, such as work in agriculture, in domestic service in private homes, in the sale and distribution of newspapers and magazines. Thus, even within a state, a child-labor law may not apply equally to all children." [35] It is noteworthy that the majority of state child-labor laws in the United States place the minimum age for the employment of youth in factories below 16. Only four states have a 16-year minimum for all employment during school hours.

The most significant aspect of the "human costs" of production is the fact that they are avoidable. Competent authorities have estimated that from 70 to 90 per cent of all work injuries could be prevented by proper safety devices. If instead of being prevented they are permitted to occur and to cause social costs of considerable magnitude, this is due to a combination of ignorance of the actual costs of work injuries and unwillingness and inability of the individual firm to bear, under conditions of competitive enterprise, the costs of adequate safety and accident-prevention programs. As it is, therefore, it may be said that to the extent of the social losses caused by the impairment of the human factor private enterprise has been subsidized by the men and women who make up the labor force employed in modern industry. While there is at least a presumption that the value of the original capital equipment is being kept intact through the use of depreciation charges, the "capital value" of the human factor of production has certainly not been maintained in the relatively short history of industrial society. If instead of 20,000 workers, 20,000 head of cattle were exposed to certain death due to an epidemic and recurrent disease, there would be an easily calculable incentive to adopt required preventive measures. It is the fact, then,

---

[35] L. Manning and N. Diamond, *State Child-Labor Standards,* U. S. Department of Labor, Child-Labor Series, No. 2 (Washington: U. S. Government Printing Office, 1946), p. 5.

that the human factor of production has no capital value, which places it in a market economy in a less favorable position than non-human means of production.

Summarizing the preceding discussion, it may be said that modern industrial production tends to give rise to a serious impairment of the physical and mental health of the individual worker. Among the more important of these human costs of production are the ill effects of industrial accidents, occupational diseases and the employment of women and children. In its economic implications, such impairment of the physical and mental health of human beings does not differ from the deterioration of nonhuman durable agents of production. And yet, whereas the depreciation of the latter tends to be translated into entrepreneurial outlays by means of depreciation charges, damages to persons would remain unaccounted for in private costs if the competitive process were left to itself. As a matter of fact, in the absence of protective labor legislation and compulsory social insurance, these human costs of production not only would be shifted to and borne by the individual but would also be considerably greater than they are at present. Workmen's compensation acts, by placing upon the employer the financial responsibility for work injuries regardless of fault, have had the effect of translating some of these human costs of production into entrepreneurial expenditures. Despite the fact that a considerable extension of protective labor legislation has taken place in recent decades, all available evidence points to the conclusion that the present scope and operation of existing laws still permit the shifting of the major part of the human costs of production to the injured worker and his dependents, or to the community.

5

THE SOCIAL COSTS OF AIR POLLUTION

IN CONTRAST to the widespread recognition of the losses caused by the impairment of the human factor, the social costs of air and water pollution have attracted much less attention. This is probably due to the fact that the causal relation between productive activities and air and water pollution is more complex and less easily seen than the relatively clear connection that exists between private production and, say, industrial accidents. Moreover, whereas the impairment of human health by industrial accidents and occupational diseases tends to affect a relatively well-organized group of persons all of whom have a strong interest in the prevention of the risks and dangers to which they are exposed in their daily work, the harmful consequences of the pollution of the atmosphere and the contamination of water by various kinds of industrial waste products are usually felt by a highly heterogeneous, unorganized group of persons. Their reaction is, therefore, less articulate than that of injured workers in the case of industrial accidents and occupational diseases. Nevertheless, there can be no doubt that the social costs of air and water pollution are considerable. In the United States these costs may well reach several billion dollars annually. The present chapter is devoted to a study of the social costs of air pollution; the problem of water pollution will be discussed in the following chapter.

The pollution of the atmosphere by smoke antedates the era of modern industrial production. In fact, evidence of the smoke nuisance resulting from the domestic use of coal can be found as early as the fourteenth century, and later, in Queen Elizabeth's reign, when the burning of coal in private houses in London was prohibited—at least "while Parliament was sitting." [1] While the domestic use of coal continues to be a contributing cause of atmospheric pollution, it is primarily the emanations of smoke and gas from industrial establishments, railroads and large heating plants which, at present, cause most of the prevailing air pollution. Indeed, the large-scale replacement of man and horse power by such energy resources as bituminous coal and oil has made air pollution a common and characteristic phenomenon around many industrial centers. Nor can it be assumed that the replacement of coal and oil by atomic energy may one day eliminate the pollution of the atmosphere. On the contrary, recent experiments with radioactive disposal systems seem to indicate that radioactive waste materials—solids, liquids and gases —may get into the air and represent not only short-lived but long-lived risks for neighboring cities and countries. In fact, if not properly controlled, the problem of air pollution in the atomic age may well become world-wide.

The manner in which present industrial production tends to give rise to air pollution need not occupy us to any great extent. Suffice it to point out that the formation of smoke and other gaseous emanations is almost invariably a sign of improper and incomplete combustion of fuels;[2] in other words, the existence of smoke is always

---

[1] Sir F. E. Smith, "Coal, Power, and Smoke," *The Journal of the National Smoke Abatement Society,* VII, No. 25 (1936), p. 19.

[2] Thus, the combustion of raw bituminous coals is incomplete if the construction and operation of the furnace, or the method of firing and the supply of draft, interfere with the development of proper heat. Under these conditions, the volatile content—i.e., the gaseous portion of bituminous coals, the distillation of which takes place even at temperatures below the ignition point—burns with an improper mixture of air, or may strike cooling surfaces that will reduce its temperature below the ignition point. In both cases, the unconsumed parts of the coal will be entrained by the upward rush of hot air and form, in association with carbon and tarry matter condensed by premature chilling of flame together with dust and ash, the visible smoke. According to the kind of fuel and the manner in which it is burned, this coal smoke will consist of greater or smaller amounts of gases (such as carbon dioxide,

indicative of technical inefficiencies in the use of energy resources. Such inefficiencies fail to be eliminated whenever the private returns (or savings) obtainable from their elimination are not high enough to cover the private costs involved. The fact that the resulting pollution of the atmosphere may cause substantial losses to other people will not and cannot normally be considered in the cost-return calculations of private enterprise.

In order to obtain a clear idea of these social costs of air pollution it is helpful to distinguish between the effects of smoke on property values, on human health and on plant and animal life.

1. Destruction of Property Values

The most obvious of the ill effects of smoke are those evidenced in the progressive destruction and premature deterioration of building materials, metals, paint coatings, merchandise, etc. Thus the various sulphur compounds contained in smoke have a destructive effect on stone and metals, corroding or disintegrating "practically all kinds of building materials (slate and granite possibly excepted); marble tends first to turn green and then black, limestone deteriorates very rapidly, turning to gypsum owing to its great affinity for sulphur. The absorption of sulphur causes the stone to expand, thus rendering it soluble and powdery so that particles are constantly washed or

---

carbon monoxide, oxygen, nitrogen, ammonia, sulphur dioxide and other sulphur compounds, unburned or partly burned fuel in the form of coke, mineral matter or ash, tar, and very fine particles of free carbon. Though not all these smoke elements are necessarily air pollutants, they may, nevertheless, become harmful under certain conditions. It is also noteworthy in this connection that the better-grade solid fuels such as anthracite and coke contain little or no volatile matter and can be burned almost completely and without smoke emission. The combustion of liquid fuel, such as oil, is generally better controlled because it takes place in a specially designed burner "which atomizes the oil and feeds it in a uniform stream and which also provides for the introduction and mixing of air in, or close to, the burner where the mixture is ignited." Nevertheless, under certain conditions the combustion of oil, too, may be incomplete, with the result that smoke is produced. "Such smoke is a tarry, greasy pollutant which coats whatever it touches, and which can also carry along with it any sulphuric or sulphurous acid with which it comes in contact, whether these resulted from the sulphur which was in the oil or came from outside sources." This summary is based upon H. B. Meller and L. B. Sisson, *The Municipal Smoke Problem* (Pittsburgh, 1935), pp. 8–16 (for quotations see p. 14).

blown away." [3] Materials such as stone, mortar, concrete, etc., are "soiled by soot and the necessary cleaning by wire brush and detergent chemicals, a sandblast or other drastic methods, is not only costly, but injures the stone itself." [4] Metals, if exposed to smoke-polluted air, suffer not only from soot and tar but also from the presence of obnoxious gases and acid vapors. While "the destruction of iron is most noticeable, for it is the metal in most common use and it is more readily corroded than the majority of metals," [5] there is hardly any metal which is not susceptible to the corrosive action of smoke. In fact, "the sulphuretted hydrogen in smoke blackens, disfigures or tarnishes nearly all metals. Copper and bronze rapidly darken . . . aluminum is affected by vapors and acids, many metals become pitted from electrochemical action and even gold and gilded articles become dull." [6]

Protective paint coatings applied to metallic surfaces and other materials are subject to contamination by atmospheric carbon and dust which tends to reduce their protective efficiency and makes necessary frequent washing.

Experiments made in England showed "the corrosion of unprotected iron work to be six times as rapid in town air as in the pure country air." [7] Further evidence of the destructive effect of smoke on metals may be found in Appendix V, which shows data concerning the relative length of time different sheet metals last in Pittsburgh and in a smoke-free atmosphere. These data indicate that metals in Pittsburgh must be renewed in one-half the time that would be necessary if there were no smoke. Metallic surfaces in Pittsburgh are painted about twice as often as is necessary in such cities as Washington, D. C.

---

[3] Smoke Investigation, University of Pittsburgh, Department of Industrial Research, Bulletin No. 3, *Psychological Aspects of the Problem of Atmospheric Smoke Pollution* (Pittsburgh, 1913), p. 36.

[4] H. B. Meller, "Air Pollution from the Engineer's Standpoint," *Heating, Piping and Air Conditioning,* Journal Section (January, 1931), p. 2.

[5] *Ibid.,* p. 3.

[6] Smoke Investigation, Bulletin No. 3, p. 37.

[7] Smoke Investigation Bulletin No. 6, *Papers on the Effect of Smoke on Building Materials* (Pittsburgh, 1913), p. 46.

Furthermore, smoke-polluted air affects the interior of buildings and interior decorations. Air-conditioning and ventilating equipment in particular are subject to corrosion and have been seen to fail within a period of three months owing to smoke-polluted air.[8] Similarly, factory smoke is responsible for the deterioration of the quality and value of all kinds of merchandise, causing substantial losses to wholesale and retail businesses. In addition, air pollution causes social losses as a result of the necessity of more frequent household cleaning and washing.[9]

2. Smoke and Human Health

The social costs of atmospheric pollution go far beyond the losses resulting from the more rapid deterioration of building materials, metals, and paint coatings. Several students of the problem of air pollution have pointed to the injurious effects which the loss of daylight and of ultraviolet light may have upon human health. The most important damages to persons seem to be caused by the inhalation of smoke-polluted air. The poisonous compounds and soot particles contained in smoke-polluted air may serve "as carriers of the obnoxious products of human fatigue which irritate the sensitive membranes of the eyes, nose, throat, lungs, and gastro-intestinal tract, increase the susceptibility of gastro-intestinal pulmonary and nasopharyngeal disorders, diminish the potential reserve, working capacity, and well-being of the individual, increase fatigue, irritability and malcontent, and may tend to hasten premature decay."[10]

Other less direct effects of air pollution on human health are re-

[8] H. B. Meller and L. B. Sisson, "Effects of Smoke on Building Materials," *Industrial and Engineering Chemistry*, XXVII (November 1935), p. 1311.

[9] This was demonstrated by a comparison of costs of household washing in Manchester—a smoky town—and Harrogate—a clean town. The comparison made by the Manchester Air Pollution Advisory Board in 1918 showed "an extra cost in Manchester of $7\frac{1}{2}d.$ a week per household for fuel and washing material. The total loss for the whole city, taking the extra cost of fuel and washing materials alone, disregarding the extra labour involved and assuming no greater loss for middle-class than for working-class households (a considerable under-statement), works out at over £290,000 a year for a population of three-quarters of a million." See A. C. Pigou, *The Economics of Welfare*, p. 185, n. 4.

[10] Smoke Investigation, Bulletin No. 3, p. 41.

vealed by the following brief analysis of the influence which factory smoke may have upon weather and general meteorological conditions. To be exact, air pollution and weather conditions influence each other. The presence of smoke in the atmosphere tends to increase the relative humidity and affects adversely the character of daylight; and similarly, high temperatures, low winds and high relative humidity add to the intensity of air pollution in any given locality. In particular, it was found that "smoke lessens the duration and intensity of sunshine; reduces the intensity of daylight, the limit of visibility and the diurnal winter temperature; increases humidity, mists, the frequency and duration of fogs[11] and possibly alters the electrical potential." [12] Moreover, "fogs may become mixed with smoke to such an extent that their color is changed from white to brown, or even black and prevent sunlight from penetrating to the level of the street. Heat rays as well as light rays are thus stopped so that evaporation of the fog is retarded." [13]

There is no lack of evidence of these adverse influences of smoke on general weather conditions. Investigations in such towns as Leeds, Sheffield and Manchester show that the duration of sunshine "is in winter months less than half that in outlying districts. In summer, the deficiency is less marked, but the intensity is at all times impaired, particularly in respect to the ultraviolet rays." [14] More recent investigations of the loss of light due to smoke in Great Britain compare the intensity of daylight in two centers of Halifax during the year April 1931–March 1932 and point to the fact that "the more heavily polluted centre received 20 per cent less light than the other, the loss being greater in the winter months and amounting in December 1931 to nearly 50 per cent." [15] Similarly, it has been estimated that 20 per cent of all London fogs are due to smoke.[16]

[11] This is apparently due to the fact that "smoke . . . contains hygroscopic particles which act as nuclei for the condensation of water vapor and tend to produce wet fogs in chilled air . . . ," "Smoke and Smoke Prevention," *Encyclopaedia Britannica* (ed. 14, 1929), vol. 20, p. 841.
[12] Smoke Investigation, Bulletin No. 3, p. 41.
[13] H. B. Meller and L. B. Sisson, *The Municipal Smoke Problem,* p. 18.
[14] "Smoke and Smoke Prevention," p. 841.
[15] F. E. Smith, "Coal, Power, and Smoke," p. 21.
[16] J. W. Graham, *The Destruction of Daylight,* pp. 6 and 24 (quoted from A. C. Pigou, *The Economics of Welfare,* p. 184, n. 3).

Investigations of the smoke nuisance and its effects on light in the United States established the fact that "city fogs are more persistent than country fogs, principally because of their increased density due to the smoke that accumulates in them." [17] This, in turn, leads to less intense sunshine as well as to "fewer hours of sunshine in the cities than in the surrounding country." [18]

A special study of the loss of light due to smoke on Manhattan Island emphasizes that "in some cases the average hourly or daily percentage loss was greater than 50. The average percentage loss for the whole year was 16.6 for clear days, 34.6 for cloudy days, and 21.5 for all days. The percentage loss on cloudy days was, therefore, about twice as great as on clear days." [19]

In the light of these findings it is not difficult to understand why a smoke-filled atmosphere may have far-reaching effects upon human health and all animal and plant life. The loss of sunshine and the exclusion of ultraviolet radiation reduces physical vitality and makes the human body more susceptible to colds and other bacterial infections.[20] Moreover, humidity intensified by smoke increases the solid poisonous contents of the air, aggravates various pathological conditions of the body, reduces the sensibility of some organs and depletes the vital potential.[21] Fogs likewise "increase the prevalence of diseases and augment the death rate." [22] Still other disadvantages accrue from the fact that artificial light made necessary by the loss of sunshine has injurious effects on human health inasmuch as colorless daylight is superior for visual efficiency, and optical health.[23]

It must be noted, however, that the gradual absorption by the human system of the poisonous products of imperfect combustion

[17] Smoke Investigation, Bulletin No. 5, *The Meteorological Aspects of the Smoke Problem* (Pittsburgh, 1913), p. 30.

[18] *Ibid.*, p. 30. See also H. B. Meller and M. E. Warga, "Effects of Air Contaminants on the Natural Light of Cities," *American Journal of Public Health*, XXIII, No. 3 (March 1933), pp. 217–224.

[19] J. E. Ives, "A Study of the Loss of Light due to Smoke on Manhattan Island, New York City during the Year 1927," U. S. Public Health Service, *Studies in Illumination*, Public Health Bulletin No. 197 (1930), p. 38.

[20] H. B. Meller, "Air Pollution from the Engineer's Standpoint," p. 5.

[21] Smoke Investigation, Bulletin No. 3, p. 42.

[22] *Ibid.*, p. 42.

[23] *Ibid.*, p. 41.

does not necessarily "give rise to any definitely recognizable acute disorder or specific disabilities. But the process of slow poisoning may insidiously eat away like a mild cancer at vital tissues and thus in time deplete our potential reserve . . ." [24]

3. Effects upon Plant and Animal Life

The effects of air pollution upon plant and animal life have been the subject of careful investigations carried out under the auspices of the International Institute of Agriculture in Rome. According to these studies, the sulphur and sulphur dioxide[25] in coal smoke affects the fertility of the soils and attacks the metabolic system of plants. By washing out of the soil such important elements as potash, calcium and magnesium, the pollution of the atmosphere tends to affect practically all garden and field vegetation in and around industrial districts. Animals are affected by air pollution not so much as a result of inhalation as by ingestion of forage exposed to gaseous emanations. For "plants attacked by toxic emanations . . . themselves become toxic, and their consumption, continued for a certain time, may cause fatal chronic toxic conditions in animals." [26]

Evidence of the harmful effects of smoke on the fertility of the soil is found in the fact that the soil of all smoke districts tends to become poor in potash, calcium, and magnesium—"a fact particularly noticeable in the mining districts of Czechoslovakia." [27] Dr. Stoklasa emphasizes that careful observations in the mining and factory districts of Czechoslovakia

[24] Ibid., p. 8; H. B. Meller, "A Modern Plan for a Community Campaign against Air Pollution," American Journal of the Medical Sciences, No. 2 (August 1933), pp. 157 ff. After the present study had been completed, a thorough investigation into the effects of smoke on health and other aspects of air pollution was made and published under the auspices of the U. S. Public Health Service. The investigation was undertaken after twenty persons died and several thousand became ill during the smog that enveloped the town of Donora, Pa. in October 1948. See Air Pollution in Donora, Pa., Public Health Bulletin No. 306 (Washington: Federal Security Agency, 1949).

[25] These substances are encountered primarily "in the manufacture of sulphuric acid from pyrites, also in foundries, chemical works, ultramarine, soda sulphite, cellulose and glass factories, tile works, lime kilns, coke ovens, slag heaps, and in coal and all other mines." See H. Cristiani and J. Stoklasa, The Loss to Agriculture Caused by Factory Fumes (International Institute of Agriculture, Rome, 1927), p. 19.

[26] Ibid., p. 14.

[27] Ibid., p. 25.

showed that "the soil is gradually losing all its fertility and yearly produces smaller crops." [28] Similar evidence of the harmful effects of smoke on soil fertility is found in the United States. In Pennsylvania, severe erosion is reported to have resulted from factory fumes which "caused such high acidity in the soil as to retard and later prevent the growth of vegetation." [29]

Evidence of the injurious effects of air pollution on vegetation is revealed by chronic damage to garden, field and forest plants in the presence of a small amount of sulphuric acid in the air, which may lead to a complete destruction of the plants if the acid content of the air increases. According to Dr. Stoklasa, "it can safely be said that the presence of 0.002 per cent sulphuric acid may cause chronic mischief to all useful cultivated plants in the widest sense of the word, such as wheat, rye, barley, oats, maize, buckwheat, peas, lentils, vetch, horse beans, beans, tares, rape for seed and for oil, poppies, mustard, hops, tobacco, flax, hemp, potatoes, sugar beets, lucerne, red clover, meadow grasses." [30] More delicate plants are seriously damaged by the presence of a smaller amount of sulphuric acid in the atmosphere.

Interesting illustrations of the injurious effects of air pollution on animal life were brought to light by a series of studies, observations and experiments made in the environment of a large factory producing aluminum, nitric acid and its own electrodes for the electrolysis of the ore containing aluminum. Emanations from this plant (smoke as well as gases) poisoned the grass which farmers in the vicinity of the factory used either for cattle feeding or as litter. Animals which eat these damaged forage plants (even in small quantities) all die. "It is not even necessary to feed these animals with the damaged forage; it suffices to use it as litter. In these cases, the animals consume small quantities when the litter is renewed and also ingest fragments of hay . . ." [31]

Even the foregoing lengthy analysis does not convey a complete picture of the social losses caused by smoke and other emanations from factories and industrial centers. No mention has been made, for example, of the effects which smoke may have upon real estate

[28] *Ibid.*, p. 25. See also J. Stoklasa, *Die Beschädigungen der Vegetation durch Rauchgase und Fabrikexhalationen* (Berlin, 1923).

[29] A. F. Gustafson, H. Ries, C. H. Guise and W. J. Hamilton, Jr., *Conservation in the United States* (Ithaca: Comstock Publishing Co., 1939), p. 85.

[30] H. Cristiani and J. Stoklasa, *The Loss to Agriculture Caused by Factory Fumes*, p. 20.

[31] *Ibid.*, p. 10.

values.[32] Nor has any reference been made to the higher costs of artificial lighting[33] made necessary by the loss of daylight as a result of smoke. Other losses involved in air pollution are costly delays in transportation, especially air transportation (loss of flying days) and shipping, and higher accident rates bound up with the increased intensity and duration of city fogs as a result of smoke.[34]

4. Evidence of Air Pollution and Quantitative Estimates of the Social Costs Caused Thereby

Numerous investigations by private and public agencies have yielded a wealth of evidence and quantitative estimates of the social losses caused by air pollution in different industrial localities. Careful studies have been made with a view to measuring the amount of carbon, ash, tar, iron oxide and sulphur dioxide in the air which in the form of dust settles in and around industrial communities. For example, it has been found that 1,800 tons of dust settle per square mile per year in the center of the city of Baltimore, while three miles

[32] The *Report of the St. Louis Committee on Elimination of Smoke* calls attention to the fact that smoke with its grime and dirt and unhealthful conditions has had a "potent hand in persuading thousands of our citizens that St. Louis, under these conditions, is no longer the best place of abode for them. The result has been an appalling shrinkage in real estate values to the point that real estate no longer holds its former eminent place in the investment field. No longer will our citizens seek to to own their home in a market of crumbling real estate values. Many citizens have lost their homes (already owned) because of their inability to properly protect loans on their properties which only a few years ago were considered conservatively mortgaged. The city, likewise, is losing taxes on dwellings and commercial buildings which have been torn down to avoid taxes, and if the deterioration continues, the result will be more and more serious. Once more we say that not all of this condition is due to smoke, but again we say that a substantial part is due to it and that the loss in value from that part due to smoke alone is staggering." *Report of St. Louis Committee on Elimination of Smoke,* presented to Mayor B. F. Dickmann, February 24, 1940, pp. 1–2.

[33] Estimates of the Smoke Investigation placed the cost of artificial lighting in Pittsburgh due to the loss of daylight as a result of smoke at $734,000 yearly. See Smoke Investigation, Bulletin No. 4, *The Economic Cost of the Smoke Nuisance to Pittsburgh* (Pittsburgh, 1913), p. 44.

[34] The growing significance of these losses is emphasized by current experiments designed to develop practical methods of dispersing fogs over harbors and airports. Indeed, smoke-induced air pollution and the resulting reduction of visibility in and around large cities may well become an important hindrance to the large-scale development of air transportation in the future.

from the center only 800 tons of settled dust was recorded, and ten miles out in the country the settled dust was 340 tons per square mile per year.[35]

Several monetary estimates of the social costs of air pollution have been made; the earliest and most detailed of these estimates are those of the Mellon Institute of Industrial Research of the University of Pittsburgh in 1913. According to the Smoke Investigation of the Mellon Institute, the smoke nuisance costs the people of Pittsburgh approximately $9,944,740 per annum.[36] This figure applies to conditions pervailing in 1913. More recent estimates place the losses caused by smoke in Pittsburgh at $9.36 per person per year.[37] Later investigations in Pittsburgh convinced the Institute "that we were safe in estimating the cost to each man, woman and child in the city at about $15 each year." [38] Studies made in other places, among them New York, Chicago, Cincinnati, Salt Lake City, Boston and Baltimore have revealed losses amounting to "from $10 to $30 per capita." [39] Estimates for Cleveland range as high as $80 for each family.[40] The total costs of the smoke nuisance in New York City are placed at about $100,000,000 per year.[41] For the country as a whole "the annual bill for smoke . . . lies in the neighborhood of $500,000,000, of which $140,000,000 is said to represent the cost of

[35] J. H. Shrader, M. H. Coblenz, F. A. Korff, "Effect of Atmospheric Pollution upon Incidence of Solar Ultraviolet Light," *American Journal of Public Health and the Nation's Health,* No. 7 (July 1929), pp. 717–724. For other and more detailed estimates of the smoke content in the atmosphere in industrial centers in Great Britain, see W. N. Shaw and J. S. Owens, *The Smoke Problems of Great Cities* (London, 1925) and J. R. Ashworth, *Smoke and the Atmosphere* (Manchester: Manchester University Press, 1933). These and other available estimates of the amount of dust deposited per square mile per year in both industrial and nonindustrial American cities are summarized in Appendix VI.

[36] Smoke Investigation, Bulletin No. 4, p. 44. For more complete data, see Appendix VII.

[37] J. E. Ives and R. R. Sayers, "City Smoke and Its Effects," *U. S. Public Health Reports,* Vol. 51 (January 1936), p. 16.

[38] According to estimates by H. Meller quoted by W. B. Courtney, "Our Soiled Cities," *Collier's Weekly* (January 27, 1934).

[39] J. E. Ives and R. R. Sayers, *op. cit.,* pp. 16–17.

[40] Smoke Investigation, Bulletin No. 1, *Outline of the Smoke Investigation,* p. 8.

[41] H. Obermeyer, *Stop That Smoke* (New York: Harper and Brothers, 1933), pp. 48–49.

spoiled merchandise and of building cleaning." [42] H. W. Wilson of the U. S. Geological Survey likewise placed the loss which the country as a whole suffers as a result of smoke at over $500,000,000 "in damage done to merchandise, defacement on buildings, tarnishing of metals, injury to human life and to plant life, the greatly increased labor and the cost of housekeeping and the losses of the manufacturers due to imperfect combustion of coal." [43]

Other quantitative estimates of total losses due to air pollution are available for Great Britain and Czechoslovakia. In Great Britain, the additional costs of maintaining buildings and making good the results of atmospheric impurity are estimated to have reached a figure of from £20,000,000 to £60,000,000 for a period of twenty-five years.[44] Repair work on the Houses of Parliament necessitated by the attack of atmospheric acids during the past sixty years is estimated at $5,000,000. In the British Museum 10,000 leather-bound volumes have had to be rebound with a leather specially treated to withstand the sulphur in smoke. The total losses caused by smoke in Britain are estimated to approach a figure of $400,000,000.[45] In Czechoslovakia the injurious effects of smoke (due to the presence of sulphur dioxide and sulphuric acid) are said to have caused a yearly loss of 250 to 300 million kronen. The decrease in crop production in industrial and mining areas as a result of smoke and other factory fumes amounts to 30 to 90 per cent in the territory of the Czechoslovak Republic.[46]

It is probable that further investigations into the effects of air pollution will bring to light additional evidence of social losses. Such evidence would lend further support to the conclusion that air pollution represents another important case of social costs of modern industrial production. The social losses caused thereby are reflected

[42] *Ibid.*, p. 47.

[43] Quoted from Smoke Investigation, Bulletin No. 1, p. 10.

[44] Sir Frank Baines, *An Examination into the Effects of Atmospheric Pollution on Buildings* (Pamphlet, 1933), quoted from F. E. Smith, "Coal, Power, and Smoke," p. 23.

[45] H. Obermeyer, *Stop That Smoke,* p. 49.

[46] H. Cristiani and J. Stoklasa, *The Loss to Agriculture Caused by Factory Fumes,* p. 19.

in destructive effects of smoke upon property values, human health, and plant and animal life. None of these social losses, which seem to be far greater than is usually realized, is reflected in entrepreneurial outlays. As a matter of fact, in the absence of legislative prohibitions and restrictions, there is nothing which would induce the individual producer to take the necessary steps to prevent the pollution of the atmosphere by smoke and similar emanations from industrial establishments. On the contrary, as long as it does not pay (in terms of private savings resulting from greater efficiency in combustion of coal) to take precautionary measures with a view to eliminating or controlling the emanation of smoke, the individual producer is likely to disregard the social losses which the discharge of smoke into the atmosphere causes to virtually all members of the community. A further elucidation of some of the economic aspects of the problem of air pollution is contained in the following discussion of the problem of water pollution, which in many respects is similar.

6

THE SOCIAL COSTS OF WATER POLLUTION

THE POLLUTION of streams, rivers and lakes by industrial waste products is strikingly similar in its effects to air pollution. Like the latter, the contamination of water affects human health and property values and causes losses for which neither custom nor law afford as yet either full or reasonably adequate compensation to the persons injured. In the case of water pollution, it is true that courts have definitely and repeatedly established the responsibility of pollutors to pay damages to those who sustain losses as a result of pollution. However, as in the case of air pollution, the damages caused by water pollution in most instances are distributed among many individuals, who may have so small an interest at stake that they do not feel impelled to initiate or partake actively in court action. Another reason why injured persons may fail to defend themselves against the damages of water pollution is the fact that it is usually difficult and expensive to prove liability for damages in court. "Judicial precedent requires the demonstration of specific damage rather than general damage, and further requires quantitive estimates of the amounts of damage experienced by specified individuals. Variations in the natural quality of water and polluting substances make the process of marshaling such evidence lengthy and intricate." [1] Furthermore, even if liability and damages are proved, it is also necessary

[1] National Resources Committee, Third Report of the Special Advisory Committee on Water Pollution, *Water Pollution in the United States* (Washington: U. S. Government Printing Office, 1939), pp. 67–68.

to demonstrate that practicable means of abatement exist before an injunction may be obtained. This entails additional expense and further delay. It is for these reasons that court action and legal responsibility to pay damages to injured persons have failed to eliminate water pollution and to allocate the social losses resulting therefrom to individual pollutors.

1. Public Sources of Water Pollution

The most frequent sources of water pollution are (a) municipal sewages, (b) mining wastes and (c) industrial wastes. As far as the first of these sources is concerned, it might be argued that the harmful effects resulting from the improper disposal of municipal sewages and domestic wastes arise in the public sector of the economy, and not as a result of private processes of production. This is doubtless correct, and to the extent to which losses are caused by the pollution of rivers and streams through municipal and domestic wastes, these losses are not social costs in the sense in which this term is being used in this study. However, in a more general respect such losses may well be regarded as "social costs" insofar as they tend to be shifted to persons entirely unrelated to those responsible for the damage. Thus, by failing to provide for adequate sewage-disposal plants, municipalities cause serious losses to the members of other communities, mostly those living further downstream.

According to available estimates, slightly more than 50 per cent of the population in the United States dispose of their domestic wastes through public sewage systems.[2] Of this municipal sewage only 50 per cent receives primary and secondary treatment before it is discharged into water bodies. The remaining half is discharged untreated and may thus become an active source of water pollution.[3] Municipal sewage and domestic wastes insufficiently treated promote the spread of typhoid and other water-borne diseases; they affect the taste, odor and color of the water and impair its usefulness for domes-

[2] The remainder "of the total population which is not served by sewers is located on farms, in small villages, and on the outskirts of larger towns and cities. It does not contribute a substantial amount of sewage to water bodies." *Ibid.*, p. 5.
[3] *Ibid.*, p. 1.

tic and livestock uses and recreational purposes. Moreover, such wastes tend to deplete the oxygen in the water and thereby injure or destroy fish and lower forms of aquatic life.

2. Mining and Industrial Wastes as Sources of Water Pollution

Unlike municipal sewages, mining and industrial wastes originate in the private sector of the economy. The principal offenders in the field of mining are the producers of petroleum and coal. In order to understand fully the manner in which the production of oil may give rise to water pollution, it is only necessary to realize that "many subsurface formations of sandstone and limestone are saturated with salt water or brine. When these strata are penetrated by wells drilled for oil and gas or other purposes, the brines are released and, unless proper precautions are taken, may be brought to the surface through the wells or may find their way into formations containing fresh water." [4] Older wells usually produce substantial quantities of brines and may eventually go to water, especially "in those fields where brines underlie the oil in the extraneous parts of the oil-bearing reservoirs . . ." [5]

The relative amount of salt water produced varies considerably between different oil fields and wells. While some wells are reported to produce only one barrel of water to 27 barrels of oil, other wells may produce as much as 100 barrels of brines to every barrel of oil produced.[6] According to estimates of the U. S. Bureau of Mines, the midcontinent and Gulf coast oil fields produce approximately 10,000,-000 barrels of brine daily—that is about 3 barrels of brine for every barrel of oil.[7]

---

[4] L. Schmidt and C. J. Wilhelm, *Contamination of Domestic Water Supplies by Inadequate Plugging Methods or Faulty Casing* (Report prepared under a coöperation agreement between the U. S. Bureau of Mines and the Kansas State Board of Health), p. 1.

[5] H. C. Miller and G. B. Shea, *Recent Progress in Petroleum Development and Production* (Washington: U. S. Bureau of Mines, 1940), pp. 374–375.

[6] L. Schmidt and J. M. Devine, *The Disposal of Oil Field Brines* (U. S. Department of Mines, reprinted February 1937, R. I. 2945), p. 1.

[7] H. C. Miller and G. B. Shea, *Recent Progress in Petroleum Development and Production*, p. 375; see also L. Schmidt and J. M. Devine, *The Disposal of Oil Field Brines*, pp. 1–2.

In the absence of adequate precautionary measures (such as the use of buttonhole plugs, the cementing and repair of wells or the proper disposal of brines at the surface) these salt waters are likely to find their way into streams, rivers and lakes, where they may give rise to a serious contamination of fresh-water supplies. While it is impossible to trace all the possible consequences of improper disposal of oil field brines,[8] it may at least be pointed out that the resulting pollution of the surface streams may make such waters unpalatable to humans and livestock. Brines may also become destructive to fresh-water fish life; they may even affect the quality and fertility of the soil and kill vegetation "when . . . allowed to flow for a considerable time over the surface of the ground."[9] Finally, they may render the water unattractive for recreational uses and cause a higher corrosiveness of the water, thereby impairing its usefulness for industrial purposes.

In coal mining, certain washing processes yield a wash water "which carries fine particles of coal and refuse, known as culm, into the streams."[10] Moreover, water pumped from operating mines and draining from abandoned mines often has a high acid content, which may become an active source of water pollution. Although detailed estimates of the amounts of culm and acid currently pouring from coal-mining regions into stream systems are not available, it is an established fact that such mining wastes have contributed to the filling of stream channels, thereby decreasing their navigable depth and increasing the height of flood flow. Like oil brines, mine drainage increases the acidity and also affects the taste, odor and color of water, thereby impairing or destroying its usefulness for domestic, industrial and livestock uses. Surface waters polluted by such drainage are known to corrode boilers, bridge piers,

[8] For a summary of some of these effects ascertained by scientific observers see L. Schmidt and J. M. Devine, *The Disposal of Oil Field Brines*, pp. 3–8; L. Schmidt and C. J. Wilhelm, *Contamination of Domestic Water Supplies*, pp. 2–5; and V. G. Heller, "The Effect of Saline and Alkaline Waters on Domestic Animals," *Oklahoma Agricultural and Mechanical College, Agricultural Experiment Station, Bulletin No. 217* (December 1933).

[9] L. Schmidt and J. M. Devine, *The Disposal of Oil Field Brines*, p. 3.

[10] National Resources Committee, *Water Pollution in the United States*, p. 12.

piping, barges and other metal structures; they are toxic to all aquatic life.

Hydraulic mining and dredging operations give rise to other kinds of mining debris which, if discharged into rivers and streams, contribute materially to the silting and pollution of stream channels. For example, debris from gold mining operations in California once constituted a source of serious silting of streams and threatened the use of channels downstream. While various control measures required under Federal regulation (such as the construction of storage dams, levees, and barriers) have substantially reduced these harmful consequences of water pollution in California, hydraulic mining and dredging operations in parts of Idaho and some other Western states are still reported to contribute materially to the silting of stream channels.

The most important industries giving rise to water pollution are those that produce and process foods and beverages, textiles and tanning products, petroleum-refining products, iron and steel, non-ferrous metals, rubber, paper and illuminating gases.[11] These industries discharge a wide variety of industrial wastes into rivers and streams and must be regarded as major sources of water pollution in and around all regions of large-scale manufacturing. Waste materials arising in the production of food products deplete the oxygen content of the water and, as a result, kill or injure fish or other forms of aquatic life. Some meat-packing waste may even carry human or livestock diseases. Industrial wastes arising from the production of chemicals, textiles and tanning products likewise impair quality of water for domestic, industrial and livestock purposes by affecting its taste, odor or color; like mining wastes, these industrial wastes also lead to the corrosion of bridge piers, boilers and other metal structures, and are toxic to some fish and lower forms of aquatic life. Paper and oil-refining wastes contain solids which make it necessary to subject the waters to special treatment at water-purification plants. Wastes from metal works and metallurgical operations increase the turbidity of the water, affect its taste and color, and impair its quali-

[11] *Ibid.*, p. 4.

ties in other ways. Water pollution may thus have the most far-reaching effects upon life, property and other less tangible values. "Human health may be impaired and life may be lost; the supply of aquatic life may be reduced, the suitability of water for domestic and industrial use may be impaired; the life of bridges and other structures may be shortened; and recreational use of water bodies and adjacent lands may be hampered or prevented." [12]

The disposal of waste radioactive solids, liquids or gases in waterways, as in the air, creates hazards of world-wide dimensions. The possible magnitude of the dangers resulting from the disposal of untreated radioactive material may be indicated by the fact that some of the materials are long-lived and may be as hazardous a century hence as they are today. Also there seems to be no assurance that plants will not pick up radioactive atoms and thus concentrate them. Clays and some minerals strongly absorb some of the radioactive elements. While the search for possible means of protection against these hazards seems to be under way, the magnitude of the dangers involved in the disposal of radioactive waste material is one further reason why the development of atomic energy can take place safely only under public auspices.

3. Evidence of the Magnitude of the Pollution Problem and the Social Costs Caused Thereby in the United States

It is difficult if not altogether impossible to estimate with any degree of accuracy the magnitude of the social costs of water pollution resulting from private production in monetary terms. This difficulty arises from a number of factors. In the first place, it is not easy to determine the extent to which the contamination of any given river or stream is due to public or private sources. Moreover, some of the values destroyed by water pollution are highly intangible in character. This applies, for example, to the impairment of the aesthetic and recreational values of streams and lakes, as well as to the destruction of wildlife (insofar as it is not valued for commercial purposes). In view of these facts, we shall have to be satisfied with a few

[12] *Ibid.,* p. 31.

quantitative estimates of some losses. A survey jointly carried out by the State Boards of Health of Minnesota and Wisconsin placed the annual losses to commercial fishing and clamming caused by the contamination of the upper Mississippi River at $95,000; the annual damage done to sport fishing and attendant industries was placed at $35,000, while decreased property values in the Twin Cities was estimated a $2,000,000 and damage to lands for recreational purposes at $1,500,000. Evaluations of similar losses in other states, such as Indiana, Iowa, and Virginia, are reported to aggregate millions of dollars annually.[13]

Other estimates cover the annual losses caused by water pollution as a result of its corrosive effect upon bridge piers, piping, barges, and metal structures. Thus "in 1925 the Corps of Engineers estimated that the annual losses from acid pollution in the Pittsburgh district—an area having exceptionally acute problems—amounted to $8,000,000. In 1915, they were estimated at $11,000,000." [14] In 1934 railroads running east from Pittsburgh were reported to spend from 12 to 20 million dollars annually for the repair and replacement of locomotive boilers corroded as a result of mine drainage and the concomitant depreciation of the quality of water in that district.[15]

As far as the relative severity of water pollution is concerned, all available evidence indicates that the problem is most serious in the northeastern part of the country, that is, in the area which corresponds closely with the concentration of manufacturing and the greatest density of population. It stretches westward from the seacoast, lying between the Merrimac and James rivers. According to the Report on *Water Pollution in the United States,* "all the larger streams and many sections of the coastal waters along the Atlantic seaboard are polluted to a serious degree. Most of the shorter streams

[13] National Resources Committee, *Report on Water Pollution by the Special Advisory Committee on Water Pollution* (mimeographed; July 1935), p. 41.

[14] National Resources Committee, *Water Pollution in the United States,* p. 37.

[15] National Resources Board, *A Report on National Planning and Public Works in Relation to Natural Resources and Including Land Use and Water Resources with Findings and Recommendations* (Washington: U. S. Government Printing Office, 1934), p. 315.

are polluted from municipal and industrial wastes throughout most of their lengths." [16]

"The Merrimac, Penobscot, Connecticut, Mohawk, and Hudson Rivers are all heavily polluted for considerable distances above their mouths. New York Harbor and the waters in its vicinity have reached a state of gross pollution which has been a scandal for years. The Delaware River and the contributing larger rivers, the Lehigh and Schuylkill, are all grossly polluted although an effort has been made by the Sanitary Water Board of Pennsylvania to control further contamination of these streams. All these water courses receive large volumes of domestic and industrial wastes, and the Lehigh and Schuylkill are contaminated also by coal-mine drainage. The aggregate pollution discharged into the Susquehanna River is also extensive." [17]

"The Fox, Milwaukee, Chicago, Calumet, and Maumee Rivers are lined with industrial plants and so contaminated that usefulness for any other purpose is destroyed. In addition, the large cities are centers of intense and diverse industrial development. Among the major waste problems are: wood pulp, tanneries, canneries, and creameries in Wisconsin and Michigan; meat packing, corn products, tanneries, paint and chemicals in Chicago; coke and steel mills around the southern tip of Lake Michigan and the southern shore of Lake Erie. This region is very highly industrialized, and the sewage and trade-waste disposal problems will continue to increase in magnitude, particularly as more and more demands are made for clean streams and lakes for water supply, swimming, and recreational uses. An enormous amount of trade waste is contributed to the upper Mississippi River Valley by the creameries, canneries, pulp and paper mills, and slaughtering and poultry-dressing establishments which have located in this populous area. The Chippewa, Black, Wisconsin, Rock, Des Moines, and Illinois Rivers carry large quantities of industrial wastes. The seriousness of the stream-pollution problem in this highly industrialized area is probably as great as in any other section of the United States." [18] The industrial wastes in the lower Mississippi River region ". . . are very scattered, consisting principally of oil and brine from the oil fields of Kansas and Oklahoma, beet sugar wastes along the upper reaches of the Arkansas River in Colorado, and packing-house waste at Oklahoma City." [19]

[16] National Resources Committee, *Water Pollution in the United States,* p. 40.
[17] National Resources Board, *Report on National Planning and Public Works,* p. 336.
[18] *Ibid.,* p. 8.
[19] *Ibid.,* p. 337.

Industrial pollution within the Missouri River Valley "is concentrated at St. Louis, Kansas City, and some centers in Nebraska, consisting principally of trade wastes from packing houses, breweries, paint and chemical plants, canneries, and beet-sugar refineries . . . The many industrial wastes of the Ohio Basin are greatly diversified, having their greatest concentration around the Pittsburgh area. Mine drainage on the Monongahela River neutralizes the natural alkalinity of the water and causes an acid condition during the greater part of the year and over most of its length . . . Other major sources of industrial waste in the Pittsburgh area are the steel mills, chemical plants, tanneries, and distilleries. The paper industry on the headwaters of the Ohio contributes large volumes of waste to the streams." [20]

Other areas affected by serious water pollution are located on the Pacific Coast around Los Angeles, San Francisco, and Portland. Whereas pollution in the Los Angeles and San Francisco districts is largely caused by municipal wastes, the sewage discharge, the lower Willamette River in Oregon is primarily affected by pulp and paper mills and canneries "to such an extent that there is no dissolved oxygen at the mouth of the river at certain times. It is reported that these wastes account for half of the oxygen-consuming impurities in this river." [21]

Another method of indicating the relative magnitude of the problem of water pollution is to estimate the money outlays required for the prevention and abatement of such pollution. Although outlays of this kind do not measure the social costs of water pollution, they convey at least an idea of the price at which it would be possible to eliminate and avoid the contamination of surface waters and the resulting social losses. Moreover, detailed estimates of such outlays for each industry tend to reveal the financial burden which a program of pollution abatement might place upon business concerns; such estimates are therefore a prerequisite for the determination of the relative worthwhileness of practical measures in this direction. Estimates made by the Special Advisory Committee on Water Pollution of the U. S. National Resources Committee place the capital expenditure required for an adequate national pollution-abatement program at more than $2,000,000,000, spent over a period of more

[20] *Ibid.*, pp. 337–338.
[21] *Ibid.*, p. 338. See Appendix VIII for a map of the United States illustrating the geographical distribution and relative severity of the pollution problem.

than 10 to 20 years. To these capital outlays would have to be added approximately 240 million dollars representing the annual costs of operating, maintenance, interest, depreciation and insurance involved in the pollution-abatement program of the recommended proportions.[22] About half the total capital outlay would be required for the construction of sewers, interceptors and treatment plants for the safe disposal of municipal wastes. The abatement of mining waste, including oil brines, would cost not less than $150,000,000 and reasonably adequate alleviation of pollution from industrial sources would involve capital outlays of approximately $900,000,000.

A more detailed breakdown of these figures according to major waste-producing industries is given in Table 2, which also indicates the total output value of these industries in 1935. Although this table conveys only a general picture of the total output value and estimated capital outlays required for the prevention of water pollution according to major industrial groups, it reveals, nevertheless, great differences in the financial burden which these costs would place upon individual industries. Thus, the estimated costs of waste treatment in the manufacture of paper amount to almost one-seventh of the annual value of the total output. In the textile field, costs would reach one-fifth of the total output, whereas the manufacturers of rubber goods would be able to provide for the necessary waste treatment at a cost equal to 1/469 of their total output.

Even more significant than these over-all comparisons are estimates of the cost of industrial-waste treatment in individual plants and manufacturing processes in relation to total capital investment and annual costs of production. Such estimates not only disclose the relative financial burden which the required corrective measures would place upon individual manufacturers, but they also indicate which industries would be likely to experience difficulties if they had to bear the costs of waste treatment. The great practical significance of such a distinction led the Special Advisory Committee to draw up the following preliminary and tentative classification of the chief waste-producing industries according to whether the costs of ade-

[22] National Resources Committee, *Water Pollution in the United States*, p. 42.

quate waste treatment would be "not burdensome," "sizable" or "extremely high."

1. *Industries for which waste-treatment could be provided at a cost which would not be burdensome:* "Small isolated food establishments producing dairy products and canned goods; small laundries; certain chemical industries with small volumes of wastes; some textile industries in which separation of wastes may reduce the volume for which final treatment may be provided; petroleum refineries; metallurgical industries with small volumes of acid pickling wastes and large receiving

TABLE 2

COMPARISON OF ESTIMATED VALUE OF PRODUCTS MANUFACTURED WITH ESTIMATED COST OF INDUSTRIAL-WASTE TREATMENT FOR MAJOR INDUSTRIES CONTRIBUTING TO THE POLLUTION OF SURFACE WATER IN THE UNITED STATES[1]

Product	Total Value (1935)	Estimated Costs of Waste Treatment[2]
Food and beverages............	$ 8,830,896,000	$205,400,000
Textiles.....................	2,516,157,000	54,000,000
Chemicals...................	1,366,311,000	28,300,000
Petroleum (refining)...........	1,823,793,000	30,000,000
Ferrous metals...............	1,902,909,000	20,000,000
Nonferrous metals............	382,526,000	21,600,000
Rubber......................	469,400,000	1,000,000
Paper.......................	822,719,000	129,000,000
Gas.........................	203,751,000	5,000,000
	$18,318,461,000	$494,300,000
Miscellaneous waste treatment		100,000,000
Added for contingencies......		100,000,000
Total costs................		$694,300,000

[1] Compiled for the volume of production indicated by the 1935 Census of Manufacturers and based upon the judgment of engineers who have had wide experience in the treatment of industrial waste. See National Resources Committee, *Water Pollution in the United States*, pp. 31, 53-54.

[2] These estimates do not cover the costs of industrial-waste treatment for all manufacturing processes within each particular industry. In other words, the actual cost of an adequate waste-treatment program exceeds these estimates. The Committee considers that the total costs may reach at least $800,000,000 and may well amount to $900,000,000. (*Ibid.*, p. 55.)

bodies of water available . . . ; waster-gas manufacturing plants near ample dilution water . . . ; and miscellaneous plants producing wastes which can be partially treated at point of origin and safely discharged into sewage-treatment works."

2. *Industries for which waste-treatment works would involve equipment of considerable magnitude and constitute a sizable item in the cost of production:* "Meat-packing plants; large canneries, beet-sugar plants; distilleries; breweries; certain cereal-processing industries, particularly corn-products plants; textile mills; tanneries; coke ovens and other units producing phenolic wastes; paper mills not producing sulphite or sulphate pulp; and smelting and refining plants producing nonferrous metals."

3. *Industries for which the cost of corrective measures would be extremely high:* "Sulphite and sulphate paper pulp mills; certain distilled-spirits industries; certain chemical-process plants producing wastes high in concentration and complex in character; and steel mills producing large volumes of pickling liquors." To these industries must also be added the petroleum industry, inasmuch as capital outlays required for the proper treatment of oil-field brine waste are estimated conservatively to amount to at least $100,000,000 exclusive of the annual operating costs, which would likewise be excessively high (perhaps as much as 18 to 33 per cent of the capital investment).[23]

If more detailed and up-to-date cost studies should confirm the relative accuracy of the above classification and establish the fact that the burden of constructing and maintaining the required waste-treatment works would cause serious financial disruptions in certain well-established lines of manufacturing, such evidence would offer an interesting illustration of the fact that entire industries might be able to occupy and to maintain their present economic position only because they do not bear the full costs of production but find it possible to shift a substantial part of these costs to other persons and to the community at large.

4. *The Pollution of the Sea*

A special kind of water pollution is the pollution of the sea and coastal waters through the discharge of oil and oily mixtures by oil-burning or oil-carrying ships. At one time the losses resulting from

[23] *Ibid.,* pp. 47–50.

the pollution of ocean and coastal waters were considered so significant that their prevention was sought by means of an international agreement among the chief maritime countries of the world.[24] Although these attempts proved unsuccessful, they revealed important information regarding the effect of oil pollution and the extent of the losses caused thereby. According to a committee of experts from various countries assigned to study the subject for the League of Nations, "the damage caused by oil pollution related to the destruction of sea birds, . . . to the destruction of fish, particularly shellfish, and of the marine grasses which form the staple food of fish and birds."[25] The committee also pointed out that the pollution of beaches resulted in damages to bathers and the depreciation in value of seaside resorts generally, and constituted a menace to public health; and finally, that the accumulation of oil which, in many cases, drifted into harbors from outside territorial waters created a danger of fire.[26]

The extent of the damage caused in various countries by the pollution of the sea is indicated in the following passage from the memorandum which the Committee of Experts submitted to the Communication and Transit Organization of the League of Nations:

These evils [of oil pollution] occur to a greater or less extent in various countries. In the United Kingdom and in the United States they are all still present to a serious extent, though conditions have improved on certain parts of the coast of those countries in recent years. In Japan, though pollution is not very serious at the present time, oil discharged or escaping from vessels along the coasts has caused damage to fisheries, particularly shell-fisheries, and has also jeopardized the cultivation of

---

[24] In fact, the question formed the subject of an international conference in Washington, following an invitation by the Government of the United States in 1926, and was studied by the competent organs of the League of Nations, in 1935, preparatory to an international conference to be called on the subject in 1936. See League of Nations, Organization for Communications and Transit, *Pollution of the Sea by Oil*, Official No. A 20 1935 VIII. (See also the following documents of the League of Nations: *Draft Convention Relating to the Pollution of the Sea by Oil*, Official No. C 449 M 235 1935 VIII; and *Replies of Governments Relating to the Draft Convention and Draft Final Act*, Official No. A 18 1936 VIII.)

[25] *Pollution of the Sea by Oil*, p. 3.

[26] *Ibid.*, p. 3.

edible sea weed which forms one of the most important industries on portions of the coast. In Italy, the damage has not been very serious; it has principally affected the sea beaches, and there is also the danger of fire in certain harbors from the presence of oil washed in from beyond territorial limits. In France, the chief damage has been to fisheries and to seaside resorts and bathing stations. In Denmark, there have been only a few cases of pollution, but it is feared that as oil-burning and oil-carrying vessels increase in numbers, the damage may become more serious.[27]

It is interesting to note the reasons for the failure of the chief maritime nations to arrive at an international agreement on the prevention of oil pollution and the resulting damages. The official replies which the League of Nations received to its questionnaire on the subject indicate clearly that the shipping industries objected to the financial burden involved in the compulsory fitting of separators (designed to separate oil from water) on oil-burning and oil-carrying ships. Consequently, the draft convention on the prevention of oil pollution was never adopted.

Summarizing the preceding discussion, it may be said that by discharging their waste products into waterways without adequate previous treatment a great number of more or less clearly defined industries set the cause for substantial social losses resulting from water pollution. Such pollution has been shown to have far-reaching harmful effects on human health and wild life; it destroys recreational values and is responsible for premature corrosion of metallic structures, bridges, boilers, etc. The individual producer is not interested in the prevention of these social losses; indeed, their prevention could only add to his costs and thus affect adversely his competitive position as well as the profitableness of his concern. In this case, too, the competitive process, if left to itself, tends to generate important social damages not accounted for in entrepreneurial outlays.

[27] *Ibid.*, p. 3. For a more detailed picture of the effects of oil pollution on birds, fish and fishing industries, resorts and harbor installations in different countries, see the summary of the official replies which the League of Nations received to a questionnaire on this subject (*ibid.*, pp. 11–18).

7

DEPLETION AND DESTRUCTION
OF ANIMAL RESOURCES

THE PRECEDING CHAPTERS have dealt with simple cases of social costs. The impairment of the human factor by modern industrial processes, the pollution of the atmosphere by smoke and other wastes, and the contamination of water by industrial-waste products are all relatively clear examples of social losses not reflected in entrepreneurial outlays. The present chapter introduces the analysis of social costs whose origin and nature are less easily ascertained, namely, the losses likely to arise in the competitive exploitation of natural resources.

1. The Competitive Exploitation of Natural Resources

Natural resources have all the characteristics of income-yielding capital assets. They differ from other capital goods only in so far as their capacity of yielding returns normally extends over a greater period of time—often beyond the life span of one generation. Moreover, the nature of some natural resources is such that private ownership rights can be established only after their "capture." Both these factors are of great importance for the explanation of the social losses resulting from the competitive exploitation of natural resources.

The fact that the income-yielding capacity of natural resources extends far into the future makes their evaluation subject to the operation of the principle of "time preference." Both consumers and producers tend to attribute greater value to present enjoyments and incomes than to the same amount of enjoyment and income in the more or less distant future. In other words, the present value of all future goods and incomes is lower than their anticipated future value. In fact, the more distant the future enjoyment, the lower will be its present value. This preference for present consumption may give rise to a general "distortion" of the market value of natural resources and consequently to a serious neglect of the possible consequences of their premature exhaustion. Thus, consumers will demand the products of natural resources without taking fully into consideration that they may have to forego the use of such products in the future once the available stock of resources has been exhausted. Producers, likewise, in their preference for present income as compared with the same amount of income in the future, will tend to intensify the exploitation of natural resources in spite of the fact that such production may reduce the income-yielding capacity of their capital asset in the years to come. This interaction of consumers' and producers' time preference accounts for the fact that private competitive exploitation of natural resources tends to take place with an almost complete disregard of the capital losses caused thereby. In other words, the private costs of recovery do not take into consideration the rapid decline of the income-yielding capacity of the particular asset. Hence they tend to fall short of the actual total costs of production of natural resources and their products.

This outcome is particularly evident in the case of those natural resources which are legally "free" commodities prior to their capture as, for example, wildlife and petroleum. The fact that these resources are "free goods" from the point of view of the individual producer makes them subject to particularly wasteful practices of exploitation and recovery. This is especially true in the case of animal resources which are both free and self-renewable. If the natural process of reproduction of wildlife resources is not disturbed by their commercial exploitation—that is, if the rate of capture does not exceed the actual replacement rate—the income-yielding capacity of these resources, and consequently their capital value, may be kept intact indefinitely. The competitive process of the market economy offers, however, no assurance that the exploitation of wildlife resources will be kept within the limits required to permit the normal reproduction of animals. In fact, there is no guarantee whatsoever that the exploitation of animal resources will stop at the point at which a further intensification of hunting and fishing tends to lead to the gradual depletion and complete exhaustion of the capital asset. Even if individual hunters and fishermen want to pursue a policy of reasonable conservation, they can hardly be expected to do so as long as cost-price conditions make it profitable for their competitors to continue production. Indeed, far from preventing the depletion and possible extinction of renewable resources, a policy of conservation pursued by individual hunters or fishermen would in effect merely permit competitors to take their place and to produce a larger share of the legally "free," although practically limited, animal resources. As a matter of fact, not even depressed prices and lower returns resulting from excessive production will necessarily lead to a curtailment of output. Quite on the contrary, lower yields may actually prove an incentive to greater efforts on the part of the individual fisherman or hunter, inducing them to make up for their declining returns by still greater output. In these efforts they will be aided greatly by highly efficient modern methods of fishing and hunting by which available animal resources can be depleted and extinguished within a remarkably short time.

In the light of the foregoing analysis it becomes clear that the destruction of animal resources under conditions of unregulated competition does not differ fundamentally from the depreciation and deterioration of other capital assets. But, whereas the depreciation of privately owned capital assets tends to be translated, by means of depreciation charges, into entrepreneurial outlays, the depletion of animal resources remains largely unaccounted for in the cost-return calculations of the individual hunter or fisherman. What appears to be a highly remunerative exploitation of fisheries and game resources may in reality be an extremely costly and wasteful process of capital consumption. The social losses caused by the depletion and destruction of animal resources thus resemble the social costs resulting from the impairment of the human factor in the course of modern industrial production. Unlike the latter, however, the social losses caused by over-fishing and excessive hunting can be measured, at least approximately, in monetary terms. Thus, "at an interest rate of 5 per cent, an annual yield of $100 worth of fish represents a capital value of $2,000; if by taking $200 worth of fish we prevent them going up the river to spawn so that the flow completely stops, then we have destroyed a $2,000 capital asset to obtain a present income of $100." [1]

The following section presents evidence and estimates of the social losses caused in the past by the competitive exploitation of animal resources on the American continent. It was only after depletion and in some cases complete destruction began to be felt in the form of steadily decreasing monetary returns, that conservational regulations were enacted. By severely restricting the most destructive practices of over-fishing and hunting, these protective regulations have had the effect of preventing the complete extinction of many species and have even led to a gradual restocking of the menaced animal resources.

2. Evidence and Estimates of Social Losses Caused in the Competitive Exploitation of Animal Resources

There is no lack of evidence for the fact that the unrestricted competitive exploitation of animal resources in the past has been responsible for considerable social losses. One of the most outstanding examples in this respect is the decline of the shad and salmon fisheries on the Atlantic and Pacific Coasts. The breeding habits of these two species make them especially vulnerable to destruction. While their feeding grounds are in salt water, both salmon and shad must leave the sea and enter rivers to spawn. This is the time when they are caught in substantial numbers. From Northern California to Western Alaska packing plants are located along the coast, usually near river mouths. "By means of traps, purse seines, and gill nets,

---

[1] A. C. Bunce, "Time Preference and Conservation," *Journal of Farm Economics,* XXII (August 1940), p. 541.

the fish are caught by the thousands and taken to canneries where machinery . . . does most of the work." [2] Some of the streams of Alaska "were blocked so completely by traps that practically no fish ascending to spawn escaped. After a few years of heavy packs but scant returns of young salmon, the runs stopped and the canneries had to be abandoned." [3] The following data showing the decline of output are of interest in this connection: "Salmon canning along the small coastal rivers of northern California, Oregon and Washington reached a peak of about 250,000 cases in 1911; the 1936 pack in the same area was 29,000 cases. The Columbia river, a steady producer for over sixty years, reached its maximum of 634,000 cases in 1895. Since then, the teeming sockeye runs in the Columbia have shrunk to a fraction of their former size." [4]

The shad fisheries along the Atlantic littoral from Florida to Newfoundland offer another example of overfishing: "So severe were the inroads upon the shad that as early as 1880 there was a marked decline in the catch. Gill netters in the Chesapeake Bay and at the mouths of the Potomac and other tributaries cut down the escape of spawning adults to such an extent that the level of replacement began to suffer. With thousands of fry destroyed by sewage and industrial wastes, the runs have grown steadily smaller. The catch, about 50 million pounds in 1900, is now a little more than 10 million, with resultant higher prices for shad and particularly the ever-popular shad roe." [5]

Similar evidences of decline could be cited with respect to the Pacific halibut, the haddock and the giant sturgeon of Chesapeake Bay, "which was slaughtered indiscriminately for the roe, the bodies frequently being left to rot along the shore," [6] and which is now in

---

[2] Reprinted by permission from A. E. Parkins and J. R. Whitaker, *Our Natural Resources and Their Conservation* (New York: John Wiley and Sons, Inc., 1939), p. 517.

[3] *Ibid.*, p. 518.

[4] *Ibid.*, p. 517. More recent reports, however, seem to indicate an improvement of the situation at least as far as the salmon catch in the Columbia River is concerned (see *The New York Times*, September 15, 1941).

[5] *Ibid.*, pp. 515–6.

[6] *Ibid.*, p. 515.

danger of extinction. Fresh-water fisheries have suffered in a similar manner. "Valuable native game fish such as the black bass, striped bass, perch and crappie have almost disappeared from the Mississippi." [7] The Great Lakes, too, are reported to have suffered a noticeable decline in the abundance of fish.

Of course, it must not be overlooked that other factors than excessive commercial fishing have contributed to this decline of formerly abundant fish resources. Chief among these contributing factors has been the progressive pollution of rivers and streams which so reduced the oxygen content of the water that fish could not survive. Erosion of upstream lands makes for muddy rivers detrimental to all aquatic life. Moreover power dams not provided with special fish ladders have proved impassable barriers to migratory fish; unscreened irrigation ditches likewise have been responsible for the loss of a substantial percentage of young salmon returning to the sea.[8] However, although the destructive effects of these contributing factors cannot be denied, one of the dominant causes of the depletion of the fisheries, according to the concurring opinion of serious students of the problem,[9] has been wasteful and excessive fishing.

Unrestricted, competitive exploitation of natural resources by large factory ships of many nations has been responsible for the depletion of fur seals and whales and has caused the decline of formerly prosperous industries. Fur seals once existed in great numbers on the Pribilof Islands. Thus "it is estimated that before the purchase of Alaska by the United States in 1867, several million fur seals inhab-

[7] *Ibid.*, p. 515.

[8] "Millions of young fish accidentally enter mill races and canals. A survey was made in Washington a number of years ago, in which it was found that about 4,000 young salmon had been stranded in the irrigation ditches of a 200-acre tract. This occurrence could be multiplied many times in a single season." A. F. Gustafson, H. Ries, C. H. Guise and W. J. Hamilton, Jr., *Conservation in the United States* (Ithaca: Comstock Publishing Co., 1939), p. 275. On these and other contributing causes of the depletion of marine resources, see F. Tomasevitch, *International Agreements on Conservation of Marine Resources* (Food Research Institute, Stanford University, 1942), p. 232.

[9] See P. G. Redington and E. Higgins, "Wildlife," in C. Van Hise and L. Havemeyer, *Conservation of Our Natural Resources* (New York: The Macmillan Co., 1930), p. 482; A. E. Parkins and J. R. Whitaker, *Our Natural Resources*, pp. 513–521; A. F. Gustafson, *et al.*, *Conservation in the United States*, p. 273.

ited these islands in a single season." [10] As a result of excessive slaughter, "the animals were much reduced and actually threatened with extinction" [11] until the taking of fur seals in the North Pacific was regulated by an international agreement between the United States, Japan, Russia and Great Britain in 1911. Since that time, "the seals have increased from approximately 125,000 animals in 1911 to more than 1,800,000 in 1937." [12]

In contrast to this policy of conservation with respect to fur seals, the progressive depletion and rapid extinction of the whale is still going on. It is illustrated by "the shift of whaling centers . . . from Norway and Iceland to the shores of New England, thence to the North Pacific, with headquarters in the Hawaiian Islands, and finally south to New Zealand, the Falkland Islands, and the Antarctic." [13] The practical extinction of whales in regions where they formerly abounded merely reflects the growing efficiency of the international whaling industry. How "efficient" modern methods of whale hunting have become may be indicated by the fact that nowadays whales are "located and reported by wireless-equipped airplanes and killed by electric harpoons." [14] Moreover, the competing whaling industries of Great Britain, Norway, Germany, and the United States consist of "large steel vessels . . . [which] have been turned into veritable floating factories . . . Each of these mother ships employs a number of small but high-powered chaser boats. Equipped with a Norse invention, the Foyn harpoon gun which shoots a harpoon carrying a bomb in its tip, the chaser hunts down the whale, then tows it back to the mother ship. The carcass is dragged up a runway to the cutting floor inside the vessel, where it can be completely processed in two hours . . . A single successful whaling season in

[10] A. F. Gustafson, et al., Conservation in the United States, pp. 290–291.
[11] Ibid., p. 291. For details see F. Tomasevitch, International Agreements, pp. 77, 88–90.
[12] A. F. Gustafson, et al., Conservation in the United States, p. 291.
[13] A. E. Parkins and J. R. Whitaker, Our Natural Resources, p. 525. Estimates place the whale population of the globe at not more than 350,000—"a mere remnant of the hordes which once frequented the seas" (ibid., p. 526).
[14] A. F. Gustafson, et al., Conservation in the United States, p. 289.

the Antarctic may result in products worth $2,000,000 per vessel." [15]
Though highly profitable in terms of outlays and returns from a
short-run point of view, such methods of hunting have been responsible for a rate of killing far in excess of the natural replacement
rate of the animals, thereby preventing their natural reproduction.
This international scramble for valuable animals and their ultimate
extinction can be prevented only by means of an *international* conservation treaty.

Similar evidence of the depletion and even complete extinction
of other valuable wildlife and especially of game and fur resources
in the course of competitive exploitation could be cited almost at
random. In the United States, the fur-bearing animals were among
the first to fall under the competitive process. As Veblen pointed
out: "Business enterprise has run through that range of natural resources [the fur-bearing animals] with exemplary thoroughness and
expedition and has left the place of it bare. It is a . . . concluded
chapter of American enterprise." [16] The social consequences of this
extinction of fur-bearing animals went far beyond the destruction of valuable capital assets. For "indirectly and unintentionally,
but speedily and conclusively, the traffic of the fur traders converted a reasonably peaceable and temperate native population to
a state of fanatical hostility among themselves and an unmanageable
complication of outlaws in their contact with the white population." [17] In the course of this process, "remote trading posts in a
few years garnered a fabulous wealth of fur and left to posterity
scarcely more than scattered remnants of what had been a tremendous resource. Traffic in game as food flourished after the Civil War
and probably reached its peak in the 1880's. During that time un-
counted millions of passenger pigeons, prairie chickens, grouse,
ducks, geese, upland plover, snipe, woodcock, quail, and other food
species were annually sent to market by gunners who, except for a

[15] A. E. Parkins and J. R. Whitaker, *Our Natural Resources*, pp. 526–7.
[16] T. Veblen, *Absentee Ownership and Business Enterprise in Recent Times* (New
York, The Viking Press, Inc., 1923), p. 168.
[17] *Ibid.*, p. 169.

few months in midsummer, shot and snared game the whole year round." [18] How effective the competitive exploitation of animal resources has been in the past is perhaps best illustrated by the devastating effects which certain methods of hunting and trapping had upon wildlife.

The literature on conservation and game management is replete with evidence on this point. Suffice it to cite only two examples: "In Southern California during the winter of 1902, two hunters armed with automatic shotguns killed 218 geese in one hour and their bag for the day was 450 geese." [19] "Night hunting was formerly the cause of great killings. A boat could be poled into the midst of flocks of sleeping ducks and dozens killed with a single discharge. Many more were hopelessly crippled but died where they could not be recovered by the market hunter." [20]

No elaborate analysis is required in order to show that these and similar highly effective hunting methods made not only for an abundant supply of game but also for low prices[21] of meat and furs which, in turn, stimulated the demand for these products of hunting and trapping. The depletion of animal resources thus tended to become cumulative and self-sustaining.[22]

The results of this cumulative process of depletion may be seen from the following nostalgic account of the present wildlife situation in the United States: "The great herds of buffalo no longer blacken the plains . . . The antelope millions have been greatly reduced until they number thousands rather than millions. Elk have long disappeared from the East, and are largely restricted to the western mountains. Moose are so rare in the East that their occur-

---

[18] I. N. Gabrielson, *Wildlife in New World Economy* (mimeographed; Washington: Bureau of Biological Survey, U. S. Department of the Interior, 1940), p. 3.

[19] A. F. Gustafson, *et al., Conservation in the United States,* p. 301.

[20] *Ibid.,* p. 311.

[21] In western markets wild turkeys are reported to have been sold for 25 cents, wild geese for 10 cents and ducks could be obtained three for a quarter; skins of buffalo sold for as little as 50 cents each (*ibid.,* p. 301).

[22] A similar tendency for the depletion of natural resources to become cumulative under conditions of unregulated competition will be observed also in connection with the private exploitation of energy resources such as oil and coal. See the following chapter, pp. 110, 112–3.

rence brings about newspaper comment. Our fur bearers have been greatly reduced. Marten, fisher and otter are now scarce. The wolverine is almost gone from our forests. Beavers have disappeared with the cutting of the forests. Such common fur animals as muskrat, mink, racoon, and skunk, have declined. The wonderful and impressive spectacle of immense flocks of passenger pigeons is but a memory . . . The great armies of wild fowl are seen no more, but only the survivors of their broken ranks. The very last of the once abundant heath hen died in 1931. The whooping crane and trumpeter swan seem destined to go." [23]

Of course, it would be fallacious to believe that the abundant wildlife resources of America might have been preserved undiminished. The gradual settlement of the continent was bound to destroy the habitats of many species of wildlife. Drainage of swamps and marshes wiped out the breeding and resting grounds of migratory waterfowl. The removal of the virgin forest cover for farm and town sites and the transformation of prairie areas into grain- and cattle-producing regions made these former domains of wild animals unsuitable for practically all kinds of wildlife. However, there can be no doubt that the competitive exploitation of fish and most game and fur animals went far beyond the extent to which wildlife had to be sacrificed in the course of the settlement of the country.

While direct monetary estimates of the social losses caused by the unrestricted competitive exploitation of animal resources in the past are difficult to obtain and, indeed, subject to a number of qualifications,[24] it is, nevertheless, possible to get an idea of the present value of existing wildlife resources. Thus, "the annual value of wildlife has been estimated for humid districts of the United States at 14 cents an acre for meat and fur production, and at 22.6 cents an acre for destruction of insects and other pests. For arid regions in the United States these estimates have been placed at 4 cents and 13.3 cents an acre. Fish production has been rated at 44 cents per acre of

[23] A. F. Gustafson, *et al., Conservation in the United States,* p. 300.
[24] For some of these reservations, see the general observations regarding the magnitude of the social losses caused by the premature depletion of energy resources, *infra* pp. 114–5.

fresh water." [25] The present commercial values of existing wildlife resources may also be indicated by the fact that "the investment in the fisheries industry is approximately 1 billion dollars. Production of fish totals about 4 billion pounds annually, worth 90 million dollars to the original producers. The annual catch of furs is estimated at 40 million dollars." [26] To these commercial values of existing animal resources must be added certain less tangible recreational benefits. The Chief of the U. S. Fish and Wildlife Service estimates the "minimum monetary worth" of these recreational benefits of wild life at around $150,000,000 annually, considering the fact that hunters have been willing to pay that amount for license fees, transportation, board, etc., in some years in the United States.[27]

In the light of the foregoing analysis it is safe to assert that a substantial proportion of these commercial and noncommercial values and benefits of wildlife resources would be subject to destruction if society did not place a check upon their competitive exploitation through the enunciation and enforcement of public property rights with respect to these resources. The objective of this policy is the public regulation of fishing, hunting and trapping in such a manner as to assure normal reproduction and, if possible, propagation of wildlife which would otherwise be endangered by free and unregulated exploitation.

To summarize: Natural resources represent income-yielding capital assets whose capacity to yield an income normally extends over long periods of time. This makes their competitive exploitation subject to the principle of time preference, which accounts for the fact that consumers and producers alike are inclined to neglect the possible effects of the early exhaustion of natural wealth. As a matter of fact, under the influence of the preference for present consumption, the competitive recovery of natural resources tends to take place with almost complete disregard of the capital losses caused by their premature depletion. This general tendency is accentuated

[25] I. N. Gabrielson, *Wildlife in New World Economy*, pp. 2–3.
[26] National Resources Planning Board, *National Resources Development, Report for 1942* (Washington: U. S. Government Printing Office, 1942), p. 94.
[27] I. N. Gabrielson, *op. cit.*, p. 3.

by the fact that some natural resources are "free" commodities prior to their capture. In these cases, any incentive to consider the depletion of the available stock as a deterioration of a valuable capital asset is lacking and even the complete destruction of the resource remains substantially unaccounted for in private outlays.

The present chapter has been devoted to a particularly clear example of the depletion or exhaustion of natural wealth to which private ownership rights are established and recognized only after its appropriation by capture. In addition to being "free" commodities prior to their capture, animal resources are also self-renewable if and as long as their commercial exploitation does not interfere with the natural process of reproduction. There is, however, no assurance under competitive conditions that hunting, trapping and fishing will not be intensified beyond the point at which they begin to interfere with the natural replacement of the resources upon which these activities draw. The history of the seal and whaling industries and the depletion and partial extinction of certain types of wildlife in the United States are clear illustrations of the fact that the competitive exploitation of these natural resources in the past has been accompanied by a serious consumption of capital which remained entirely unaccounted for in private costs. The following chapters will demonstrate that the competitive depletion of animal resources is not the only case where the economy tends to give rise to unpaid social costs taking the form of a deterioration or complete destruction of valuable capital assets.

8

THE PREMATURE DEPLETION
OF ENERGY RESOURCES

THE COMPETITIVE EXPLOITATION of energy resources involves even greater social losses than those discussed in the preceding chapter dealing with wildlife. Unlike wildlife, energy resources (with the exception of water power) are not self-renewing. For all practical purposes they are limited in quantity and consequently exhaustible. Moreover, their great importance for modern production makes the rate of recovery and the possible premature depletion of energy resources a more serious matter than the destruction of most animal resources. The present chapter analyzes the manner in which the competitive exploitation of such energy resources as petroleum, natural gas and coal gives rise to considerable social costs not reflected in entrepreneurial outlays.

To speak of the premature depletion of energy resources raises automatically the problem of atomic energy as a source of power for industrial purposes. Even more generally, it raises the whole question of the discovery of new energy resources which might take the place of the present ones. As will be shown in the third section of this chapter, the possibility of finding new sources of power and their utilization for industrial purposes affects only the relative magnitude of the social losses caused by premature depletion of present resources. It does not alter the fact that the competitive exploitation of natural resources tends to give rise to substantial social losses.

Even so, it may be advisable to deal with the problem of atomic energy as a substitute for the conventional energy resources of coal and petroleum before analyzing in detail the economic and technological factors which tend to give rise to social losses in the recovery of petroleum and coal.

There seems to be no doubt that nuclear fission offers potentialities of an abundant supply of energy for industrial purposes. Atomic energy could provide power and heat for cities and large industrial plants, for ships, and for remote places where the costs of oil and coal are prohibitive. The advantages of atomic power seem to rest primarily upon the "extraordinarily low rate at which fuel is consumed in proportion to the energy released, the consequent low first cost of fuel considering the energy available in it, and the wide flexibility and easy control of the rate at which power is developed. The insignificant weights of uranium as compared with coal or other nonatomic fuel for equal amounts of heat energy may also play a role in areas of high transportation costs." [1] It has been calculated that if the cost of coal were to increase from $7 per ton to $10, "equality of operating costs between coal power plants and nuclear power plants would be reached." [2]

However, the same experts who are responsible for these calculations are realistic enough to point out that the use of atomic energy for industrial purposes still depends upon the solution of many technical problems. The application of atomic energy to peacetime uses is in its earliest beginning. Much more must be known about the technology and economy of atomic power plants before it is possible to make the controlled release of atomic energy economically feasible. Not the least important among these problems which tend to delay the application of atomic energy to industrial uses is the need for heavy protective shields against radioactivity which, at least at present, eliminates the use of atomic energy for such purposes as driving motor cars or airplanes of ordinary size.[3] While it

---

[1] U. S. Department of State, *The International Control of Atomic Energy* (Washington: U. S. Government Printing Office, 1946), p. 84.

[2] *Ibid.*, p. 126.

[3] *Ibid.*, p. 84.

is impossible for the social scientist and perhaps even for the physicist to foresee the possible development of atomic research, it seems probable that the economical application of atomic energy for industrial purposes may well be delayed for years and even several decades. But even if unforeseen progress in atomic research should shorten this period considerably, it seems safe to say that atomic energy is not likely to replace coal and petroleum resources completely in all areas in which they are needed at present. These considerations, together with the fact that available petroleum resources in the United States may be exhausted in not much more than a decade, make the premature depletion of energy resources a source of substantial social costs, irrespective of the potentialities of atomic energy.

1. The Competitive Exploitation of Petroleum Resources

Like wildlife, petroleum and natural gas are "migrating" resources in the sense that they are capable of changing their location. Crude oil tends to flow "toward any point where the pressure is reduced below the equalized natural pressure throughout the reservoir. This means it flows toward any well that penetrates the structure." [4] Moreover, crude oil and natural gas are also "free" resources, inasmuch as property rights to these resources are recognized only after their "capture." Just as game belongs to the hunter who kills it, crude oil belongs to the owner of the oil well from which it is produced, regardless of whether or not the oil migrated from beneath land to which some one else had title.[5] "Consequently, when a new pool is discovered, each operator races to drain the field before the oil migrates and is produced through a neighboring well." [6] Even if an individual owner should prefer to postpone production in an-

[4] M. W. Watkins, *Oil: Stabilization or Conservation* (New York: Harper and Brothers, 1937), p. 38.

[5] In fact, this so-called "rule of capture," which still determines the ownership of crude oil, was first laid down in strict analogy to the case of wild game whose fugacious character made the establishment and enforcement of property rights prior to its capture difficult, if not impossible.

[6] National Resources Committee, *Energy Resources and National Policy* (Washington: U. S. Government Printing Office, 1939), p. 201.

ticipation of higher prices in the future, he is unable to do so "because postponement of capture means loss of the resource altogether." [7]

It is, therefore, not surprising that the discovery of new reserves usually gives rise to a competitive drilling campaign in the course of which wells tend to be drilled and spaced in such a manner as to maximize their offsetting effect upon each other. In other words, not only will an excessive number of wells be drilled in each newly discovered dome but the position and spacing of these wells will be governed by the desire of each operator to capture as much oil as possible.[8] As a matter of fact, the more the ownership of the surface land is scattered, the more accentuated will be the general rush to withdraw oil from as many "offset" wells as possible. This practice of draining oil pools as rapidly as possible receives additional impetus from the fact that oil wells are often operated under a leasing system. In the majority of cases the owner of the oil-bearing tract receives a royalty on the oil produced and therefore is materially interested in the technique and volume of oil recovery from his property. Not infrequently, special stipulations in the leasing contract compel the operating company to produce and to drill offset wells. In other words, if the lessee decided to retard production he would not only "suffer . . . the loss of oil captured from him, but also forfeit the lease itself for neglecting the interests of the lessor." [9]

As a result of the general rush to recover crude oil from all existing fields, production may be so far in excess of demand that construction of extensive new storage facilities is required.[10] The relative oversupply of oil resulting from the competitive expansion

[7] From *The Decline of Competition,* by A. R. Burns, copyright, 1936, p. 23. Courtesy of McGraw-Hill Book Company.

[8] For an interesting illustration by maps of the location of oil wells designed to offset the draining of oil from adjacent tracts under competitive conditions, see G. W. Stocking, *The Oil Industry and the Competitive System* (Boston, 1925), pp. 140–164.

[9] F. E. Pogue, "Economics of Conservation and Proration in the Petroleum Industry," *Petroleum Industry,* Section I, Part 14, Hearings before the Temporary National Economic Committee, Seventy-Sixth Congress (Washington: U. S. Government Printing Office, 1940), p. 7439.

[10] If open pits or open tanks are used, the storage of surplus quantities of oil is bound up with certain losses due to evaporation, seepage and heavy rains.

of oil-producing facilities tends to depress prices and may cause the shutdown and even complete abandonment of marginal wells.[11] The social losses resulting therefrom go far beyond the usual capital losses involved in any shutdown of overexpanded plant capacity. For the premature abandonment of pumping wells may cause oil and gas to migrate from productive strata to beds from which the fluids cannot be reclaimed or may be due to the invasion of the oil sands by surface and underground water. Furthermore, "once oil wells are plugged, it may be impossible to open them again [even if] prices rise above their costs of operation." [12]

Moreover, low prices of oil and oil products force operating companies to save on their capital outlays by producing with cheaper and less efficient equipment than they would use if prices were higher. In order to avoid losses, producers might have to resort to technically wasteful methods of recovery. Finally, unduly low and depressed prices tend to stimulate the use of oil and its products for purposes for which other nonexhaustible resources would have been used if the price of oil had been maintained at a higher level.

Other social losses arise as a result of the fact that oil is often produced together with natural gas. In many cases, oil and natural gas are actually produced at joint costs, that is, "the production of gas with oil cannot be avoided and the gas cannot be shut in entirely without shutting in the oil as well." [13] As often happens in cases of

---

[11] It must be emphasized, however, that "once a well has been sunk, the marginal cost of production, consisting of labor to watch the well and power to pump it (if it needs pumping) is extremely small. The price at the well can, therefore, fall to almost nothing without discouraging production" (A. R. Burns, *The Decline of Competition*, p. 23). According to Professor Ise, millions of barrels of oil are reported to have been sold for as little as 10 cents a barrel (T.N.E.C. Hearings, p. 7102).

[12] National Resources Committee, *Energy Resources and National Policy*, p. 193. The impossibility of reopening abandoned wells may be due to the fact that the "well casings corrode when wells are shut in, and in some areas the rate of corrosion in shut-in wells is at least three times as great as when wells are producing. Corrosion causes well casings to collapse, and redrilling and clean-out jobs are imperative if the wells are to be pumped again." U. S. Bureau of Mines, Third World Power Conference, Transactions, Vol. VI, Paper 12, pp. 768–9 (Washington: U. S. Government Printing Office, 1938).

[13] *Petroleum Investigation,* Hearing before a Subcommittee of the Committee on Interstate and Foreign Commerce, House of Representatives, 76th Congress (Washington: U. S. Government Printing Office, 1939), p. 400 (quoted as *Petroleum Investigation,* 1939).

production at joint costs, profit considerations may require a level of production at which one or several of the joint products have to be sacrificed, owing to the lack of proper marketing facilities or even the absence of demand. Thus, if, at any given time, more gas is produced than can be absorbed by consumers, the profitability of the production of oil may induce the operator to waste the "useless" gas entirely. In other instances, oil wells have been "blown into production" and gas has been permitted to blow into the air in order to appropriate as much oil as possible in the shortest possible time from the common reservoir. Instead of providing first for adequate storage and marketing facilities (such as reservoirs, pipe lines and processing plants) for gas, one of the two joint products is wasted entirely. The social waste involved in this practice is not measured merely by the loss of so many cubic feet of gas discharged in the air. It goes much further because the loss of natural gas reduces the pressure in the oil reservoir and thereby "greatly increases the cost of recovering oil, because pumping has to be initiated sooner. Not only that, but the obtaining of the remainder of the crude requires a much longer period of time, which means more labor and a greater use of capital." [14] The premature loss of pressure in the oil reservoir also increases the proportion of the oil deposits which will have to be left underground in strata from which they cannot be recovered at all. In spite of these facts, the practice of permitting gas to blow into the air may be more profitable for the private operator than any other procedure. This again is due to the fact that slower production would result in the migration of oil and gas to neighboring fields and thus their complete loss for the owner of the tract of surface land.

2. The Competitive Exploitation of Coal Reserves

Before examining in greater detail the social losses arising from the competitive exploitation of oil resources, it might be well to consider briefly the case of coal reserves. The recovery of these important energy resources takes place under conditions which differ only slightly from those prevailing in the petroleum industry. In

[14] National Resources Committee, *Energy Resources and National Policy*, p. 190.

contrast to crude oil and wildlife, coal reserves are not "migratory" but have a fixed location, and property rights can, therefore, be clearly delimited and established before the coal is recovered. Consequently, it is not possible for one producer to take the coal from beneath a neighbor's land without committing an act of robbery and without exposing himself to his neighbor's claim for damages. In other words, there is generally no danger that coal not mined by its owner will be recovered by other producers from adjoining mines and thus be lost for the private owner.

Nevertheless, the economic and technological conditions under which coal is being produced at the present time tend to bring about a rate of production and methods of recovery which are in many respects similar to those prevailing in the petroleum industry. Scattered private ownership of the surface land and the relatively great number of mines in operation, the desire of private owners and commercial operators to realize upon their property now rather than in the future, the private costs (in terms of interests and taxes) of holding undeveloped coal land, the extension of railroad facilities to remote coal regions together with maintenance of special freight rates for such regions and highly mechanized methods of mining—all these factors[15] have been responsible in the past for the opening of mines and the development of coal fields with a capacity to produce coal in excess of actual requirements. Needless to say, such overexpansion has accentuated the periodically depressed state of affairs in the American coal industry prior to World War II.

The social losses resulting from such overdevelopment of the coal industry are not merely reflected in a rapid depletion of irreplaceable coal reserves with varied harmful consequences in the future. These social losses find their expression in excessive capital outlays, depressed prices and an uneconomical inducement to employ coal for less urgent uses. More than this, low prices and the general un-

---

[15] For a more detailed analysis of the effects of some of these as well as other factors, see Committee on Prices in the Bituminous Coal Industry, *Conference on Price Research* (New York: National Bureau of Economic Research, 1938), pp. 12–27.

certainties of the industry make it often impossible to plan and carry out mining operations as economically as would have been feasible had coal prices been higher. Thus, under the pressure of competition, individual operators find it profitable to minimize current outlays "by mining only the most readily available portion of the reserve . . . although the ultimate result is either higher costs of mining or a compulsory shift of operations to a new location." [16] The objective of reasonable conservation is likewise defeated when recovery of coal from underlying thicker beds makes it impossible to mine overlying thinner beds. "These beds, if of minable thickness, are likely to be so broken and crushed by the settling of the rocks forming the roof of the thicker bed and the floor of the thinner bed that the overlying thin bed cannot be recovered at all or only at very great expense." [17] Furthermore, during depressions "numerous mines have not been operated at a sufficiently high percentage of capacity to maintain them in good condition." [18] Depressed prices likewise account for the use of mining methods that fall short of certain minimum standards of technical efficiency which it would be possible to maintain if conditions in the industry did not make for accelerated expansion of operations.[19] A general demoralization of prices may finally cause marginal mines to be shut down with the inevitable choice of either heavy maintenance costs or premature abandonment, or both. In addition, premature abandonment makes coal mines, like oil wells, subject to progressive deterioration and destruction. For "pillars may then crumble and stopes cave in, haulways break down, waters collect and in a relatively few years, the accumulative effects may be so bad that the life hazards alone may make the reopening highly questionable." [20]

[16] National Resources Committee, *Energy Resources and National Policy*, p. 100.
[17] *Ibid.*, p. 341.
[18] *Ibid.*, p. 99.
[19] For a comprehensive and descriptive analysis of certain wasteful mining practices, see National Resources Committee, *Energy Resources and National Policy*, pp. 93–95, 338–345.
[20] A. E. Parkins and J. R. Whitaker, *Our National Resources*, p. 416.

3. General Considerations Regarding the Magnitude of the Social Losses Arising from the Premature Depletion of Energy Resources

Our analysis thus far has shown that the social losses resulting from the competitive exploitation of energy resources are reflected in

(1) An unnecessary duplication of capital outlays;

(2) The loss of reserves as a result of the fact that surplus capacity and depressed prices force operators to make use of technically less efficient methods of production and to abandon wells and mines prematurely;

(3) The premature depletion of oil and coal reserves and the negative consequences thereof upon future generations.

As far as the losses resulting from the premature depletion of energy resources are concerned it is impossible to estimate their precise magnitude. This is partly due to the fact that it is not known how long present reserves of energy resources will last. For obviously their "life expectancy" is dependent upon such unpredictable factors as new discoveries of reserves, improvements in methods of their recovery and use, the development of substitutes and future demand. The magnitude of the social losses caused by the premature depletion of irreplaceable oil and coal reserves is largely dependent upon the value which these resources will possess in the future. This future value cannot, however, be ascertained since it depends largely upon the extent to which substitutes and other potential power resources (such as atomic energy, water, wind, and the tides) may become active energy resources. And even if the future value of present resources were known, the magnitude of the social costs would still depend upon the importance which the present generation attributes to the interests and values of its descendants. In any event, the determination of the magnitude of these social losses is quite beyond the realm of statistical investigation and scientific inquiry; it is a matter of social evaluation.

Although the foregoing considerations introduce elements of uncertainty into all problems related to the depletion and conservation of natural wealth, it would be an illusion to believe that the present depletion of energy resources will affect only future generations. In the first place, such a belief fails to take into consideration that long before the point of complete exhaustion may be reached, their recovery will become increasingly costly, because oil production and mining will have to shift to deposits with leaner and leaner contents and will have to be undertaken at greater depth and in more inaccessible regions. For example, it has been estimated that drilling costs mount more or less geometrically as wells go deeper. This rapid increase in costs is due to various factors such as the need of more and heavier equipment, greater hazards, loss of drilling equipment and all sorts of tedious and expensive delays.[21] In other words, continued recovery of oil and coal and the production of their derivatives is possible only at constantly increasing costs.

Second, it has been estimated that "the known recoverable domestic deposits of petroleum have at no time since 1913—one might say, since the advent of the motor age—exceeded twenty years' supply at the current rate of consumption. In 1934, the United States Geological Survey estimated the known reserves at 13.5 billion barrels or approximately 15 years' supply."[22] More recent estimates place the reserves at 15,507 million barrels which "is equivalent to a 12 years' supply at the rate of production in 1937 (1,277 million barrels). Such a volume of oil cannot, however, be extracted in this length of time from the present fields because of the normally declining rate of production that takes place from year to year."[23] These are peacetime estimates based upon prewar findings and assumptions as to production and consumption.

The present situation is best illustrated by a number of data made public in 1943 after the enormous wartime increase of the demand for petroleum and its products and the danger of an acute shortage in the near future began to attract nationwide attention in the

[21] National Resources Committee, *Energy Resources and National Policy*, pp. 150–151.

[22] M. W. Watkins, *Oil: Stabilization or Conservation*, p. 30.

[23] National Resources Committee, *Energy Resources and National Policy*, p. 292.

United States. Despite strenuous efforts to increase the rate of discovery of new fields it was found that while the number of newly discovered fields increased from 224 in 1937 to 346 in 1941 and to a substantially higher figure in 1942 "the reserves of oil found in these discovered fields are much smaller on the average than those found in previous years. In 1935 the average size of new fields discovered was about 18,000,000 barrels; in 1941 the proved reserves of the new fields discovered averaged about 1,000,000 barrels." [24] The total of new reserves discovered each year is reported to have dropped from 2,119,000,000 barrels in 1937 to 317,000,000 barrels in 1942, even though the number of wildcat wells drilled has increased.[25] These figures tend to confirm the opinion of many petroleum technologists that the better fields are already being drawn upon. At the same time it has been estimated that the proved reserves which are equivalent to only 12 to 15 times the annual volume of peacetime production "could not be produced in toto in less than half a century." [26]

In contrast with petroleum, available coal reserves are estimated to be sufficient to meet requirements for a much longer period—in fact, for several centuries.[27] However, these predictions are based upon past and present consumption of coal only. They do not take into consideration the possibility that future requirements of coal may increase substantially owing to the fact that coal is one of the most important basic materials for numerous lines of synthetic production. In any event, it is generally agreed that "the best coal beds are being mined at a rapid rate and many are nearly exhausted." [28] For example, it has been estimated that "the high-quality smokeless coals of southern West Virginia in beds three feet or more thick

[24] *The Oil Weekly,* quoted from *The New York Times* (July 11, 1943).

[25] *The New York Times* (July 15, 1943).

[26] From a letter of the Secretary of the Interior, Mr. Ickes, to the Office of Price Administration; see *The New York Times* (July 11, 1943). For a summary of more recent data regarding the state of exhaustion of commercial mineral reserves, see Appendix IX.

[27] National Resources Committee, *Energy Resources and National Policy,* pp. 281–286.

[28] *Ibid.,* p. 64.

will last only about 85 years at the 1929 rate of mining. The life of the great Pittsburgh bed in Pennsylvania is limited to 100 years at the 1929 rate of production and the Connellsville coking coal in the Pittsburgh bed, which contributed heavily to the development of the American iron and steel industry, probably will be sufficient for only 20 to 30 years." [29]

It is hardly necessary to emphasize that energy resources, such as petroleum and coal, play a strategic role in modern industrial economies in connection with both the requirements of peacetime production and the provision of airplanes, tanks and ships in the emergencies of war. This fact alone, it would appear, tends to make it hazardous for any country to look with equanimity upon the depletion of energy reserves as long as satisfactory and cheaper substitute power resources are not available. At any rate, organized society can hardly base its attitude and policy toward the depletion of irreplaceable resources upon the doctrine that the future will take care of itself and that shortages in times of emergency will lead to the development of the required substitutes for scarce resources and materials.

In contrast with the social losses resulting from the premature depletion of energy resources, the social losses caused by the unnecessary duplication of capital outlays and the loss of reserves arising from technically inefficient methods of production are subject to more accurate computation. The following section summarizes various estimates of the relative magnitude of these social costs arising from certain clearly defined competitive practices in the oil and coal industries.

4. Evidence and Estimates of Losses in the Petroleum Industry

Unnecessary Wells. As already pointed out, the competitive exploitation of petroleum reservoirs is bound up with the drilling of wells far in excess of the number necessary for the recovery of the

---

[29] *Ibid.,* p. 64.

oil underground. These "unnecessary wells" [30] constitute duplications of capital outlays, which from the point of view of society must be regarded as social losses. Estimates of the magnitude of these losses have been advanced by the oil industry itself as well as by independent investigators. Thus, after careful investigation of the matter, the Independent Petroleum Association of America placed the total number of unnecessary wells in the East Texas field "conservatively" at 12,500 up to 1936. Assuming "that the average cost of drilling a well in the East Texas field over a three-year period is $13,000 . . . the total unnecessary expense merely for the drilling of the 12,500 unnecessary wells is in round figures $162,000,000." [31] Since 1936 more than 4,000 additional wells are reported (by the U. S. Bureau of Mines) to have been drilled in the East Texas field "so that the expenditure for unnecessary wells drilled in that field to date likely exceeds $200,000,000." [32] More recently, Professor McLaughlin, in his testimony before the Temporary National Economic Committee, referred to estimates that "3,000 wells [in the East Texas field] would have been sufficient for production and that in the drilling of 21,000 additional wells perhaps $300,000,000 has been wasted up to the middle of 1937. Moreover, new and unnecessary wells are being added to the field at an additional cost of about $13,000,000 to $20,000,000 per year." [33] In the Oklahoma City field it was estimated that 360 instead of 677 actually drilled wells would have been ample to recover the oil. At an average cost of $100,000 the total unnecessary expenditures for the 317 wells amounted to $31,700,000.[34]

An even more striking example of the high costs involved in com-

[30] "An unnecessary well is one that will fail to increase ultimate recovery of oil from the pool by an amount sufficient to return the cost of investment, plus the cost of operation and royalties and a reasonable profit" (*Petroleum Investigation,* 1939, p. 353, note 67).

[31] *Ibid.,* p. 354.

[32] *Ibid.,* p. 300.

[33] T.N.E.C. Hearings (Part 17), pp. 9529 ff.

[34] *Petroleum Investigation,* 1939, p. 354. Professor McLaughlin refers to estimates according to which the unnecessary expenditures in the Oklahoma City field are placed at $67,000,000 up to the middle of 1930; see T.N.E.C. Hearings (Part 17), p. 9529.

petitive drilling was found in the case of the so-called Golden Lane field in Mexico. "The competitive part of that field is reported to have produced oil at a cost of 19.3 cents per barrel in comparison with the cost in the noncompetitive part of the field of 5.9 cents per barrel." [35]

In the light of these figures for individual fields, it would not be surprising if the annual unnecessary capital outlays of the oil industry in the United States reached an amount of almost $100,000,-000. Indeed, Ely places the *total* number of unnecessary wells drilled each year in the United States at 4,000 to 5,000, with an annual cost of $80,000,000 to $100,000,000.[36] "This annual cost of unnecessary drilling is equivalent to a self-imposed gross production tax of about 10 cents per barrel of oil produced." [37] These are said to be conservative estimates. More recent evaluations of the total losses involved in the drilling of unnecessary wells go much further. Thus, R. J. Watkins, testifying before the Temporary National Economic Committee, presented the following estimate of the total annual losses resulting from excessive drilling of wells in the United States: On the assumption that only 50 per cent (as against the much higher percentage in the East Texas field) of the 60,000 wells drilled in the United States during 1937–38 were excess wells, one would "secure an estimated loss of capital of $300,000,000 a year, calculating the cost of an average well at $20,000. No allowance is made here for the loss of operating and maintenance costs on these assumed excess wells." [38]

Loss of Natural Gas. No less striking than the costs involved in the drilling of unnecessary wells are the losses resulting from the waste of natural gas. In 1934 the daily loss of gas in the Panhandle

---

[35] See E. L. Estabrook, *Unit Operation in Foreign Fields* (A.I.M.M.E. Petroleum Dev. Tech., 1931), p. 44 (quoted from National Resources Committee, *Energy Resources and National Policy,* p. 191 n).

[36] N. Ely, *Legal Restraints on Drilling and Production,* Reprint of address delivered before Section of Mineral Law of the American Bar Association, Kansas City, September 28, 1937, p. 47 (quoted from *Petroleum Investigation,* 1939, p. 353, note 68).

[37] *Petroleum Investigation,* 1939, p. 353.

[38] T.N.E.C. Hearings (Part 17), p. 9513.

field of Texas amounted to an average of one billion cubic feet.[39] As recently as 1938, the volume of natural gas permitted to go unused in all Texas still totaled 137.2 billion cubic feet, which constitutes "approximately 12.5 per cent of the total gas produced . . ."[40] Approximately the same percentage of losses is reported for California, where "gas blown into the air at the wells totaled 38.2 billion cubic feet in 1938, or 10.2 per cent of all gas produced."[41] Data on the loss of natural gas in other fields seem to be unavailable.

The total volume of natural gas blown into the air in the United States averaged 1½ billion cubic feet per day or nearly 6 trillion cubic feet for the period 1922 through 1934.[42] This loss of gas equaled nearly one-third of the total volume utilized.

Losses Resulting from the Premature Reduction of Reservoir Pressure. Closely bound up with the drilling of unnecessary wells and the blowing into the air of millions of cubic feet of natural gas are the losses resulting from the premature dissipation of energy pressure. As already pointed out, the loss of natural gas reduces the energy pressure in the oil reservoir. As a result the costs of recovering the oil are increased because vacuum pumping has to be introduced sooner and huge outlays have to be made on various methods of artificial pressure restoration[43]—outlays which could have been to a large extent avoided if the gas had not been permitted to blow into the air in the initial stages of competitive drilling.

In addition, as previously explained, the premature reduction of oil-reservoir pressure renders impossible the recovery of a substantial proportion of the oil under ground (thereby increasing the per-

---

[39] *Petroleum Investigation,* 1939, p. 401. See also *Petroleum Investigation,* Hearings before a Subcommittee of the Committee on Interstate and Foreign Commerce, House of Representatives, 73rd Congress, 1934 (quoted as *Petroleum Investigation,* 1934), pp. 1233–34.

[40] *Petroleum Investigation,* 1939, pp. 400–401.

[41] *Ibid.,* p. 401; for more complete and detailed figures on gas losses in Texas and California, see pp. 400–406; see also p. 302. Cf. also *Petroleum Investigation,* 1934, pp. 1234–35, 1244.

[42] T.N.E.C. Hearings (Part 17), p. 9529.

[43] For various practices designed to stimulate oil production after oil wells have ceased to flow owing to earlier wasteful extraction methods, together with some indications of losses, see *Petroleum Investigation,* 1934, pp. 1193–1226.

centage of the reserve which cannot be recovered at all even with the most efficient methods of extraction). While the magnitude of the losses of underground reserves caused by the dissipation of reservoir pressure is not subject to accurate measurement, it has been estimated that the wastage of gas in the Texas Panhandle field alone led to the permanent loss of roughly 400 to 500 million barrels of oil.[44] Similar conclusions have been reached with respect to other fields. Thus, operations in the Cromwell field, Oklahoma are reported to have recovered only two-thirds of the amount of oil which could have been produced if the field had been operated as a geological unit in accordance with generally accepted engineering principles.[45]

On the basis of the available data, it is impossible to say whether or not these figures are representative of the average underground losses under conditions of competitive operation of oil fields. It is, however, interesting to note that the above evidences of social losses under competitive conditions are in striking contrast with the results obtained in Persian oil fields under unit operation. This is illustrated by the following account of the Temple of Solomon field in Persia which was opened in 1912.

As in American pools, "gas was found on top of the structure, but the gas wells were closed in, and the gas is permitted to escape only through the wells drilled into the oil zone. It thus drives oil ahead through the pores of the reservoir rock to the point where pressure is relieved by an oil well. The initial production of wells averaged 8,000 barrels per day and production rates remained high until the gas-oil level in the well lowered and the wells started producing large amounts of gas. The upstructure wells then are closed in and wells lower on the structure are allowed to produce . . . The pool has produced 300,000,000 barrels of oil and has many years proved reserves at the present rate of extraction. The oil wells have flowed, and continued to flow, their production at all times, as the owners express 'with no more trouble than opening a tap to draw water for the bath' . . . It will be noted that in this pool oil wells are permitted to flow until they change to gas wells, whereas under com-

[44] *Ibid.*, p. 1240.
[45] *Ibid.*, p. 1253; for other fields and estimates, see pp. 1254–58.

petitive development, gas wells are permitted to flow until they change to oil wells." [46]

5. Evidence and Estimates of Losses in the Coal Industry

Important social losses in the coal industry arise in connection with its general tendency to generate excess capacity, depressed prices and the premature abandonment of mines.

Surplus Capacity and Premature Abandonment of Mines. The existence of excess capacity in the American coal industry is revealed by the first census that gives an intelligible picture of the situation, namely, that of 1880.[47] In the ensuing years "capacity continued to expand, always outstripping requirements, and in the 25 years immediately preceding the World War, the bituminous mines of the country operated on the average only 213 days a year." [48] A period of coal shortage and high prices during the war and reconstruction period (1916–1923) led to a further expansion of mining capacity, only to result in drastic liquidation and acute crises long before the outbreak of the depression in 1929. As a result, "the average sales realization, f. o. b. mines, declined from $2.68 per ton in 1923 to $1.78 per ton in 1929. More than 200,000,000 tons of mine capacity was forced out of production, and 3,274 mines . . . were shut down or abandoned. The closing of these mines involved the premature abandonment of several hundred million tons of . . . finest coals, much of which was left under ground under conditions which render its subsequent recovery possible, if at all, only at great increase in cost." [49] During the period from 1923 to 1932, no less than 4,802 mines were abandoned east of the Mississippi River and outside Ohio alone before the reserves in the holdings were exhausted.[50]

Such premature abandonment of mines, together with the general uncertainty of the industry, has been responsible for widespread unemployment of miners and the familiar pattern of "ghost towns" in

[46] *Ibid.*, p. 1255.
[47] National Resources Committee, *Energy Resources and National Policy*, p. 15.
[48] *Ibid.*, p. 15.
[49] *Ibid.*, p. 17.
[50] *Ibid.*, p. 97.

mining districts. The resulting social losses involved therein need not be taken up in this connection, as they will be discussed in Chapter 11.

Proportion of Coal Left Underground. Another and more direct measure of the social losses arising from wasteful coal mining is the proportion of coal left in the ground in different coal fields of the United States. It is of course true that even the best technical mining methods could not be expected to recover 100 per cent of the original coal content of mines—to say nothing of the fact that optimum technical efficiency is not, in most cases, identical with economically worthwhile production. In other words, some of the social losses represented by abandoned coal mines and not fully recovered coal reserves are unavoidable. Nevertheless, it is interesting to note that engineers working for the U. S. Coal Commission in 1923 were able to distinguish between these unavoidable and reasonably avoidable losses and came to the conclusion "that bituminous-coal losses could be reduced from 34.7 per cent of the content of the workings to 15.3 per cent, and anthracite losses from 38.9 to 30 per cent." [51] In other words, the avoidable losses of bituminous coal amounted to 19.4 per cent of the total physical resources in the beds worked, or 150,000,-000 tons a year—a figure which equals the total annual bituminous production of postwar Germany.[52]

Undermining and Subsidence. Another type of social loss closely connected with coal mining is the damage sustained by farmers and home owners as a result of subsidence of surface land. The greatest danger of subsidence arises where the top beds are mined first and where the recovery of coal is uneven and incomplete. Whereas uniform and full recovery of the bed would make for a more or less uniform subsidence of the surface land and thereby simplify the problem of restoration, the current practices of mining only the more

[51] *Ibid.*, p. 96.
[52] *Ibid.*, p. 17. "Evidence [of losses] for earlier years, although less complete than for 1923, indicates higher ratios of loss. In 1850, 64 per cent of the bituminous coal and 75 per cent of the anthracite is believed to have been lost in the process of mining. The loss ratios in 1880 were 50 per cent for bituminous coal and 60 per cent for anthracite, a level considerably above the 1923 ratios" (*ibid.*, p. 95).

readily available portion of the underground reserves causes sags, pit-holes and cracks of the surface land despite the fact that supporting pillars are left underground.[53] Over-all estimates of the magnitude of these damages and the extent to which mine operators are able to shift these losses to other persons are not available. Damages to homes due to two specific surface crackings and cave-ins in Pennsylvania in 1940 and 1949 are estimated at $2,000,000 and $100,000 respectively.[54]

The foregoing analysis has shown that the unrestricted exploitation of energy resources is bound up with substantial social losses in the form of unnecessarily high capital and operating costs; in addition, this unrestricted exploitation tends to reduce available oil, gas and coal reserves, with complete disregard of the inevitable exhaustion of such resources and the subsequent economic, social and political consequences upon future generations. A number of factors are responsible for this outcome, namely, the migratory character of crude oil, the fact that ownership rights to oil are recognized only after its capture, the resulting rush to drain newly discovered oil reservoirs as rapidly as possible, scattered ownership of coal reserves, and above all the tendency of each owner to realize upon his property as quickly as possible. Far from preventing the premature depletion of energy resources, the price mechanism of the market economy actually tends to accelerate the exhaustion of available resources. Private outlays do not include an adequate depreciation charge for the gradual depletion of the resources, nor do depressed prices of oil and gas lead necessarily to a contraction of production, since the operation of oil wells is possible at extremely low (marginal) costs. Indeed, low prices of energy resources and of their products tend to increase rather than decrease the rate of depletion of available reserves. For such prices will not only induce consumers to use oil and coal for relatively less urgent purposes, but they will also make it unprofitable for the individual producer to apply technically efficient methods of production which would permit a higher rate of total recovery of given reserves.[55]

In recent years, the method of restricting the production of oil and gas on a quota basis known as "proration" has often been referred to as a measure designed to do away with some of the harmful effects resulting from the competitive exploitation of these resources. While such quota restrictions of output seem to have contributed to a reduced pace in the exploitation of petroleum reserves, it would be a mistake to consider prorationing as an effective method of eliminating the social costs of their competitive recovery. The primary aim of all quota restrictions of output under a proration system seems to be the maintenance of prices in times of excess supply and declining demand. The objective is a monopolistic one, namely, to stabilize prices at a higher level than would prevail under free competition. This is easily proved by the fact that practically all quota restriction of output is based upon market conditions (as determined by the ratio of aggregate demand at prevailing prices to potential output, supply in excess of the physical capacity of pipeline facilities, etc.) and not upon such criteria as the prevention of wasteful practices, the maintenance of reservoir pressure and the maximization of ultimate recovery. Indeed, under conditions where the quotas "are based simply on a constant amount per well, production restriction may lead to further drilling and thus to waste of the reserve rather than to conservation." [56]

Although it may well be that "on the whole, there has been dis-

[55] The depletion of other mineral resources constitutes a less serious problem than the exhaustion of such energy resources as oil, natural gas and coal. This is due to the fact that many mineral resources, for example, the metals, while also exhaustible and not renewable are, at least, recoverable in the sense that the same piece of metal may be used over and over again. In fact, with respect to certain metals it has been estimated that up to 60 per cent of annual production originates from the re-use of scrap. Were it not for the re-use of scrap iron, for example, "the iron situation might become serious in the relatively near future." See A. E. Parkins and J. R. Whitaker, *Our Natural Resources*, p. 418.

[56] National Resources Committee, *Energy Resources and National Policy*, p. 198.

cernible, particularly within the past three or four years, an increasing emphasis on the conservation aspects of proration and waste prevention" [57] proration offers no satisfactory substitute for a clearly defined public policy of conservation. Such a policy would not merely imply a curtailment of production but would have to provide, at the same time, for the proper spacing of wells, the determination of drilling procedures, and the enforcement of methods of well casing and cementing, with a view to reducing costs of operation and maximizing ultimate recovery. In one word, it requires the operation and exploitation of oil fields as geological units, and according to sound engineering principles.

[57] L. S. Lyon and V. Abramson, *Government and Economic Life*, Vol. II (Washington: The Brookings Institution, 1940), p. 1007.

9

SOIL EROSION, SOIL DEPLETION, AND DEFORESTATION

As WAS POINTED OUT by Fourier, and more systematically by Liebig, agricultural production and the competitive exploitation of forest land offer dramatic illustrations of the fact that private productive activities may give rise to substantial social losses that are not reflected in entrepreneurial outlays. Both agriculture and private forestry draw upon natural resources which are subject to depletion and destruction. Just as the fertility of the soil may be depleted if proper care is not taken to maintain it, so may timber resources be destroyed if lumbering operations are permitted to interfere with the normal renewal of trees and other plants. The fact that both soil fertility and forest growth (unlike petroleum and coal) would remain dependable "flow resources" as long as certain ecological relationships are not disturbed tends to emphasize the wasteful character of productive activities leading to their destruction. However, whereas the social losses arising from the destruction of wildlife and the premature depletion of energy resources are largely confined to, and measured by, the value of the capital asset which they represent, soil-depleting methods of cultivation and forest depletion may have consequences which exceed in importance those bound up with the loss of soil fertility and forest resources. In particular, they may give rise to social damages such as floods, the silting of streams and reservoirs, the diminution of ground-water stores, the pollution of rivers, the destruction of irrigation schemes, the harmful effects of dust storms and the disappearance of wildlife. It is the purpose of the present chapter to trace these social losses resulting from wasteful farming and private forestry.

Nothing in the following discussion should be interpreted to imply that soil erosion and soil depletion are social costs which occur only in competitively organized market economies. It is well known that precapitalist societies have suffered from similar social losses, and the decline of whole civilizations can in fact be traced to an over-utilization of land.[1] However, whereas these earlier cases of social costs arising from the destruction of land resources were unavoidable, inasmuch as they resulted from overpopulation or destruction by enemy forces, and were rarely fully understood in all their implications, they are now not only understood but susceptible to control by appropriate conservation practices.

1. Social Costs in Agriculture

In order to explain the manner in which the competitive process in agriculture and private forestry tends to cause social losses, it is necessary to stress the close interdependence and relationship which exists between the land and its natural vegetative cover at any given place. For anything that upsets this interrelationship may lead to costly disturbances of several kinds. In fact, a combination of natural factors such as the topography of the land, its surface configuration, the quality of the soil and the amount and distribution of rainfall all determine the vegetation in any given area. For instance, "long droughts or rainfall so light as to leave the subsoil dry may exclude forest growth." [2] Under these conditions, grassland will be dominant, the natural forest being found chiefly along the streams. On the other hand, "trees can grow on slopes far too steep for farming, and most species do not make great demands on soil fertility,

---

[1] F. Osborn, *Our Plundered Planet* (Boston: Little Brown and Company, 1948), chaps. 6 and 7.

[2] A. E. Parkins and J. R. Whitaker, *Our National Resources*, p. 230.

but nearly all are rather exacting in their moisture requirements." [3]
The vegetative cover of any given area of land performs important
soil-protecting functions. For vegetation determines the capacity of
the soil to absorb rainfall, regulates infiltration of water, keeps
ground-water stores at the proper level and equalizes runoff and
stream flow. Normal geological erosion of the land is thus kept at a
minimum, or at least reduced to a pace at which it does not seriously
interfere with natural vegetative growth and the slow process of soil
formation.

Anything that destroys this natural balance is likely to interfere
with the protective influence which the vegetative cover exercises
upon the land. Such interference may come even before the land is
being used for farming and forestry. Indeed, the very process of
bringing virgin land into cultivation by plowing under the natural
sod, by removing the forest cover or by draining ponds and other
wet lands may have harmful effects which are usually ignored by
those interested only in increasing the area of tillable land. If carried
out on a large scale in response to a rapidly growing demand for
farm products, the process of bringing virgin soil into use may endanger the very prosperity which it seeks to promote. Thus, the
removal of the virgin sod and forest cover tends to accelerate the
flow of water to the seas, with the possibility of further harmful consequences to be discussed later in this chapter. Drainage for both
agricultural and transportation purpose (e.g., for highway and railroad construction) also has contributed to accelerated runoff of rainfall and a substantial diminution of ground-water stores, "which
once gradually fed their waters to the streams by seepage and springs
through the dry season . . ." [4] This, in turn, has caused streams,
ponds, and lakes to become low during the dry season and in some
instances to disappear entirely, thus creating "serious problems of

[3] *Ibid.,* p. 230. For a more detailed discussion of the influence of natural conditions upon the vegetative cover, see U. S. Department of Agriculture, Miscellaneous
Publication No. 388, *Living and Forest Land* (Washington: U. S. Government Printing Office, 1940), pp. 2–12.

[4] H. S. Person, *Little Waters, A Study of Headwaters, Streams and Other Little
Waters, Their Use and Relations to the Land* (Washington: U. S. Government Printing Office, 1936), p. 24.

pure water supply for agricultural and municipal uses, and . . . excessive pollution of streams no longer sufficient in flow to carry the burden which public works placed upon them at a time when their capacity appeared adequate." [5] Another consequence of ill-considered drainage has been the fact that with the decreasing and irregular level or complete disappearance of streams, fish and wildlife have partly died out because of increasing difficulties in finding breeding, feeding and resting places. Although most of these losses cannot be measured in dollars and cents, the fact remains that the worthwhileness of bringing new land into use is inadequately appraised if the social losses resulting from the removal of virgin vegetation and drainage are completely disregarded.

It may be assumed that the danger of social losses is considerably reduced once the land has been taken into cultivation and methods of organized farming are being applied. Indeed, the question may well be asked whether the farmer will not, in his own interest, avoid all destructive methods of cultivation which would reduce the fertility of the soil and thus not only the value of the land but the very basis of his prosperity and existence. The answer is: not necessarily. For instance, the declining physical productivity of the land (as a result of its overintensive utilization) might be obscured for a considerable period of time by increasing or constant economic returns under conditions of rising farm prices in response to an increasing demand for farm products of a rapidly growing population. Moreover, as long as returns exceed costs it might simply be profitable to continue soil-depleting methods of cultivation. Or the farmer may be ignorant of better methods of cultivation and continue to destroy the fertility of the land because of lack of knowledge.[6] And even if the farmer realizes that he is gradually destroying the soil, he is not likely to apply soil-conserving methods of cultivation as long as worn-out land can

---

[5] *Ibid.*, p. 24.

[6] However, not too much importance should be attributed to this factor inasmuch as the effects of destructive methods of cultivation have not only been known for a considerable period of time but have also been given wide publicity. See A. R. Hall, *Early Erosion Control Practices in Virginia* (U. S. Department of Agriculture, Miscellaneous Publication No. 256; Washington: U. S. Government Printing Office, 1937).

be abandoned for less depleted land or virgin soils. Under these conditions—which were, incidentally, those which obtained in America
until recently—the utilization of agricultural land may be accompanied by a gradual and widespread deterioration of soil fertility
even though the individual farmer may be earning an annual profit.

Other factors responsible for overintensive and destructive methods of land utilization may be heavy taxes and tenancy. Under conditions of constant increases in the demand for land and its products, land values not only tend to rise, but at any given time are
likely to reflect not the present, i.e., actual, but rather the future, i.e.,
anticipated, income-producing capacity of the land. Heavy taxes
levied upon land in accordance with this assessed capital value make
for intensive utilization. Indeed, in their desire to make the most of
their investment and to reduce the relative burden of taxation to a
minimum, farmers may intensify the utilization of their land to the
point where actual soil depletion sets in. Similarly, destructive methods of cultivation may prevail under conditions of tenancy, especially
if short-term tenancy contracts are the rule and if no provision is
made for the tenant's compensation for improvements that he may
add to the land. Obviously, "the tenant who has no assurance of
permanent occupancy can rarely afford to apply fertilizers beyond
the amount which will give him most immediate returns, or to plant
soil-building crops." [7] Finally, in still other cases, soil depletion, like
the depletion of other natural resources, may simply be due to ex-
cessively low prices which make the use of soil-conserving methods
of cultivation unprofitable and impossible.

Even more detrimental and far-reaching in its effects than the
losses resulting from soil depletion may be the damages caused by
man-induced soil erosion. As long as the land is protected by its natural vegetative cover, no serious erosion is likely to take place. As
already pointed out, such vegetation permits proper absorption and
infiltration of precipitation. Moreover, the roots of the plants possess
the required soil-binding capacity and prevent any excessive runoff

---

[7] National Resources Committee, *Farm Tenancy* (Washington: U. S. Government
Printing Office, 1937), p. 6.

of rainfall. However, if this protective cover is removed, the absorp-tive capacity of land and infiltration of water are reduced and the soil is exposed to, and may be carried away by, water and wind. For example, "when an excessive number of cattle and sheep are per-mitted to graze on pasture land, or on native grassland, or in forest openings, the vegetative cover is destroyed to the very roots, runoff is accelerated and [water] erosion begins its destructive work." [8] The same thing is likely to happen if sloping land is plowed so that fur-rows run up and down the hill, especially when the land is cultivated with clean-tilled crops such as corn and cotton. In all these cases accelerated runoff may start "dissolving [the soil], carrying soil par-ticles in suspension, or merely . . . rolling them along the surface of the ground." [9]

Of course, these destructive farming practices are not the only fac-tors which determine the intensity of soil erosion in any given case. The extent and harmful consequences of soil erosion depend upon such natural factors as the composition of the soil, the amount and distribution of rainfall and topography of the land. Thus, the sandier the soil, the more intensive the precipitation, or the steeper the slope of the land, the more pronounced will be the effects of erosion. These natural factors are, however, given and not subject to human con-trol. In other words, in order to avoid soil erosion, methods of culti-vation have to be adapted to the conditions of the natural environ-ment. If the farmer fails to do so and if rapid erosion sets in as a result of a combination of natural factors and farm practices, it is obviously the latter which must be considered as the cause of the devastation of the land and not the high rainfall or the steepness of the slope.

Fundamentally, there are two kinds of erosion: water and wind erosion. Water erosion implies a more or less complete destruction of the top soil. Severe gully erosion, which develops primarily in hilly regions, may render the land permanently unsuited for any kind

[8] H. S. Person, *Little Waters*, pp. 33–34.
[9] C. Van Hise and L. Havemeyer, *Conservation of Our Natural Resources* (copy-right, 1910, 1930 by The Macmillan Company and used with their permission), p. 360.

of utilization, be it for farming, pasture or forests. Even more far-reaching are the indirect effects of water erosion. The lowered permeability of eroded soils increases the frequency and height of floods and reduces the natural replenishment of ground-water stores, thereby affecting the water supply for domestic and irrigation purposes. Finally, the deposition of erosion debris may lead to the sedimentation of bottom lands, reservoirs and stream channels.

Wind erosion, which tends to develop primarily in semiarid regions where the annual rainfall is less than 25 inches, may affect land of any topographic character. As in the case of water erosion, "the major factor favoring accelerated wind erosion is the alteration of the surface soil by cultivation and overgrazing. The loose sandy lands generally begin to drift immediately after plowing. The finer grain soils, however, are much more resistant. Nevertheless, these with continuing cultivation lose their firmness . . . Winds sweeping across the bare, dry surface lift the smaller, lighter particles into the high pathways of air currents, and carry dust great distances as was the case in the great dust storm of May 1934. The coarser, less productive particles left by this process of wind assortment roll or leap along the surface until stopped by some obstacle in the pathway, thus covering fields of good soil and burying fences and other structures." [10] Such wind erosion is "typified in the atmosphere by drifting dust particles ranging in density from yellow clouds that turn day into night, to a barely discernible haze, with occasional moving dust 'twisters.' " [11] Other important social damages of wind erosion are evidenced "not only by impoverishment of land through stripping and covering, but by obstructive accumulations in fields, along fences, highways, and railroads; and by filling of ditches and covering of farm machinery and buildings. Also considerable damage is caused through the cutting off of young grain by the abrading sand, and by covering of pasture grasses to be followed by weedy vegetations. Fine material sifting into dwellings and shops damages the furnishings and other contents. General discomfort and menace to

[10] National Resources Board, *Soil Erosion* (Washington: U. S. Government Printing Office, 1935), p. 10.

[11] *Ibid.,* p. 10.

the health of the population are among other undesirable features of all wind-eroding areas." [12]

Needless to say, the destructive effects of wind erosion not only will be felt by farmers responsible for it but may be carried into regions located at considerable distances from the original erosion area. One of the outstanding examples of erosion is the development of the so-called dust bowl in the arid regions of the American plains and the subsequent migration of hundreds of thousands of impoverished farmers from the central states to the Pacific coast. These conditions were brought about by certain farm and grazing practices of the early settlers, the lowering of the ground-water level by drainage of swamps several hundreds of miles away, and the removal of the natural grass cover during the first World War in response to the increasing demand for bread grains and the use of the land for the growing of wheat. While the individual farmer may have been able to recover his private outlays in these cases, his production caused substantial social losses which the price mechanism failed to record entirely.

Before presenting more detailed evidence and estimates of the social costs in agriculture, it will be convenient to consider briefly the case of private forestry.

2. Social Costs of Private Forestry

The depletion of American timber resources within a relatively short period of time strongly suggests that private forestry may also give rise to social losses of considerable magnitude. Here too, however, it is necessary to keep in mind the special conditions which characterized the American scene until recently. Forests were at first obstacles to the development and proper utilization of the land. In fact, the early settlers viewed forests with a certain hostility which, it is said, became "ingrained in the American spirit," [13] and hastened the removal of forests even long after the forests had ceased to be barriers to the settlement of the country. Moreover, the depletion of

---

[12] *Ibid.*, p. 13.
[13] A. E. Parkins and J. R. Whitaker, *Our Natural Resources*, p. 237.

forest resources was also encouraged by two misconceptions: first, the common assumption that all forest land was fundamentally suited for agriculture, and second, "the firm conviction that our timber resources were inexhaustible. The early settlers came from countries where woodland was scarce, to a land of untold forest riches. It was only natural that they should have firmly believed that the forests of America could never be brought visibly close to exhaustion. The nineteenth century was nearly over before this misconception was seriously challenged." [14] As a result of these ideas, the removal of the forest cover proceeded rapidly and by 1880 "about 24 per cent of the original eastern forest had been cleared for farms . . . most of the timber being burned or left to decay in heaps on the ground or in the valley bottoms." [15] And yet, it must be realized that the clearing of the land in response to the growing need for farm land alone could never have produced the present depletion of the great forest resources on the American continent. It was only when lumbering operations began to be carried out on a large-scale commercial basis that serious deforestation of vast areas began to develop. The desire of private owners of forest lands to realize as quickly as possible a maximum income upon their initial investment resulted in a rapid expansion of lumbering and tended to intensify the competitive struggle for producing timber. Indeed, competition between different timber-producing regions soon became ruinous and led to depressed prices which, in turn, caused the use of destructive methods of production. Instead of applying methods of selective logging and systematic tree renewal, without which forest resources deteriorate and sooner or later tend to be exhausted, lumber companies found it more profitable, at least in the short run, to cut trees indiscriminately. Thus, in some cases only the best trees were taken, whereas in other instances it was found more profitable to cut even smaller and younger trees, especially if the latter were found in more accessible regions. Moreover, low and depressed prices of lumber made it impossible to apply con-

[14] *Ibid.*, p. 237.
[15] *Ibid.*, p. 236.

servational practices such as proper disposal of slash (a substantial fire hazard), the elimination of insect pests and plant diseases, and the prevention of forest fires. That many of the destructive practices in private forestry stem directly from the small-scale and competitive character of the industry is revealed by the fact that three-fourths of the forest land is owned by more than four million small owners and that it is primarily the small owner who finds it difficult to adopt yield-sustaining cutting practices. Whether this is due to the lack of capital, the pressure for current earnings, the uneconomic size of the holdings or the lack of skill with which these holdings are handled, the result is the same: timber-cutting practices on about 71 per cent of the small holdings have continued to be poor and destructive and no solution seems to be in sight for this central dilemma of America's private forestry (see Appendix X).

The resulting progressive deforestation had the direct effect of raising the costs of timber, especially that of high quality, and made it necessary to use inferior woods. Furthermore, lumbering operations had to be shifted to areas far removed from the principal markets—a procedure which not only involved higher freight charges but also caused the migration of entire wood industries. As a result of the transient nature of the lumber industries, whole forest communities have suffered and not infrequently were left stranded. At present, it is not so much the large private holder, such as the big pulp and lumber manufacturers, but farmers and other small owners whose cutting practices leave the land either without or with limited means for natural reproduction. Here, as in the case of other social costs, it is the more highly competitive sector of the industry, consisting mostly of small-scale operators, which is the greatest offender.

The full extent of the social losses which arise from the competitive exploitation of private forest resources is realized only if we consider once more that forests, in addition to being a source of timber, also perform important protective and economic functions. More than any other vegetative cover "forests retard runoff during heavy rains and periods of rapid melting of snows, and increase the amount of water that percolates into the ground."[16] This quality of forest vegetation, together with the soil-binding capacity of the plant roots, not only prevents erosion and minimizes the sediment load of rivers and lakes, but, at the same time, equalizes the flow of streams and thereby reduces the frequency and height of floods.[17] In addition, forests provide habitat, feeding ground and refuge for wildlife with its important economic and recreational values. To these values must be added the utility derived from the use of the forest ranges for grazing livestock[18] and the income which thousands of persons obtain from the commercial exploitation of various minor forest by-products, such as turpentine, nuts, fruits, sugar, syrup, tan bark, cascara bark, dyestuffs, pharmaceuticals, etc.[19] It has even been suggested that forests are conducive to favorable weather conditions by exerting a beneficial influence on wind velocity, humidity and temperature. However, these beneficial influences of forests on climate are in no way definitively established, and, indeed, it is more likely that climatic conditions determine the existence and location of forests. Nevertheless, the importance of forests as windbreaks has been emphasized by experiences in Soviet Russia and the systematic establishment of tree belts at the Western border of the American plain.[20]

Most of the aforementioned utilities and protective functions of the forest remain inappropriable by the private owner of the forest land. He is not able to exact a remuneration for the soil-binding and flood-preventing capacity of his trees. Nor does he usually receive

[16] *Ibid.*, p. 244.

[17] For a more detailed and highly interesting discussion of these protective functions of forests, see H. H. Bennett, *Soil Conservation* (New York: McGraw-Hill Book Co., 1939), pp. 421–422, and A. E. Parkins and J. R. Whitaker, *Our Natural Resources,* pp. 244–248.

[18] This is of importance for about 342,000,000 acres of forest land which are grazed seasonally by domestic stock. In some regions the agricultural economy depends upon the forage from forest ranges, the crop land being used for the production of hay and grain to carry flocks and herds during the winter. See Report of the Joint Committee on Forestry, *Forest Lands of the United States* (Washington: U. S. Government Printing Office, 1941), p. 13.

[19] National Resources Board, *Report on National Planning and Public Works,* p. 137.

[20] *Ibid.*, p. 137.

any returns from those who gather the various minor forest by-products mentioned above. It is, therefore, not surprising to find that private management of forests tends to neglect these inappropriable utilities in its economic decisions and may sacrifice them completely in the course of intensive lumbering operations.

Such neglect and disregard of the protective functions of forests may have all the far-reaching harmful consequences which we have just discussed in connection with the problem of erosion. Thus, after the progressive clearing of the land of its forest cover, infiltration of precipitation is reduced, water runoff is increased and valuable soil elements begin to be washed away. Such "sediment is carried into streams where it silts up reservoirs used for irrigation, for water-power development and for water supply; impairs the navigability of streams; injures their habitat value for fish; and spoils the recreational qualities of the water. During flood periods, moreover, the sediment may be spread over fertile low land farms ruining or seriously injuring them." [21] Furthermore, forest depletion and the subsequent excessive runoff in periods of torrential downpours and melting snow tend to increase the extent and magnitude of floods. In addition, if lumbering operations clear the land faster than it can be taken into cultivation vast areas of cutover land or "slashing" are created.[22] These slashings are especially susceptible to fire which destroys not only the remaining scrub but causes damage to litter and humus under timber.[23] The destructive effects of such fires again open the way for an acceleration of runoff which, in turn, may cause serious damage to the soil by exposing it to erosion. Finally, deforestation of coastal dunes in the past menaces present-day harbor installations, transportation systems, agricultural lands, summer homes and other improvements. If to these social damages caused by deforestation are added the losses resulting from the destruction of forest grazing ranges and the disappearance of valuable forest by-

[21] A. E. Parkins and J. R. Whitaker, *Our Natural Resources,* pp. 247–248.

[22] The area of cutover land in the South of the United States is estimated at 110 million acres; it will take 250 years to reduce this area to farms. Similarly "it will take about 380 years to settle the cutover and forest area of Michigan." C. Van Hise and L. Havemeyer, *Conservation of Our Natural Resources,* p. 342.

[23] H. S. Person, *Little Waters,* pp. 25–26.

products,[24] one finally obtains an approximate idea of the possible social losses resulting from the competitive exploitation of forest resources.

3. Evidence and Estimates of the Social Costs of Agricultural Production and Private Forestry in the United States

Specific estimates of the social losses resulting from the afore-mentioned wasteful practices in American agriculture are not available. Nor is it possible to measure accurately the losses resulting from the depletion of a substantial part of the American timber resources in the course of their competitive exploitation during the last 150 years. Because of the scarcity of relevant data and the difficulties inherent in any measurement of the direct social losses caused by the depletion of natural resources, the following paragraphs present only an incomplete summary of the social costs of agriculture and private forestry.

Evidence of Soil Erosion. The most important social losses of agricultural production are those reflected in soil erosion. The Reconnaisance Erosion Survey of the U. S. Department of Agriculture of 1934 found evidence of accelerated erosion as a prevailing condition on a total area comprising nearly 1.1 billion acres. Of the three types of soil erosion, sheet erosion was most extensive, "occurring on 855,-260,347 acres, distributed, generally, over the entire country, in varied degrees of severity." [25] Serious sheet erosion with a total loss of over three-fourths of the topsoil and some subsoil was found to exist on 192 million acres or 10.1 per cent of the total land area. "The major part of this type is now unsuited for tillage." [26] In addition, "there were 663,199,473 acres, comprising 34.8 per cent of the entire country, which has lost from one-fourth to three-fourths of the topsoil, generally." [27] Severe gullying ("embodying frequent and deep dissection on agricultural, cutover and abandoned land") was found to have

---

[24] The total value of these products may reach substantial proportions, as is indicated by recent estimates placing the returns obtained from various forest by-products at $100,000,000; see *Forest Lands of the United States*, p. 13.

[25] National Resources Board, *Soil Erosion*, p. 23.

[26] *Ibid.*, p. 23.

[27] *Ibid.*, p. 24.

affected an area of 337.3 million acres, whereas wind erosion prevailed on approximately 322 million acres.[28] More recent estimates put the area either ruined or seriously impoverished in the United States as a result of erosion at approximately 282 million acres.[29] "From an additional 775 million acres, erosion has stripped away varying proportions of the fertile topsoil. Considering only crop land, it is estimated that erosion has ruined about 50 million acres for further practical cultivation. Another area of crop land approximating 50 million acres is bordering on the same condition. Nearly 100 million acres more, still largely in cultivation, has been severely damaged by the loss of from one-half to all the topsoil. On at least another 100 million acres of crop land, erosion is getting actively under way." [30]

Reduced Soil Fertility. The most immediate consequences of both water and wind erosion are to be found in the reduction of the fertility of the soil. This reduction is due not only to the loss of plant nutrients in the eroded soils[31] and their deficiency in organic matter but also to the depletion of ground-water stores which result from the accelerated flow of water to the seas. Although an accurate measure of the nation-wide reduction in soil fertility as a result of erosion is not available, it is noteworthy that average yields per acre for a number of important crops are increasing only slowly despite substantial improvements of farm methods in recent decades. Thus, technical and educational assistance have been rendered to the farmer with a view to improving methods of crop rotation and soil and water conservation, and sizable sums have been spent on fertilizers and farm machinery "designed for more efficient tillage, seeding, placement of fertilizer, and distribution of manure . . ." [32] There is, indeed, reason to assume that "these changes and improve-

---

[28] *Ibid.*, p. 24.

[29] H. H. Bennett, *Soil Conservation*, p. 7.

[30] From *Soil Conservation*, by H. H. Bennett, copyright, 1939, p. 7. Courtesy of McGraw-Hill Book Company.

[31] It is estimated that erosion washes away annually at least 3 billion tons of solid material which contain huge quantities of the most valuable plant nutrients such as phosphorus, potassium, nitrogen, calcium and magnesium (*ibid.*, p. 9–10).

[32] *Ibid.*, p. 225.

ments should have raised acre yields considerably—how much, it is difficult to say exactly, but we believe an increase of 40 to 60 per cent would have been conservative . . . There can be but one explanation for the stubbornness with which acre yields have resisted the farmer's efforts to improve them. *The natural productive capacity of the land has been deteriorating at a rate almost fast enough to offset all of these improvements in soil and crop management.* With every step ahead we have slipped back almost if not quite as far." [33]

No conclusive evidence exists as yet on the relation between the depletion of soil fertility and malnutrition of man and animals. However, "the supposition cannot be dismissed that the alarming increase of degenerative diseases, including psychological and neurological illnesses, may be related, in a manner yet to be defined, to the steady deterioration and waste of top soil . . ." [34]

Damages Due to Sedimentation and Erosion Debris. As pointed out above, other losses of erosion result from the accumulation of erosion debris, either on adjoining, low-lying agricultural land or in reservoirs, stream channels, irrigation ditches, etc. Vast areas of fertile land are known to have been ruined and costly water-utilization facilities injured or destroyed. Special sedimentation studies of the U. S. Soil Conservation Service estimate that the annual losses resulting from "damage and maintenance costs chargeable solely to the effects of soil erosion on water-utilization facilities run into tens of millions of dollars." [35] Similar investigations into the silting of reservoirs seem to indicate that about 39 per cent of all reservoirs "will be useful for less than fifty years from the date of their construction, 25 per cent will be useful for fifty to one hundred years, 21 per cent for one hundred to two hundred years, and only 15 per cent for more than two hundred years." [36] The possible magnitude of the losses involved in the silting of reservoirs may be indicated by the total amount of public and private investments in storage reservoirs. Ac-

[33] R. M. Salter, R. D. Lewis and J. A. Slipher, *Our Heritage, The Soil* (Bulletin No. 175, Agricultural Extension Service, The Ohio State University, ed. 3, 1941), p. 5.

[34] See F. Osborn, *Our Plundered Planet*, p. 86.

[35] H. H. Bennett, *Soil Conservation*, p. 253.

[36] *Ibid.*, p. 265.

cording to Bennett, these investments exceed 2 billion dollars. In addition the aggregate investments in or dependent on all forms of water utilization must be counted in terms of tens of billions.[37]

Floods. It would be a mistake to assume that all floods are the result of accelerated runoff caused by deforestation and farm practices which opened the way to erosion. There exists conclusive evidence "that the Eastern tributaries of the Mississippi and the lower section of the master stream suffered from great floods before the land was settled and the forest was largely removed." [38] Nevertheless, the severity and frequency of floods seem to increase steadily, as may be seen from available estimates of the losses caused by major floods in the United States in the course of the last four decades (see Appendix XI). In the light of the foregoing analysis there can be hardly any doubt that improper methods of land utilization and especially the denudation of formerly forested areas must be considered as one of the reasons for this increasing severity of floods on the American continent.

Evidence of Depletion of Timber Resources. That American timber resources continue to be depleted at a rapid rate is indicated by the results of a recent nation-wide survey of the management status of forest lands carried out by the Forest Service of the U. S. Department of Agriculture. According to this survey, 64 per cent of the timber cutting on privately owned forest lands is classed as poor or worse, 28 per cent as fair, and only 8 per cent as good and better. Only 4 per cent of the small-owners' cutting can be classed as good or better (i.e., designed to build up and maintain quality and quantity yields consistent with the full productive capacity of the land) as contrasted with 29 per cent on large holdings. The bearing which these cutting practices have upon the country's future supply of timber becomes clear if it is realized that privately owned forest lands "contain 75 per cent of the commercial forest acreage; they contain much more than that proportion of the better site-class lands . . . Until recently, something like 90 per cent of the timber cut has come

[37] *Ibid.,* p. 253.
[38] A. E. Parkins and J. R. Whitaker, *Our Natural Resources,* p. 386.

from private lands." [39] Thus, 4,200,000 farmers and other small owners whose cutting practices are up to 71 per cent "poor" and "destructive" (i.e., not yield sustaining) hold 76 per cent of all private forest land. Furthermore, 37 per cent of all privately owned commercial forest land has either poor (less than minimum standard) or no fire protection.

In the light of these data, earlier estimates of the annual excess of cutting over natural replacement of forest resources are significant. According to the U. S. Forest Service, the American timber industry is taking 50 per cent more saw timber each year than is being replaced by growth. "In 1936 the total drain through cutting and losses by fire, insects, disease, etc. on our combined forest capital of saw timber and cordwood-size material exceeded growth by 2,200,000,000 cubic feet. The drain on saw timber, estimated at 47,800,000,000 board feet, exceeded total saw timber growth by 15,800,000,000 board feet or by 50 per cent. This drain exceeded growth in every major forest region except the North East. Because of poor quality, species and remote location not all growth really counts. Drain exceeded effective growth by an additional 4,500,000,000 board feet." [40]

Ghost Towns. It has been pointed out that the premature depletion of timber resources in certain regions and the subsequent shift of lumber operations to other regions frequently left entire industries and whole communities stranded. Evidence of the possible social losses caused thereby is contained in the following account of the rise and decline of lumbering in the northern part of the Lower Peninsula of Michigan:

While lumbering was flourishing in this part of Michigan, population steadily increased, villages and cities grew up, and thousands of settlers took up farms, marketing their products in the logging camps and milling centers. But after a few decades, logging and fires had destroyed all but a few scattered fragments of the original forest. The number of

[39] U. S. Department of Agriculture, Forest Service, *The Management Status of Forest Lands in the United States* (Washington: 1946), p. 5.

[40] *Forest Land of the United States,* p. 25. For a more recent over-all reappraisal of the forest situation in the United States, see U. S. Department of Agriculture, *Forests and National Prosperity* (Washington: U. S. Government Printing Office, 1948).

employees in camps and mills dropped from many thousands in 1889 to a few hundred in 1929. Many railroad lines were abandoned, leaving farmers without adequate transportation. As the cost of roads, schools, and other government services mounted, taxable rural values declined and the income of local governmental units was, perforce, greatly decreased. Many farmers, no longer able to find winter work in the woods and deprived of a local market for their produce, left the region . . . As the forest industry waned and farmers became less prosperous, the villages and towns lost their chief support and dwindled away. A desolate cutover of barren sands or scrubby second growth, abandoned or poverty-stricken farms, and ghostlike community centers have characterized this final stage in the sequence of forest exploitation of nonagricultural land, a sequence which ordinarily has required but 25 to 40 years from beginning to end.[41]

Similar social losses are reported in other areas:

In the Pacific Northwest 76 ghost towns have resulted from disorderly forest liquidation; and in another 77 communities decline of population has kept steady pace with the closing of mills due to dwindling timber supply . . . Millions of acres of cutover land have become tax delinquent and abandoned.[42]

The Ozark region of Missouri contains 35 counties originally covered with splendid stands of pine, oak and hickory. With the cutting out of timber, forest industries moved out, leaving a large dependent population unable to support itself in decent fashion. The farmers lost both nearby markets for farm produce and the opportunity for profitable winter employment. More than 20 per cent of the rural families went on relief, with the remainder eking out a sorry existence . . . In many Ozark counties 30 to 50 per cent of the land has gone tax delinquent. Expenditures for essential road, school and county government services are only a third of reasonable requirements.[43]

In conclusion, it may be said that both farming and private forestry have failed, at least in the United States, to develop methods of cultivation and production which would have kept intact the capital value of the self-renewable soil and timber resources. However, the

[41] A. E. Parkins and J. R. Whitaker, *Our Natural Resources*, pp. 242–3. See also W. T. Chamber's account of lumbering in the Pine Wood areas of Southeastern Texas, *ibid.*, p. 243.

[42] *Forest Lands of the United States*, pp. 16–17.

[43] *Ibid.*, p. 15.

social losses caused by these private productive activities tend to go far beyond the mere depletion or even complete destruction of privately owned capital values. By indiscriminately removing or changing the original vegetative cover of the land on steep slopes or in areas of rolling topography; by growing the same cash crop year in year out; by depleting forests in the course of profitable lumber operations—agricultural production and private forestry have opened the way for accelerated runoff of rainfall and caused soil erosion with all its far-reaching effects upon soil fertility, reservoirs, water-power projects, floods, and wildlife.

10

THE SOCIAL COSTS
OF TECHNOLOGICAL CHANGE

WE HAVE ALREADY DEALT with the proposition that social costs are in many instances the short-run price of economic progress and growth (see chap. 2). In this chapter we shall trace in more detail the social costs which arise in the course of the introduction of new methods of production under competitive conditions. In this connection it will be necessary to deal once more with the general thesis that the social costs of technical change are inherent in the process of dynamic change. Before taking up this point, however, we will prepare the ground for our analysis by summarizing briefly the manner in which the effects of technological progress have been treated in previous discussions.

According to Adam Smith and later J. B. Say, the introduction of new machines has the tendency of reducing costs and prices and thereby opening the way for greater output. This increase of production, Say pointed out, is not limited to those industries which produced and introduced the new machine; the subsequent reductions of costs and prices of commodities are said to enable consumers to demand more goods and services of other industries not directly affected by the new machine. The resulting increase of production in all industries, according to Say, makes possible the employment of a greater number of workers than were originally displaced by the new method of production. The effects of technological improvements are thus presented as unequivocally beneficial, not only from the point of view of society but also from that of the individual worker whose temporary loss of employment is more than offset by his gains as a consumer.[1] More than a hundred years after Say's writings, P. H. Douglas[2] and W. I. King[3] on the basis of statistical investigations arrived at substantially the same although perhaps more refined conclusions. These conclusions are summarized by King in the following words: "No facts or figures thus far discovered cast any doubt upon the approximate validity of the orthodox economic theory that the forces giving rise to technological unemployment tend, at the same time, to create a demand for new goods, and that the production of these new goods normally calls for a volume of labor roughly equaling the quantity displaced. From this premise it follows that since labor-saving devices increase production without materially decreasing the ability of workers to find jobs, such devices are decidedly beneficial rather than injurious to society as a whole." [4]

It is well known that these optimistic conclusions were not held unanimously even among classical economists. Ricardo revised his earlier contention of the impossibility of lasting displacement of labor by machinery in later editions of the *Principles* (Chapter 31). Important qualifications of the orthodox doctrine were advanced by John Stuart Mill and J. E. Cairnes. Open opposition to the doctrines of Smith and Say came from some of the earliest dissenters and critics of classical economics, namely Sismondi and Malthus.[5] It re-

---

[1] J. B. Say, *A Treatise on Political Economy* (3rd American edition, Philadelphia, 1827), chap. VII, pp. 26–31. For Adam Smith's position on the advantageous effects of machines see *The Wealth of Nations,* pp. 271–272.

[2] See P. H. Douglas, "Technological Unemployment," *American Federalist* (Vol. XXXVII, No. 8, August 1930), pp. 923–950. See also P. H. Douglas and A. Director *The Problem of Unemployment* (New York: The Macmillan Co., 1931), esp. pp. 121–141.

[3] W. I. King, "The Relative Volume of Technological Unemployment," *Proceedings of the American Statistical Association,* Vol. XXVIII (March 1933), pp. 33–39.

[4] *Ibid.,* p. 39.

[5] Sismondi's position has been indicated briefly in the discussion of the general nature and significance of social costs (see *supra,* p. 31). An excellent summary of the whole controversy is to be found in A. Gourvitch, *Survey of Economic Theory on Technological Change and Employment.* Work Projects Administration, National Research Project, Report No. G VI (Philadelphia, 1940), pp. 39–79.

mained, however, for Marx to view the introduction of technical improvements in relation to the pattern of cyclical instability of the capitalist process. Indeed, the introduction of new and improved machinery is, according to Marx, an integral part of the capitalist process and the decisive factor in the process of continuous structural change which has been the most significant feature of capitalist production since the Industrial Revolution.

Technological progress is viewed as the weapon with the aid of which the individual capitalist tends to accumulate more surplus value and to keep abreast in the competitive struggle. At the same time, technological improvements provide the outlets for an expanded investment of available surplus value (or profits). While such expansion is under way technological improvements tend to lead to a temporary contraction of the reserve army of the unemployed and raise wages above the minimum level. However, technological progress also sets into motion tendencies in the opposite direction. By increasing the amount of capital per worker (the "organic composition of capital"), new machines lower the relative demand for workers, which means a lower surplus, reduced investments and ultimately an expansion of the reserve army of unemployed with the simultaneous effect of wages falling below the minimum level. Thus, according to Marx, the displacement of workers by technological improvements not only is functionally related to the cyclical process but has ultimately the effect of swelling the ranks of the reserve army and of keeping wages at the minimum level. In other words, "it is capitalistic accumulation itself that constantly produces, and produces in the direct ratio of its own energy and extent, a relatively redundant population of laborers, i.e., a population of greater extent than suffices for the average needs of the self-expansion of capital, and, therefore, a surplus population." [6] This relative surplus population may take "the more striking form of the repulsion of laborers already employed, or the less evident but no less real form of the more difficult absorption of the additional laboring population through the usual channels." [7] In short, "the laboring

[6] K. Marx, *Capital* (Chicago, 1906), Vol. I, p. 691.
[7] *Ibid.*, pp. 691–692.

population . . . produces, along with the accumulation of capital produced by it, the means by which itself is made relatively super-fluous, is turned into a relative surplus population; and it does this to an always increasing extent." [8]

1. The Problem of Technical Change during the Twentieth Century

This is not the place to discuss in detail the special conditions which prevailed during the second half of the nineteenth century and which led to an increase rather than a decrease of employment as well as a higher rather than a lower level of living, in contradiction to Marx's anticipation. What Marx, theorizing on the basis of data reflecting the conditions during the first fifty years of mechanized production in England, did not and perhaps could not foresee were primarily four factors: first, the extraordinary expansionist effects which the extension of capitalism to the rest of the world would have; second, the special role which the economic development of America would play both as a market of goods and as an outlet (until recently) for Europe's surplus population; third, the effects which trade unions and collective bargaining would have on the intensity of competition among workers and the distribution of the national product; and fourth, the improvements of working conditions caused by government regulation. Even without a detailed analysis of these factors, it must be clear that the impact of technological change is not necessarily the same at different times. There can be hardly any doubt that the conditions which made for a rapid expansion of production during the second half of the nineteenth and first decades of the twentieth centuries were exceptionally favorable for a relatively quick reabsorption of displaced workers.[9]

Furthermore, the capacity for assimilating technical changes depends upon a number of conditions which are not always fulfilled

[8] *Ibid.*, p. 692.

[9] Whether or not the particular circumstances of the period immediately following Marx invalidated his doctrine or merely suspended temporarily the validity of his predictions is a methodological question which need not concern us here. For a detailed analysis of the favorable factors which made for a quick absorption of displaced workers up till 1914, and the obstacles to such absorption, see E. Lederer, *Technical Progress and Unemployment. An Enquiry into the Obstacles to Economic Expansion* (Geneva: International Labor Office, 1938), pp. 1–2.

in all sectors of modern industrial economies. Thus, the absorption of workers displaced by new machinery is dependent, as Say pointed out long ago, upon the subsequent expansion of production either in the same industry or in those branches of the economy which benefit indirectly from the new method of production. This capacity of expanding production and absorbing unemployed laborers is, however, determined by the extent to which the lower costs of production resulting from technical progress are actually passed on to the consumer in the form of reduced prices, on the one hand, and the responsiveness of the demand to lower price levels, on the other. The extent to which economies in the costs of production are passed on to the consumer depends upon the character of competition prevailing in the particular industry. Generally speaking, it can be said that conditions of monopoly and monopolistic competition may reduce the competitive pressure under which lower costs find their way to the consumer in the form of lower prices. In other words, such conditions are not conducive to an expansion of production in response to technical progress. In fact, all attendant phenomena of monopolistic competition, such as price policies and price rigidities (especially of cost prices), product differentiation, restrictions of output and the absence of "free entry" conditions in many industries, seem to reduce the capacity of the industrial system to reabsorb into the productive process workers displaced by technical improvements at some point. These considerations lend support to the conclusion that the obstacles in the way of a smooth readjustment of the economy after technological changes have taken place not only are considerable, but tend to increase in importance under modern economic conditions.

Another important factor which tends to obstruct the automatic and speedy assimilation of improved techniques of production is the immobility of the displaced workers. For, obviously, the more specialized the worker's skill and occupation and the more he is tied to his place of residence by family relations or home ownership, the more incapable and reluctant will he be to submit to changes and movements which new methods of production thrust upon him.

Finally, the social and economic effects of technological advances can be fully understood only if they are viewed in relation to the general phenomenon of cyclical instability of modern industrial society. Indeed, the repercussions of technological changes are so fused with the general effects of the expansion or contraction of production that it is well-nigh impossible to isolate them in practice. As a matter of fact, it is probable that the favorable effects of technological improvements upon labor actually precede, or coincide with, the introduction of the new method of production. Thus, it has been suggested that "the greatest stimulus to demand for labor is given by technological change *while it is being introduced,* while the instruments designed to embody it are under construction; and the stimulus is given through that construction, through the demand for capital goods which it implies, and through the impulses it thus gives to a general boom in business. The greater the volume of that construction and of that demand, the more powerful is the boom and the greater the demand for labor." [10] In other words, as Marx pointed out, the actual displacement of laborers after the introduction of technical changes may be felt only in the ensuing depression.

The foregoing discussion opens the way for a number of important conclusions. In the first place, it must be clear that the effects of technological improvements are far more complex and at times considerably less beneficial than is usually assumed. In any event, "a facile dismissal of the problem on the assumption that an automatic adjustment to industrial shifts is effected, with reëmployment of all displaced productive factors, is no longer possible." [11]

Second, the impact of technological advance cannot be ascertained by inspection and statistical measurements. The effects of technical change in a given industry are felt over so vast an area of allied and competing industries and become so fused with the consequences of other changes and business movements that neither unemployment surveys nor general investigations into labor productivity and the

[10] A. Gourvitch, *Survey of Economic Theory,* p. 194.

[11] F. C. Mills, "Industrial Productivity and Prices," *Journal of the American Statistical Association,* XXXII (June 1937), No. 198, p. 247.

displacement and absorption of labor by new methods of production, and still less studies based upon questionnaires and interviews of dismissed workers,[12] are capable of determining even approximately the impact of technical advances.

Third, the traditional theoretical treatment of technical changes, by concentrating its attention upon the problem of ultimate readjustment, seems to have led the entire discussion into a blind alley. For, even if the introduction of new techniques of production is ultimately followed by some kind of readjustment and even by an increase in the demand for labor somewhere in the economic system, the real question is rather how quickly and how smoothly such reabsorption and readjustment are likely to take place. Our analysis so far indicates that the disappearance of the exceptionally favorable conditions for a quick absorption of displaced workers and the development of certain monopolistic practices have considerably reduced the capacity of the market economy to readjust and adapt itself to technical changes within relatively short periods of time. It is, therefore, not only possible but probable that the introduction of technical improvements will give rise to periods of prolonged economic maladjustments and unemployment.

2. The Social Costs of Technological Progress

The foregoing conclusions gain additional support if we consider the manner in which the market mechanism determines whether or not the introduction of technical improvements is to be undertaken. Two cases may be distinguished. Under competitive conditions with no control of supply and free entry of new firms, innovations will be introduced regardless of the (private) losses resulting from the de-

[12] The industrial worker can hardly be expected to recognize either the cause of his unemployment or the reason for his reëmployment. Indeed "a little reflection will . . . show that only in a minority of cases will workmen be able to recognize the technological change responsible for their dismissal. For this it would be necessary that machines be introduced in an existent plant under the eyes of the workmen and that dismissal be affected immediately after." J. A. Schumpeter, *Business Cycles* (New York: McGraw-Hill Book Company, 1939), Vol. II, p. 514 n. Moreover, as F. B. Garver after Marx pointed out, technological change may simply make unnecessary the hiring of new workers as the old ones leave their job. *Jour. Am. Statist. Assoc.* (March 1933), Suppl., p. 40.

preciation which the new method causes to the value of existing capital equipment. Entrepreneurs who delay the introduction of new techniques until they have fully amortized the original value of their old equipment (or, what amounts to the same thing, until savings in costs expected from the new method are sufficiently great to compensate for the remaining value of old equipment) will be forced out of business by new firms not burdened by obsolete equipment. In fact, under competitive conditions technical improvements will be introduced as soon as the prospective average total costs of production (with the new equipment) are low enough to permit the recovery of the new capital in a relatively short period of time. In short, no attention is paid to the financial losses resulting from the depreciation of the value of capital already invested.[13]

When competition is imperfect, i.e., if entrepreneurs in one way or another exercise control over amounts supplied and if conditions of free entry of new firms and new investments are not fulfilled, the innovating firm does take into consideration those financial losses which result from the fact that the new technique renders obsolete the capital equipment already in use. And even though these losses are measured not by the value of the original investment but only by that part which is not yet fully accounted for by the sum total of past depreciation allowances, these losses may be substantial. That the entrepreneur will take into account the losses caused by the obsolescence of existing capital equipment in considering its replacement by new equipment is easily demonstrated if we consider the case where the original investment was financed by the issuance of bonds. For in this case it is clear that the fixed charges for interest and amortization continue regardless of whether or not new equipment is substituted for the old. Evidently, the situation is essentially the same if the financing of the original investment was made by stock issues. Hence, only if the economies expected from the new equipment are sufficient to compensate also for the financial losses caused

---

[13] For the most detailed analysis of the factors considered in connection with innovation decisions, see Eugene L. Grant, *Principles of Engineering Economy* (New York: The Ronald Press Company, 1938), chaps. 14 and 15.

by the obsolescence of existing capital will the new equipment be introduced. In other words, under conditions of imperfect competition the replacement of old techniques of production by new ones tends to be slower than under competitive conditions.

However, from the point of view of the analysis of social costs, the significant thing is that in both cases the introduction of new equipment in the market economy proceeds in terms of a cost calculation which fails to take into consideration two important kinds of social costs of technological progress: namely, those resulting from the depreciation of existing capital equipment owned by other firms and certain harmful effects of technical change upon workers.

To consider the losses resulting from the obsolescence of existing equipment as social costs calls for further explanation. The prevailing opinion is that the economic worth-whileness of cost-reducing improvements should be determined on the basis of a comparison of the prospective average costs with the costs (including repair and increased operating costs) involved in continuing the old equipment, irrespective of any possible losses due to the obsolescence of the latter. In support of this view it is usually pointed out that the loss to the owners of the old machines is offset by an equivalent gain to consumers who obtain their products at lower prices.[14] Such a comparison of gains and losses may serve the purpose of a static, i.e., timeless analysis, although it offers cold comfort and certainly no practical remedy to the individual entrepreneur to be told that the losses which forced him into bankruptcy are offset by the gains of those who are getting their goods for less than the price that would have repaid the average total costs. If the dynamic repercussions of a periodic curtailment of the earning capacity of firms operating with old equipment are considered, the introduction of improvements irrespective of the devaluation of existing equipment appears in a different light. In fact, to the extent to which such periodic curtailment of the earning capacity of existing businesses leads to bankruptcy and failure the social costs of technological progress merge

[14] A. C. Pigou, *Economics of Welfare,* pp. 188–190; Oskar Lange and F. M. Taylor, *On the Economic Theory of Socialism,* pp. 111–114.

into the social costs of depressions and cannot be distinguished from them.[15]

Nothing in the foregoing analysis is intended to suggest that durable capital equipment should be discarded only after it is worn out completely and has been fully amortized. What we wish to emphasize is the fact that under competitive conditions only a small proportion of the capital losses caused by the introduction of new machines enters into private business considerations; the bulk of these losses has to be borne by other firms in the form of a progressive depreciation of their capital equipment.[16]

[15] The nature of these repercussions resulting from the constant reduction of the earning power of older establishments has often been analyzed, especially by those authors who consider technological change and innovation as the primary cause of the business cycle. Veblen, for example, held the view that the progressive improvement of the industrial process and the resulting discrepancy between the current earning power and the accepted capitalization of older firms makes for a more or less pronounced but chronic depression under the fully developed regime of the machine industry—a state of affairs which is mitigated only by speculative movements or "through a freer supply of the precious metals or by an inflation of the currency, or a more facile use of credit instruments as a subsidiary currency mechanism." See T. Veblen, *The Theory of Business Enterprise* (New York: Scribners, 1915), p. 235; cf. pp. 227–234. Another who considers the rapid obsolescence of capital through technological progress as the principal cause of the depression is R. Liefmann, *Grundsätze der Volkswirtschaftslehre* (Stuttgart and Berlin, 1919), Vol. II, pp. 755–762. It is interesting to note that Schumpeter, whose explanation of the business cycle is based entirely upon his concept of "innovation," hardly stresses this relationship between technological improvement, obsolescence, capital losses and depression, although he describes in considerable detail the effect of innovation upon the "old" firms. See J. A. Schumpeter, *Business Cycles,* Vol. I, Chap. 4, esp. p. 134.

[16] Nor do we think that Pigou's arguments on the subject are convincing. Pigou pointed out that if allowance has to be made for the depreciation which the improvement causes in the value of existing plant, "reason would be shown for attempts to make the authorization of railways dependent on the railway companies compensating existing canals, for refusals to license motor omnibuses in the interest of municipal tramways, and for the placing of hindrances in the way of electric lighting enterprises in order to conserve the contribution made to the rates by municipal gas companies." See A. C. Pigou, *Economics of Welfare,* p. 188. The answer to this argument was given in 1913 by J. A. Hobson, whom Pigou had criticized for emphasizing the necessity of making allowance for the depreciation of existing capital equipment. Hobson replied as follows: "A municipality faced with a proposal to scrap its present expensive plant in favor of a new plant which will work at slightly lower costs, will properly take into consideration the unexhausted value of the existing plant, upon the capital value of which interest must be paid whether it is scrapped or not. If that unexhausted value is great, the new plant will rightly be substituted more slowly than if the unexhausted value is small, for the interest on this capital, if considerable,

Other elements of social costs are revealed if we consider briefly the effects of technical change upon the worker. Quite apart from the net effect which technological improvements are likely to have upon total employment and job security, one thing appears certain: innovations and the increasing use of machinery have had the effect of reducing the skill requirements in modern production. In fact, particular skills have become obsolete and occupations which formerly could be filled only by a limited number of trained workers can now be occupied by less skilled laborers. This, however, is merely another way of saying that the competition among workers tends to increase —a fact which is bound to be reflected in lower wages. The outstanding historical example in this respect will probably always remain the introduction of machinery during the initial stages of the Industrial Revolution which, by opening the way to woman and child labor in the manufacturing process, led to a continuous increase of competition among workers, depressing wages often to the level of starvation.

However, it would be a mistake to believe that the introduction of machinery had these results only during the Industrial Revolution. Virtually every new technological advance tends to render particular skills and occupations obsolete and increases the competition among workers. Laborers with obsolete skills are likely to encounter temporary, if not permanent, employment difficulties. Indeed, for older workers it may become impossible to find any employment at all; younger workers will be forced to acquire new skills through reschooling and retraining. If technical changes lead to the disappearance of entire industries and if reëmployment opportunities are available only in other localities, displaced workers not only have to acquire new skills but, at the same time, must submit themselves to costly movements to other places. In fact, technical progress in some cases left entire communities and industrial areas stranded and

---

will outweigh a slight economy of working costs in the case of the new plant. In a word, it is evident that the cost of scrapping must enter into considerations of business policy. Under competitive industry, however, it is not taken into account. The former, not the latter, represents the social policy as regards rate of improvements." See J. A. Hobson, *Gold, Prices and Wages* (London, 1913), pp. 107–108.

created the conditions of "ghost towns." [17] Needless to say, none of the aforementioned costs of transition made necessary by technical changes tend to be reflected in private costs and, therefore, fail to be taken into account in entrepreneurial decisions as to whether or not technological improvements are to be introduced.[18]

Before examining these social costs it is necessary, however, to deal once more with the proposition that the social costs of technical progress are inherent in dynamic change. Schumpeter, for example, holds with Marx that the most essential aspect of capitalism is its inherent tendency of dynamic change. In fact, according to Schumpeter, the fundamental impulse that sets and keeps the capitalist engine in motion comes from various innovations such as "new consumers' goods, the new methods of production or transportation, the new markets, the new forms of industrial organization that capitalist enterprise creates." [19] It is these "innovations" and the manner in which they are brought about by individual firms which "incessantly revolutionize the economic structure *from within,* incessantly destroying the old one, incessantly creating a new one. This process of Creative Destruction is the essential fact about capitalism. It is what capitalism consists in and what every capitalist concern has got to live in." [20]

Now if the destruction caused by technical advances is implicit in

---

[17] For factual evidence on this point see T.N.E.C. Hearings, Part 30, *Technology and Concentration of Economic Power* (Washington: U. S. Government Printing Office, 1940), pp. 17229–17232.

[18] As was pointed out in Chapter 3, this neglect and shift of the social costs of transition and adaptation to other persons or to the community is not limited to the case of technological change. It is rather a common phenomenon in the market economy and accounts, for example, for much of the persistent opposition of large groups of industrial producers and laborers to the removal of barriers to international trade in the interest of a greater international division of labor. Such opposition is based upon the realization that the competitive process offers no assurance to the individual worker or entrepreneur, whose job or business may be eliminated in the course of the transition made necessary by the importation of goods from abroad, that they will receive adequate compensation for their sacrifices either in terms of temporary financial support or in terms of an adequate share in the ultimate benefits resulting from the better utilization of resources incident upon the more effective international division of labor.

[19] J. A. Schumpeter, *Capitalism, Socialism and Democracy*, p. 83.

[20] *Ibid.*, p. 83.

the structure of capitalism and can even be called "creative," the question obviously arises whether it is still possible to speak of social costs of technical progress. Schumpeter's own position seems to be open to more than one interpretation. After emphasizing the need for judging the performance of capitalism over time, as it unfolds through decades or centuries, Schumpeter states that "a system—any system, economic or other—that at *every* given point of time fully utilizes its possibilities to the best advantage may yet in the long run be inferior to a system that does so at *no* given point of time, because the latter's failure to do so may be a condition for the level or speed of long-run performance." [21] Once more this thesis seems to challenge the whole conception of social costs. It seems to assert that social costs are the price that has to be paid for the long-run efficiency of the system which, apparently as a result of the possibility of shifting social costs to the shoulders of the community, may make possible a social performance and a degree of spontaneity and long-run progress superior to that of "less spontaneous" systems. Indeed, it may or may not. I know of no criteria in terms of which the question could be given a satisfactory and unambiguous theoretical answer. The long-run social performance of any economic system can be accounted for only in terms of many factors which are part of the whole economic, political and geographic constellation within which the system operates. The relative weight of any of these factors is not easily measured by statistical tools but is largely a matter of subjective evaluation.

The difficulty of arriving at an answer based upon empirical evidence is even greater; we would have to wait for another two or three hundred years of socialist evolution (let us say in Great Britain or Soviet Russia) before a comparative appraisal of the over-all performance of socialism could be undertaken. But let us accept Schumpeter's thesis—in other words, let us assume that the social wastes evidenced in the social costs of production at a given point of time are actually the condition for the most rapid long-run rate of growth and a high level of performance. It would still be important to trace

[21] *Ibid.*, p. 83.

the social costs as fully as possible, to measure their importance and to take account of them in the theoretical models in terms of which capitalist reality is analyzed. Furthermore, the question remains whether the shifting of social costs cannot be carried too far (so to speak, beyond the point of diminishing returns in terms of long-run efficiency and rate of growth) and whether a system whose long-run spontaneity and level of performance are bought at the price of social costs is not inherently unstable (and hence inefficient) in view of the opposition it is bound to call forth, under democratic conditions, from those who are called upon to foot the bill of social costs.

However, we need not lose ourselves in speculations of this kind. Schumpeter himself seems to provide an answer to the challenge he raises. In his subsequent analysis of monopolistic practices he shows convincingly and in opposition to the whole trend of most modern theories of monopolistic and oligopolistic competition that certain restraints of trade may perform important protective functions against the perennial gale of creative destruction. In fact, according to Schumpeter there are several situations in which restraints of trade by old concerns, whether or not directly attacked by innovations, may produce positive results. In Schumpeter's own words:

[1] Situations emerge in the process of creative destruction in which many firms may have to perish that nevertheless would be able to live on vigorously and usefully if they could weather a particular storm . . .

[2] Sectional situations arise in which the rapid change of data that is characteristic of that process so disorganizes an industry for the time being as to inflict *functionless losses and to create avoidable unemployment* . . . [italics added]

[3] There is certainly no point in trying to conserve obsolescent industries indefinitely; but there is point in trying to avoid their coming down with a crash and in attempting to turn a rout, which may become a center of cumulative depressive effects, into orderly retreat.[22]

In all these situations restraints of trade, including price regulations, "may in the end produce not only steadier but also greater expansion of total output than could be secured by an entirely uncontrolled

[22] *Ibid.,* p. 90.

onward rush that cannot fail to be studded with catastrophes." [23] In his further analysis of business practices designed to preserve capital values by delaying the application of cost-reducing new inventions, Schumpeter points out that restrictive practices of this kind, if they existed, "would not be without compensatory effects on social welfare." [24] And again, "a new type of machine is in general but a link in a chain of improvements and may presently become obsolete. In a case like this it would obviously not be rational to follow the chain link by link regardless of the capital loss to be suffered each time. The real question then is at which link the concern should take action. The answer must be in the nature of a compromise between considerations that rest largely on guesses. But it will as a rule involve some waiting in order to see how the chain behaves." [25] This is exactly the conclusion which emerges from the preceding analysis of the social costs of technological progress under conditions of competitive enterprise.

However, the most important social losses bound up with technological improvements are neither the neglected capital losses of other entrepreneurs nor the costs of transition which fall on the individual worker, but the costs of "technological" unemployment to which the introduction of new methods of production tends to give rise under certain economic conditions. The general nature of these social costs of unemployment will be discussed in the following chapter as part of the social costs of economic depressions.

The positive results of the present chapter may be summarized as follows. In introducing technical improvements, the individual entrepreneur tends to disregard completely two important types of social losses to which his innovation tends to give rise: first, the capital losses which other firms suffer as a result of the new technique of production; second, the losses which technical changes tend to cause to laborers. These losses are measured by various individual expenses involved in temporary unemployment, moving, retraining and a general reduction of skill requirements, and, more important, they may be represented by extended periods of unemployment during which (as will be shown presently) the social overhead costs of labor are shifted to the individual worker. In other words, technical improvements may appear economically justified from the point of view of the individual entrepreneur (i.e., in terms of private costs and private returns) although a more accurate calculation of the total costs of the innovation might show its introduction to be unjustified, premature and wasteful.

11

THE SOCIAL COSTS OF UNEMPLOYMENT
AND IDLE RESOURCES

THE FOLLOWING DISCUSSION of the social costs of unemployment is designed to apply the techniques of the preceding analysis to the most destructive feature of the market economy: unemployment.

This does not mean that unemployment and cyclical instability are regarded as uncontrollable or that other forms of economic organization will necessarily be free of this feature of capitalism. Even a completely planned economy may, under certain conditions, experience periods of unemployment and idle resources. However, for the purpose of our discussion, we accept the views of those economists who hold that the typical operation of the competitive market economy sets the conditions for recurrent periods of depression, and that business cycles would occur even if such special circumstances as extreme income inequalities, excessive credit elasticity, price rigidities, declining investment opportunities and "economic maturity" were completely absent.

Again, this is not to deny the basic approach of those business-cycle theories which, seeking to explain economic fluctuations largely within the theoretical framework of equilibrium economics, regard one or the other of the above-mentioned factors as the cause of recurrent deviations from an imagined norm. But any one-sided emphasis upon such factors as oversaving or price rigidity tends to overlook numerous equally if not more basic disequilibrating forces which make for instability under conditions of competitive private enterprise. The most prominent of these forces seem to be the following: the fact that the combined action of producers acting independently of each other may have the effect of distorting and rendering false their own cost and price expectations; the cumulative and self-sustaining nature of price rises and declines; the increasing relative importance of durable goods in modern economic life and the "acceleration" of the demand for and production of producers' goods; the propensity to speculate and the tendency of prices to rise or fall in accordance with speculative expectation and behavior and the disproportions created by innovations giving rise to a depreciation of capital and labor; and finally, the fact that producers, acting in response to price rises and without accurate information about future effective demand, are likely to overexpand production, especially of durable goods, in such a manner that periods of relative overproduction with corresponding disproportions between cost prices and product prices call for a readjustment of relative prices before production can be resumed again.

1. The Neglect of the Fixed Cost of Labor

In order to understand the nature of the social costs of unemployment it is only necessary to elaborate some of the ideas advanced in connection with the discussion of the social costs resulting from the impairment of the human factor of production by occupational diseases and industrial accidents. It was argued then that the impairment of the worker's physical and mental health in the course of modern industrial production does not differ fundamentally from the depreciation of nonhuman factors of production. And yet, in contrast with the calculable depreciation of privately owned factors of production, the impairment of the physical and mental capacity of the laborer fails to be reflected in entrepreneurial outlays under the customary wage system of the market economy as long as compulsory legislation does not provide for an adequate system of accident and industrial-health insurance.

Just as the human factor of production is subject to deterioration and impairment in the course of the productive process, so do its "production" and "upkeep" entail certain fixed costs. Not only are monetary outlays involved in raising the new generation of workers, but, in addition, young persons have to be provided with some kind of training, which may vary from the elementary education of the unskilled worker to the highly specialized training of the professional man and intellectual worker. In addition to this fixed investment of time and money in raising the family of the worker, there are the costs of maintaining the worker himself in proper "working conditions." These costs of bringing up the laborer and maintaining his working capacity intact are relatively constant; indeed, a certain minimum of them must be borne under all circumstances "whether the laborer works or not: that is, if it is not borne, if the maintenance is not forthcoming, the community suffers a loss through the deterioration of its working power . . ." [1] In this sense the costs of labor, or at least a substantial part of them, constitute a kind of overhead costs not only for the individual worker but also and especially for society as a whole. As a matter of fact, the costs of labor are overhead costs in an even more definite sense than are the fixed charges on capital account. Neither the laborer nor the community could escape the burden of these costs even if they wanted to do so.[2]

Under capitalism, these overhead costs of labor are translated into variable costs "in much the same way in which the constant costs of a telephone exchange are translated into a variable charge when the user pays so much per call." [3] In the case of the individual worker, this translation of overhead costs into variable costs is the result of the fact that the laborer under conditions of the present exchange economy is a free person who sells his services by means of a free wage contract. Under this system the burden of all overhead costs of

[1] J. M. Clark, *Studies in the Economics of Overhead Costs* (Chicago, 1923), p. 16.

[2] These ideas make no claim to originality. They were generally accepted by all classical economists since they form the cornerstone of the labor theory of value. See also O. Bauer, *Kapitalismus und Sozialismus nach dem Weltkrieg,* Vol. I, "Rationalisierung und Fehlrationalisierung" (Vienna: Wiener Volksbuchhandlung, 1931), pp. 166 ff.

[3] J. M. Clark, "Some Social Aspects of Overhead Costs," *American Economic Review,* XIII (March 1923), No. 1, Suppl., p. 55.

labor is bound to fall upon the individual worker; "he is, under our social system, a free being, responsible for his own continuous support and that of his family; hence his maintenance is his own burden and not an obligation of industry, except so far as he can exact wages that will cover it." [4] This is in marked contrast with the costs of machines and the fixed charges of the borrowed capital which have to be met by industry regardless of business conditions.[5]

It is at this point that the social costs of unemployment become apparent. For, once the fixed overhead costs of labor have been converted into variable costs, the entrepreneur is able to disregard the fixed costs of labor completely. A decline of business will be met first by a reduction of the "variable" costs of labor and thus tends to give rise to a wave of unemployment. This procedure is not only the most convenient for the entrepreneur, but in view of the fixity of most capital outlays it is the only method of reducing costs of production. Periods of depression will thus give rise to a general shift of the fixed burden of labor to the individual worker, his family or the community.[6]

The same disregard of the fixed overhead costs of labor marks all entrepreneurial decisions concerned with the introduction of technological improvements. In this case, too, entrepreneurial outlays are bound to fall short of the actual total costs, part of which have to be borne by the worker or the community in the form of greater expenditures for relief and unemployment. Needless to add, this is

[4] J. M. Clark, *Studies in the Economics of Overhead Costs,* p. 8.

[5] Again it must be emphasized that this difference in the behavior of the costs of capital and those of labor is not unavoidable—or something that must be accepted as being within the nature of things. It is rather the result of the different manner in which labor and capital contracts are drawn up. Although there may be "substantial reason for drawing them in the customary way . . . it would be quite possible to make labor a constant cost by putting it on a salary basis, as the higher officials are now, and to make capital a variable cost by leasing it for a payment depending upon the use that is made of it." J. M. Clark, "Some Social Aspects of Overhead Costs," p. 56.

[6] It is perhaps useful to reëmphasize that the foregoing argument does not rest upon any assumed moral obligation of industry to provide for the worker's livelihood in good and in bad times. Instead, it is based entirely upon the undeniable fact that the maintenance and training of labor has to be met as a social overhead cost if production, and with it individual and social life, are to continue.

not the result of any miscalculation by the entrepreneur but is inherent in the capitalist wage system.[7]

A similar shift and disregard of overhead costs is involved in the nonutilization of nonhuman productive resources. This becomes evident as soon as it is realized that the conversion of fixed into variable costs is not limited to the field of labor but takes place "whenever anybody who has any 'overhead costs' sells his products or his services."[8] For he then "puts the 'overhead costs' into the price he charges and thus they nearly always become a 'variable cost' to the purchaser. Thus, most of the 'constant costs' of business disappear as constant costs and are converted into 'direct' or 'variable' costs . . ."[9]

In times of depression these direct costs tend to be shifted backward all along the line along which goods move toward the consumer. As soon as business conditions begin to deteriorate, each individual firm reduces its variable expenditures by curtailing as far as possible its purchases of raw materials, semifinished articles, tools and other producers' goods. However, the overhead costs involved in the production of these intermediate goods remain substantially the same. Since their fixed costs have to be borne by a smaller volume of output and sales, unit costs are inevitably increased. It is this increase of costs resulting from any contraction of the demand for intermediate goods by producers closer to the consumer, which is not considered entirely in private business decisions and cost calculations.[10] And inversely, in deciding the question whether or not it

[7] O. Bauer, *Kapitalismus und Sozialismus*, p. 175. A guaranteed annual wage would do away with this feature of the unplanned market economy. By making the cost of labor a fixed charge for the individual firm it would not only eliminate an important source of social costs but it would at the same time create an incentive to use available resources more fully since the cost of labor would have to be paid anyway. Whether these benefits of an annual wage are offset by new elements of rigidity which such a wage system would introduce into entrepreneurial outlays is as yet an open question.

[8] J. M. Clark, "Some Social Aspects of Overhead Costs," p. 53.

[9] *Ibid.*, p. 53.

[10] This shift of "variable" costs backward to intermediate stages of production accounts also for the fact that the capital-goods industries seem to bear the brunt of the depression: while all producers closer to the consumer find it possible to shift costs to these intermediate producers and thereby force their unit costs up, the producers of capital goods have nobody to whom to shift their own costs, since modern production starts with them.

is worth while to resume production at full capacity, instead of keeping part of his plant idle, the individual entrepreneur can only disregard the entire series of savings which would accrue in all intermediate stages of production as a result of the fact that with increased production the fixed overhead costs in these industries could again be distributed over a larger total output. This is merely another way of saying that for the economy as a whole the difference in costs involved in partial utilization of available plant equipment as against those involved in full utilization is relatively small—so small, indeed, that as long as the additional products have any want-satisfying power there is a presumption that their production is worth while in terms of total costs and total returns. In other words, the cost calculations of the individual firm fail to record both the social costs resulting from enforced idleness and the economies obtainable from full utilization of productive resources.

It is this "atomistic" method of accounting which tends to distort the economic calculations of the market economy and accounts for the obviously absurd fact that no production and complete idleness are preferred to at least some output and partial utilization of available resources. Another reason for this absurdity, according to which —while millions of persons are unable to satisfy their most elementary needs—nothing seems to be preferable to at least something, is that during the initial stages of the depression many cost prices reflect what the productive resources were worth in the past and not what they are worth under existing conditions. In other words, "a wage rate of three dollars per day for making shoes ought to mean that there are other opportunities for using this labor to produce something worth three dollars per day. If the worker stands idle because he is not worth three dollars per day at making shoes, that means that the three-dollar alternative does not exist or at least is not available within the limits of existing knowledge. Under these conditions, to act on the assumption that shoes are not worth producing unless they will cover the three-dollar wage is false social accounting, flying in the face of the elementary fact that anything produced is that much more than nothing. It stands in the way of our making the best available use of our productive resources, whatever that use may be, by insisting that they shall not be used at all unless their use will cover 'costs' which changed conditions may have rendered, for this purpose, arbitrary and misleading." [11] The same applies to interest and rent. They too represent what capital and land were worth in the past in times of prosperity and not what they are worth under the new conditions after business has declined. It is, therefore, "inevitable that productive resources should go to waste, with the further result that they create no purchasing power to buy the products of other productive resources." [12]

2. Estimates of Social Losses Caused by Unemployment

Various attempts have been made to measure the social costs of depressions in terms of the potential real national income lost due to the decline of output and employment. Using this approach, W. C. Mitchell and W. I. King placed the loss of income from depression in one bad year (1914) at nearly 3,500,000,000 prewar dollars—not quite one tenth of the national income. These authors also calculated on the basis of a rough approximation that "the worst years (in a cycle period) run something like 15 to 20 per cent behind the best, and something like 8 to 12 per cent behind the moderately good years." [13] This was before the Great Depression.

In 1939, the National Resources Committee estimated that the loss of national income caused by the depression years of 1929 to 1937 amounted to over 200 billion dollars. "The significance of this figure . . . is hard to grasp, but some idea can be obtained by considering what 200 billion dollars would mean in terms of concrete goods. If all the idle men and machines could have been employed in making houses, the extra income would have been enough to provide a new $6,000 house for every family in the country. If, instead, the lost income had been used to build railroads, the entire

[11] J. M. Clark, "Productive Capacity and Effective Demand," *Preface to Social Economics*, p. 375.

[12] *Ibid.*, p. 375.

[13] From "The Economic Losses Caused by Business Cycles," *Business Cycles and Unemployment*, by W. C. Mitchell and W. I. King, p. 39. Copyright, 1923; courtesy of McGraw-Hill Book Company.

railroad system of the country could have been scrapped and rebuilt at least five times over. Of such is the magnitude of the depression loss in income through failure to use available resources. It meant a lower standard of living for practically every group in the community." [14]

With a national income running at 180 billion dollars, the average annual losses of a depression (of equal severity to that of 1929) would be roughly 45 billion dollars in current prices. (This figure is arrived at by estimating that the loss of 200 billion dollars from 1929 to 1937 represents roughly 25 per cent of the potential income during these years.) Estimates of this nature raise, however, a number of statistical problems related to trend analysis and the forecasting of the national product with which we cannot concern ourselves in this study.

It is clear that these estimates of the losses of depressions in terms of national income foregone fail to take account of certain less tangible consequences of recurrent disruptions of the productive process. It will probably never be possible to visualize fully, and even less to appraise adequately, the psychological effects of economic fluctuations which result from general insecurity and the frustration of the hopes of millions of individuals. The foregoing figures also omit the social costs of depressions which are evidenced in a general deterioration of the state of public health, higher mortality, greater incidence of crime, increased alcoholism, and lower marriage and birth rates.[15] The political consequences of depressions are likewise beyond the measuring rod of national income. Suffice it to say that a major depression in the United States might lead not only to a cessation of foreign lending (as it did in 1929) but also to a contraction of American imports. Both these developments would have the effect (as they did after 1929) of transmitting the depression to

[14] National Resources Committee, *The Structure of the American Economy*, Pt. I (Washington: U. S. Government Printing Office, 1939), pp. 2–3, 371.

[15] For a systematic attempt to measure these general social consequences of depressions see D. S. Thomas, *Social Aspects of the Business Cycle* (London: London School of Economics, 1925). This work contains also a summary of previous investigations into these questions. See also W. A. Bonger, *Criminality and Economic Conditions* (Boston, 1916).

the rest of the world. The existing "dollar shortage" would be accentuated and the process of reconstruction would be brought to a halt in all countries dependent upon American markets and supplies. It is not difficult now, as it was perhaps in 1929, to visualize the political upheavals that would follow in the various countries in the path of the depression.

Even if these broader social and political consequences of depressions are left out of account, it is safe to assert that the social losses of depressions are by far the most important social costs bound up with the operation of the private enterprise economy. They were seen to be reflected in a general shift of the overhead costs of labor to the unemployed and the community, as well as in the higher unit costs which result from the peculiar manner in which "variable" entrepreneurial outlays can be shifted backward to intermediate and primary stages of production. As soon as the demand for its own products begins to fall off, each concern finds it possible and convenient to curtail its orders and "variable" costs, irrespective of the effects which such action is likely to have upon costs and employment in the preceding stages of production. In other words, instead of contributing his "share" to the fullest utilization of available productive equipment and factors of production, the individual entrepreneur finds it more profitable, or rather less expensive, to stop producing altogether. By the same token, the private firm can only disregard the economies that would accrue, in the form of lower costs in all intermediate stages of production from any resumption of production at full capacity, owing to the fact that fixed overhead charges could again be distributed over a larger total output and turnover. In this way, private outlays tend to distort and to magnify the actual costs of production in times of depression.

12

MONOPOLY AND SOCIAL LOSSES

IN TURNING to the social costs of monopoly we are entering a field of economic analysis which is today, after controversies that have raged over centuries, just as inconclusive as it ever was. In fact, it becomes increasingly clear that we have as yet not developed an adequate theoretical framework within which the advantages and disadvantages of monopolistic restraints of trade can find a balanced appraisal. Just as the validity of the medieval accusations against "engrossing" and "forestalling" were questioned in their time and just as Luther's well-known indictment of various trading and "usury" practices of large trading companies in Germany and their successful collusion with political authorities was challenged by the trading city of Augsburg,[1] so the contemporary revolt against all kinds of restraints of trade encounters an increasing skepticism even within progressive and liberal circles. All of this points to a basic ambiguity in the theoretical treatment of monopoly which modern theories of monopolistic and oligopolistic competition have not been able to eliminate.

As pointed out in the summary of earlier discussions of social costs, the modern theory of monopolistic competition must be credited with a new realization of the ubiquity of monopolistic elements

[1] For evidence, see the documents and reports relating to two early monopoly investigations (by the Diets of Worms [1521] and of Nuremberg [1522–23]) included in *Introduction to Contemporary Civilization in the West* (New York: Columbia University Press, 1946), Vol. I, pp. 364–373.

in most market situations. In view of the fact that the new theory has brought into sharp focus the social wastes of market situations with monopolistic elements, it would be convenient to use it for a brief analysis of the social costs of monopoly. Unfortunately, this approach is open to objection on the ground that the whole trend and technique of static monopolistic competition analysis can be shown to be inconclusive for most relevant practical cases. There are three closely interrelated reasons for this inadequacy. (1) By viewing the competitive process at a point of time instead of over a period of time, the theory fails to take account of the most essential dynamic aspects of capitalist reality. (2) In its preoccupation with an essentially stationary model of competition it fails to recognize the much more effective forms of capitalist competition which result from innovations such as new technologies, new commodities, and new sources of supply. (3) Because these dynamic forms of capitalist competition are neglected, the antisocial effects of certain restraints of trade are exaggerated and their protective function against the gale of "creative destruction" is hardly seen at all.[2]

The practical implication of this unsatisfactory state of affairs in the theory of monopoly is not that we have to condone uncritically each and any kind of restraint of trade. However, the lack of an adequate theoretical framework within which the merits and demerits of contemporary business practices can be appraised means that we find ourselves on highly uncertain ground when we deal with questions of this sort. Let us illustrate this point in the following discussion.

1. Monopoly and the Over-All Efficiency of the Market Economy

The common method of approach to the theoretical discussion of the social cost of monopoly is through a juxtaposition of the two models of perfect and monopolistic competition. The first step is to show that when there is not perfect competition the most profitable price tends to be higher than under competitive conditions.

[2] For a fuller analysis of this unsatisfactory state of affairs of our monopoly theory, see J. A. Schumpeter, *Capitalism, Socialism and Democracy*, pp. 81–106.

From this it is possible to deduce a number of further propositions regarding the relative productive inefficiency of monopolistic competition. Thus, it may be argued that higher prices make for reduced sales and consequently for a smaller scale of production and unused capacity which, in turn, mean higher unit cost of production. In addition, higher prices may then be shown to divert demand and, therefore, consumption from more to less urgently desired commodities. In other words, "consumers who would be willing to purchase larger quantities of his [the seller's] product at lower prices are forced, instead, to buy goods that are wanted less. Capital and labor are thus diverted from those things which the community prefers to those which are, at best, a second choice." [3] Other inefficiencies closely bound up with a departure from the model of perfect competition are those resulting from price discrimination. Such price discrimination, whether practiced openly or under the guise of identical delivered prices through freight absorption and basing-point systems, not only assures the absence of price competition at any point of delivery but also makes for wasteful cross-hauling and prevents the most economical and decentralized location of industrial production in reasonable proximity to its markets.[4]

Finally, it may be argued that when there is power to control supply and therefore price, the pressure which forces producers under competitive conditions to reduce the margin between cost prices and product prices is absent or reduced to a minimum. Under these conditions, lower costs of production will not be passed on either to the consumer in the form of lower prices, or to the worker in the form of higher wages. In fact, it has been maintained that "monopoly inflicts no penalty on inefficiency. The monopolist may achieve economies through combination and integration; he may eliminate wastes and cut costs; but he is under no competitive com-

[3] C. Wilcox, *Competition and Monopoly in American Industry* (Temporary National Economic Committee, Monograph No. 21; Washington: U. S. Government Printing Office, 1940), p. 16.

[4] For a lucid analysis of the effects of the basing-point system in the American steel industry, see Federal Trade Commission, *Monopoly and Competition in Steel* (*T.N.E.C. Hearings*, Part 5; Washington: U. S. Government Printing Office, 1939), pp. 2192–2200.

pulsion to do so. Through inertia, he may cling to traditional forms of organization and accustomed techniques. His hold upon the market is assured." [5]

These are perhaps the most important conclusions (in nontechnical terms) which emerge from the "timeless" juxtaposition of the models of pure and perfect competition with that of monopolistic competition so characteristic of modern theory. Of course, the theory itself proceeds at a much higher level of abstraction which is due to the use of the mathematical tools and concepts of marginal costs and marginal returns typical for individual firm analysis. The task before us is not to reproduce this technique of analysis—any modern textbook may be consulted for this purpose—with a view to discovering any logical flaws in it; the problem is rather to outline the general limitations of the whole approach.

First, is it realistic to compare price and output adjustments of the two models at a given point of time? Conditions of monopolistic and oligopolistic competition do not arise overnight. They either arise gradually in old industries suffering from chronic overexpansion and cutthroat competition or are the result of the application of a new and protected method of production (including new products). In the former case, the establishment of some form of control over supply usually makes it possible to avoid wasteful duplication of plant facilities; if physical integration of equipment takes place, there is no reason why the "monopoly" should not concentrate and expand production in the most efficient part of existing facilities and eliminate the rest. In fact, the "monopolist" may endeavor to avoid all wasteful duplication of plant in an effort to take full advantage of the economies of large-scale production; he is better equipped than the small-scale concern to engage in advanced scientific research, and has every reason to apply cost-reducing inventions to the entire plant.

In the light of these considerations, the alleged inefficiencies of monopoly appear in a different light. In fact, it has been asserted that in some industries monopoly and monopolistic combinations are the conditions of efficient production in view of the fact that the

[5] C. Wilcox, *Competition and Monopoly*, p. 16.

existence of a multitude of independent small producers might prevent each of them from attaining a scale of operation at which production could take place in the most economical manner. Indeed, "if it were true in any particular industry, or industry in general, as some writers have suggested, that the optimum scale of production was infinitely large, so that an increase of scale always brought further economies, then one unit of production would always be more efficient than two smaller ones, and thus monopoly would always be more efficient in like conditions than any competitive system." [6] At the same time, it is not easy to refute the claim "that the demand for the vast majority of products is sufficiently great to enable a large number of plants, each under separate ownership, to realize the economies of size." [7] In other words, the final answer to the question whether or not monopoly and monopolistic conditions make for productive efficiency depends upon the kind of commodity and industry under consideration. As a matter of fact, there is reason to believe that general conclusions regarding the relative efficiency or inefficiency of monopoly and competition offer no satisfactory answer to our problem. Only a detailed analysis of the concrete case promises to yield significant results.

As soon as one permits the dynamic elements of change and time to enter the picture, it also becomes necessary to revise the prevailing preoccupation with forms of competition which are confined to price and quality as well as product differentiation under conditions of an otherwise stationary technology. If we agree with Marx and Schumpeter that the essential characteristic of capitalist reality is change and innovations, it becomes obvious that competition of the innovator is much more important than price competition and sales effort. "In capitalist reality as distinguished from its textbook picture, it is not that kind of competition which counts but the competition from the new commodity, the new technology, the new source of supply, the new type of organization (the largest-scale unit of control for instance)—competition which commands a decisive cost or

[6] E. A. G. Robinson, *Monopoly* (New York: Pitman, 1941), p. 109.
[7] C. Wilcox, *Competition and Monopoly*, p. 15.

quality advantage and which strikes not at the margins of the profits and the outputs of the existing firms but at their foundations and their very lives." [8] Schumpeter's analysis leads to the conclusion that this kind of competition is an ever-present threat which "disciplines before it attacks" [9] and which—although not in all cases—tends to enforce a long-run behavior "very similar to the perfectly competitive pattern." [10]

It is in the light of these considerations, which view the *modus operandi* of capitalist competition in connection with the perennial process of dynamic change, that certain restraints of trade assume the character of protective rather than necessarily antisocial devices. As such, as pointed out in the preceding chapter, some monopolies and oligopolies, though certainly not all, must be credited also with a stabilizing influence insofar as they are bound to adopt a more conservative course of action than that which emerges out of the uncontrolled competitive process with respect to technical change. The oligopolist controls a substantial portion of the total capital equipment of the industry. Consequently, in introducing technical improvements, he will consider the possible depreciation which the existing equipment suffers as a result of his innovation.

These considerations lend some support to the contention that monopolistic conditions "serve to bring about a greater control over the one disturbing factor which in a free competitive system acts to upset the tendencies to an equilibrium, namely, the sporadic appearance of innovations. For this, restraints of trade tend to substitute 'automatized progress' with a much more even rate of change and adjustment." [11] Also, in the exploitation of exhaustible resources,

---

[8] J. A. Schumpeter, *Capitalism, Socialism and Democracy*, p. 84.

[9] *Ibid.*, p. 85.

[10] *Ibid.*, p. 85.

[11] A. Gourvitch, *Survey of Economic Theory*, p. 144. This was the position Schumpeter took in 1928; see "The Instability of Capitalism," *The Economic Journal*, XXXVIII (1928), 385. It is interesting to note that in his more recent contribution to the problem Schumpeter takes a somewhat less definite position regarding the stabilizing influence of "trustified capitalism." See *Business Cycles*, Vol. I, pp. 96–97; see also, however, *Capitalism, Socialism and Democracy*, pp. 96–98.

large-scale units may follow a policy of conservation with a view
to maximizing their income in the long run. This is in marked contrast with the recovery of such resources by a multiplicity of small
firms, which, as was pointed out before, tends to be bound up with
a premature depletion of natural wealth under almost complete disregard of the interests of future generations. Nevertheless, no matter
what these results regarding the relative long-run efficiency of "monopoly" and oligopoly are in specific instances, one proposition cannot be doubted: namely, that wherever there is ability to control
price and supply there is a potential danger of exploitation and, indeed, of "plunder" of the consumer, to use an expression of John
Stuart Mill.[12] Nor is there, indeed, any guarantee that restraints of
trade will not be carried to the point where they become distinctly
antisocial. In fact, which form the "plunder" of the consumer may
take can only be surmised.

In the American steel industry it has long been customary (before
World War II) to charge prices high enough to make profits when
operating at less than 40 per cent of capacity.[13] In other cases, plundering of the consumers has taken the form of a systematic degrada-
tion of the quality of consumers' goods in the interest of a quicker
and repeated turnover. This interest of the monopolist in selling
products of a shorter life for the sole purpose of increasing sales and
profits is best exemplified by the following extract from a proposal
made to the General Electric Company to reduce "the life of flashlight lamps from the old basis on which one lamp was supposed to
outlast three batteries to a point where the life of the lamp and the
life of the battery under service conditions would be approximately
equal . . . If this were done we estimate that it would result in increasing our flashlight business approximately 60 per cent. We can
see no logical reason, either from our viewpoint or that of the bat-

[12] John Stuart Mill, *Principles of Political Economy* (London: Longmans, Green
and Co., 1940), p. 792.
[13] See Federal Trade Commission, *Monopoly and Competition in Steel* (T.N.E.C.
Hearings, Part 5), p. 2194.

tery manufacturer, why such a change should not be made at this time." [14]

It is safe to assume that other manufacturers, too, fail to see why they should not reduce the average life and quality of their products if by so doing they are able to increase the volume of their sales. In fact, such reduction and degrading, if not of the physical capacities, then of the economic value of consumer's goods, are the practical effect and purpose of many sales promotional activities, and especially of the promotion of fashions. In the automobile industry, the policy of "degrading" consumer's goods by the periodic introduction of new models has given rise to intermittent periods of peak production (and employment) and partial utilization of existing equipment with a high percentage of enforced idleness of relatively highly skilled workers and specialized capital equipment.

2. Monopoly and Defense

During the initial stages of the transition from peacetime to wartime production in England and the United States during World War II, another conflict of interests between monopolies and society was brought into the open. In so far as existing schemes of price control are based upon the ability to control and restrict production, their very existence is endangered by new procedures and by any undue expansion of production. It is, therefore, not surprising to find that price agreements and combinations, often extending over more than one country, delayed and prevented the expansion of production of essential war materials and equipment. "Looking back over ten months of defense effort," writes the Assistant Attorney General in charge of the Antitrust Division of the U. S. Department of Justice in his *Annual Report* to Congress in 1942, "we can now see how much it [the defense effort] has been hampered by the at-

---

[14] From a memorandum from the files of the General Electric Company, reported by the Assistant Attorney General to the Senate Committee on Patents; *Hearings,* 77th Congress, 2nd Session, Part I, p. 630. See also C. D. Edwards, *Economic and Political Aspects of International Cartels,* United States Senate, 78th Congress, Senate Committee Print, Monograph No. 1 (Washington: U. S. Government Printing Office, 1944), p. 16.

titude of powerful private groups dominating basic industries who have feared to expand their production because expansion would endanger their future control of industry. These groups have been afraid to develop new production themselves. They have even been afraid to let others come into the field. They have concealed shortages by optimistic predictions of supplies, and talked of production facilities which do not exist. Antitrust investigations during the past year have shown that there is not an organized basic industry in the United States which has not been restricting production by some device or other in order to avoid what they call 'the ruinous overproduction' after the war." [15] Congressional investigations of the American war program have brought to light a wealth of evidence leading to the same conclusion.[16] These facts should not be dismissed lightly because they point to one of the most important obstacles which delayed the transition from peace to war production of the market economies of the Western Powers during the last war.

Equally detrimental in their effects upon economic preparedness and security may be international cartel and licensing agreements based upon patents, especially if some of the large national corporations entering into the agreement are not even independent business concerns but instruments in the hands of their governments. All this was brought into sharp relief after the outbreak of the second World War. In particular, it was discovered that patent-licensing agreements between American, British and German firms producing important strategic materials (such as beryllium, tungsten, carbide, carboloy, plastic glass, optical equipment, etc.) provided for regular exchanges of technical information as well as for a division of world markets into noncompetitive zones. As a result, each firm enjoyed a privileged and protected position in its own territory and, in return,

[15] *Annual Report of the Assistant Attorney General Thurman Arnold* (mimeographed), p. 1. See also T. W. Arnold, *Democracy and Free Enterprise* (Norman, Okla.: University of Oklahoma Press, 1942), pp. 11–26. For a detailed presentation of evidence of how monopolistic interests hampered the defense effort, see J. F. Stone, *Business as Usual. The First Year of Defense* (New York: Modern Age, 1941).

[16] C. D. Edwards, *Economic and Political Aspects of International Cartels,* pp. 58–64.

agreed not to sell its products in the markets of its foreign partner to the agreement.

That these private agreements may have had far-reaching effects upon war production in the United States and Great Britain, and, indeed, conflicted with the declared foreign policy of these countries, is indicated strongly by the evidence presented to various Congressional Committees.[17] Thus, patent agreements between American and German firms were found to have been responsible for shortages and the insufficient development of essential war materials in the United States; after the outbreak of the war in Europe in 1939, American interests in such agreements are known to have been reminded by their German partners that the latter's sales territory included Canada. The German company requested that no information that came from Germany under the contract be given to Canada and that no instruments, built under license, be knowingly supplied to Germany's enemies. The American company is said to have given such assurance in accordance with the terms of the agreement. Moreover, as late as January 1941, one American company refused, apparently because of fear of a civil damage suit for breach of contract, to sell certain types of ammunition to the British Purchasing Commission because of its cartel agreement with a German firm.[18]

Two major conclusions emerge from the foregoing discussions. (1) Although monopoly and oligopoly have doubtless increased productive efficiency, especially in those lines of production where the optimum size is large and calls for one or a few firms instead of many, one would not be justified in assuming that monopoly is the precondition of efficiency in *all* industries. (2) Monopoly, in its constant

---

[17] W. Hamilton, *Patents and Free Enterprise* (T.N.E.C. Monograph No. 31; Washington: U. S. Government Printing Office, 1941), pp. 103–108; see also U. S. Senate, Investigation of the National Defense Program. Additional Report No. 480, Part 7, May 26, 1942 (Washington: U. S. Government Printing Office), pp. 27–42.

[18] Cf. A. Krock, "The Cartels as Parts of a German War Plan," *The New York Times* (March 27, 1942). The most complete picture of the role which international patent agreements played as a source of shortages and in the delay of American war production is contained in G. Reimann, *Patents for Hitler* (New York: The Vanguard Press, 1942).

fear of "overproduction," tends to exercise a delaying influence upon any expansion of productive facilities and thus appears to be particularly unfitted to secure the necessary transition from peace to war production in times of national emergency.

13

SOCIAL COSTS OF DISTRIBUTION

To SPEAK of social costs of distribution does not imply that it is easy to separate distribution from other phases of production. In many instances, the so-called distributive process not only precedes manufacturing but forms an integral part of the manufacturing process. Any distinction between distribution and manufacturing is, therefore, only a device of simplification.

As far as the distribution of the finished product to the consumer is concerned, one encounters two kinds of social costs, namely, those resulting from the duplication of retail outlets and the more general problem of the social losses involved in advertising and related efforts of sales promotion. These social costs will be dealt with in the present chapter. The following chapter is devoted to an analysis of the social costs arising in the field of transportation, which may be considered as a special phase of the process of distribution. In other words, this chapter does not deal with social costs arising in the distribution of raw materials and semifinished products.

1. Social Costs in Retailing

That the system of private enterprise tends to give rise to an excess of retailers to the injury of the consumers in the form of higher prices, and that these higher prices are due to monopolistic elements in retailing, was first pointed out by Wicksell in his *Lectures on Political Economy*. The passage dealing with this problem is significant also as an indication of the extent to which the elements of modern theories of monopolistic competition were anticipated in early neo-classical doctrine. It runs as follows:

Practically every retailer possesses, within his immediate circle, what we may call an actual sales *monopoly,* even if, as we shall soon see, it is based only on the ignorance and lack of organization of the buyers. He cannot, of course, like a true monopolist, raise prices at will—only in places remote from trade centers can a considerable local rise in prices occur—but if he maintains the same prices and qualities as his competitors, he can almost always count upon his immediate neighborhood for customers. The result is not infrequently an *excess of retailers,* apparently for the convenience, but really to *the injury, of the consumers.* If, for example, two shops of the same kind are situated at different ends of the same street, it would be natural that their respective markets would meet in the middle of the street. Now if a new shop of the same kind is opened in the middle of the street each of the others will, sooner or later, lose some of its customers to the new shop, since the people living round the middle of the street believe that if they get the same goods at the same price they are saving time and trouble by making their purchases at the nearest shop. In this, however, they are mistaken, for the original shops which have now lost some of their customers without being able to reduce their overhead expenses to a corresponding degree, will gradually be compelled to raise their prices—and the same applies to the new competitors who have been obliged from the beginning to content themselves with a smaller turnover.[1]

Wicksell goes on to explain that this wasteful duplication of retailers was the reason why the abolition of the tax on the entry of goods into a town never produced the expected reduction in prices. As long as buyers do not establish some form of organization among themselves to counteract the sales monopoly of the retailer—the only correct remedy, according to Wicksell—"the anomaly must remain that competition may sometimes raise prices instead of always lowering them, as one would expect." [2]

Let us trace the social losses involved in this excess of retailers in greater detail. Above all, what evidence is available to indicate an

[1] K. Wicksell, *Lectures on Political Economy,* pp. 87–88.
[2] *Ibid.,* p. 88.

excess of retailers? The existence of considerable and wasteful duplication of retail outlets is indicated by the relative number of businesses doing business on an exceedingly small scale and the extraordinarily high rate of business failures. Even in 1929, 42.7 per cent of all retail stores had sales of less than $10,000 per year. (In 1935 and 1939 the percentage had risen to 58.9 and 54.2, respectively.) In other words, even at the height of prosperity, almost 700,000 out of 1,543,158 retail stores were operating on sales of approximately $30 or less a day. According to a study of the U. S. Department of Commerce, the ratio of operating expenses to sales increases the lower the sales volume (varying between 24.1 and 41.3 per cent for retail business with sales of less than $9,999 in 1939).[3] If these percentages were applied to the figures quoted above it would mean that more than half of all retail outlets operate with exorbitant ratios of expense to total sales. By comparison the ratio of operating expenses to sales of self-service supermarkets does not exceed 12 per cent.[4] It is true that these small-scale retailers account for only 5.4 to 10.6 per cent of the total retail business transacted (see Appendix XII).

Closely connected with and indeed a special aspect of this low volume of sales and the resulting high expense ratio is the unusually high rate of failures in the retail trade. The average annual rate of business failures has been shown to vary from 9.4 to 35.9 per cent of the number of firms actually engaged in particular trades in different localities.[5] In commenting upon these figures, the Twentieth Century Fund's study *Does Distribution Cost Too Much?* points out that "retailer mortality entails a heavy loss for the economic system. Not only is the capital of proprietors wiped out but losses are also often sustained by creditors. In addition to direct money losses are many other undesirable effects. For example, stable competitors are injured by the fact that failing proprietors cut prices in

[3] *Small-Scale Retailing* (U. S. Department of Commerce, Domestic Commerce Series No. 100, 1938), p. 26.

[4] See *Distribution Services and Costs* (Washington: U. S. Chamber of Commerce, 1939), p. 34.

[5] A. E. Boer, "Mortality Costs in Retail Trades," *The Journal of Marketing*, II (July 1937), pp. 53–54.

an effort to stave off the evil day; and then, when the business is closed out, the inventory is often sold at sacrifice prices." [6]

Nor are these the only social losses arising from duplication and inefficiency in retailing. An excessive number of retailers means higher distribution costs for wholesalers and manufacturers who have to supply these outlets. "Fewer and larger stores would mean fewer and larger purchases and lower costs of physical handling and selling, as well as many collateral savings such as lower insurance and credit and collection costs." [7] Furthermore, the constant danger of commercial failure compels the small retailer (and for that matter the small businessman) to adopt practices of cutthroat and fraudulent competition of which he likes to accuse his larger competitors. Competition is thus in danger of sinking to those moral standards which prove more profitable, as J. B. Clark once pointed out.[8]

No attempt will be made to subject other areas of distribution, such as wholesaling, insurance, banking and the business of real-estate brokers, to the same type of analysis. With the exception of the business of the real-estate broker, these areas of distribution show a much higher degree of concentration and probably have avoided some of the inefficiencies and wastes found in retailing. But even so there is reason to believe that the whole superstructure of the distributive system of middlemen is liable to be overexpanded in response to the same forces which bring into being an excess of retail outlets.

It has been argued that the existence of a multiplicity of business units in the field of distribution is evidence of the need for the respective services rendered. Such reasoning, which does not deny that the existence of an excess number of middlemen prevents each from reaching the optimum scale of operation, fails to demonstrate that the various services would still be in demand if their costs were known, i.e., if the consumer knew by how much distribution costs

---

[6] *Does Distribution Cost Too Much?* (New York: The Twentieth Century Fund, 1939), p. 322; see also E. Grane, "The Social Cost of Bad Debt," *Quarterly Journal of Economics,* LIII (1939), pp. 477–486.

[7] *Does Distribution Cost Too Much?,* p. 299.

[8] J. B. Clark, *The Philosophy of Wealth* (Boston, 1904), p. 168.

could be reduced if the scale of operations were to approach the optimum size. In short, while it is true that the consumer's demand is at least partially responsible for the emergence of inefficiencies in the distribution system, it is equally true that he is also the victim of the high costs resulting therefrom. This will become even more evident in the following discussion of the social costs of sales promotion.

2. The Social Costs of Sales Promotion

The commercial promotion of sales through advertising, the use of trademarks and fashions, and various other methods of persuasion are integral parts of the modern distribution system. Increasingly, distribution has become concerned with the creation of demand and the direction of it into particular channels. That the intensity and volume of promotional efforts are still increasing in modern society—as evidenced by the steadily increasing volume of advertising expenditures—is an indication of the existence of monopolistic elements in modern economic life. For it is only under conditions of monopolistic competition that sales promotion by individual sellers becomes possible and necessary. Under conditions of pure competition, the product sold by one seller would be identical to that of the rest and the demand for each seller's product infinitely elastic. In other words, "ex hypothesi, the market will take, at the market price, as much as any one small seller wants to sell." [9] Since he can dispose of his entire output at the market price, the individual seller (and producer) under strictly competitive conditions has no inducement to spend money on advertising. However, if the fixed and specialized productive capacity of individual producers and sellers is such as to permit them to produce more than the market will take at the market price (that is, if they produce at increasing returns), or if consumers can be convinced of the superior qualities, whether real or imagined, of individual products (that is, if the elasticity of demand at the market price of their product can be reduced), then entrepreneurs will find it profitable to invest in

[9] A. C. Pigou, *Economics of Welfare*, p. 196, n. 2.

advertising and sales promotion. In fact, under conditions of monopolistic competition it is not only profitable but essential for the individual entrepreneur to engage in various kinds of sales-promotional activities. In fact, under such conditions the commercial survival of each competitor depends more and more upon his ability to increase the demand for his particular product and to make this demand as inelastic as possible. To this end, the seller must convince the consumer of special qualities of his products as compared with those of his competitors. If the entrepreneur's survival depends upon his ability to create a demand for his "differentiated" commodity, he can hardly be expected to abstain from making exaggerated or even misleading claims as to the superiority of his particular article or brand.

Various arguments have been advanced to justify the institution of sales promotion. Thus, it has been pointed out that advertisements perform certain "educative" functions in so far as they describe for the consumer the use and desirability of available commodities, together with their quality and prices. Along similar lines, economists have distinguished between "informative" and "competitive" advertising,[10] justifying the former as a means of increasing the consumer's knowledge and disapproving of the latter as merely a method of "transferring the demand for a given commodity from one source of supply to another." [11] More recently, largely under the impact of mounting criticism, advertising has been defended on the ground that it has led to lower costs by enabling producers to enlarge the scale of production; that as a result it must be credited with the benefits which have accrued to consumers in the form of lower prices and higher levels of living; that it has had the effect of widening the range of merchandise available to consumers; and that, in general, advertising promotes economic growth and progress. The author of one study went even so far as to assert that all semblance of a free society would vanish if the use of persuasion were to be

---

[10] A. Marshall distinguished between "constructive" and "combative" advertisements; see his *Industry and Trade* (London, 1919), pp. 304–307.

[11] A. C. Pigou, *The Economics of Welfare*, p. 196.

forbidden. "What significance can be attached to the designation of a society as 'free' if there is no freedom to exercise persuasion in the relationship between buyers and sellers? Persuasion and counter-persuasion are exercised freely from pulpit, press, rostrum, classroom and government agencies for information." [12] Why should they not be used by sellers? That the commercial manipulation of choice by people who have a financial interest in the consumer's decision differs in kind from the "persuasion" exercised from the pulpit, or in the classroom, did not occur to this investigator. The same author, although not a Keynesian himself, also suggests that aggressive selling efforts tend to raise the propensity to consume and thus induce fuller employment and higher income than would exist with greater saving.[13] Finally, it has been calculated that almost 50 per cent of all advertising expenditures are "returned to consumers in the form of low-cost periodicals and free radio entertainment." [14]

It is neither possible nor necessary to deal with every one of the foregoing arguments in defense of the institution of advertising. Suffice it to say that advertising which conveys information about existing commodities and their respective qualities is of great value to the consumer; it increases his knowledge, it shows him existing alternatives, it makes his demand for any given article less inelastic, in short, it offers a greater opportunity for competition, although always at an additional cost which must be covered by the price. However, the purpose of advertising and all other sales-promotional activities is to sell; in some cases this purpose is served by offering the consumer truthful and detailed information, helping him make a more reasoned choice of commodities. But in the great majority of cases, selling efforts play upon the buyer's susceptibilities; as Chamberlin puts it, they "use against him [the buyer] laws of psychology with which he is unfamiliar and therefore against which he cannot

---

[12] N. H. Borden, *The Economic Effects of Advertising* (Chicago: Richard D. Irwin, Inc., 1942), p. xxiv

[13] *Ibid.*, p. 187.

[14] *Ibid.*, p. 71. That the resulting dependence of radio and the press upon income from advertisements exposes both to the pressure of advertisers and menaces their political and cultural status is an aspect which Borden does not even mention.

defend himself, which frighten or flatter or disarm him—all of these have nothing to do with his knowledge. They are not informative; they are manipulative." [15]

Similarly, the commercial promotion of brands and trademarks— a correlate of advertising—is not necessarily helpful to the consumer. While doubtless contributing to uniformity and standardization— although rarely according to scientific specifications—brands and trademarks often give the commodity a "fictitious individuality" preventing "the consumer from comparing it with competitive products of identical composition. He [the seller] diverts attention from the weight, the quality, and the price of the article he is selling, to the shape, size, and color of the package in which it is housed. Through his advertising he creates a reputation for this package which is intended to take it out of competition." [16] Instead of describing, brand names, in many cases, misrepresent the branded commodity; instead of assisting the consumer, their great number confuses him.[17] Moreover, habits and customs often tend to bind the consumer to inferior or deteriorated brands.

As far as the effects of advertising on costs and prices are con-

---

[15] E. Chamberlin, *The Theory of Monopolistic Competition,* pp. 119–120. Another serious student of the matter comes to similar conclusions: "Advertisements are not written to help people make a reasoned choice of commodities, they are written with the object of inducing them to buy particular things, and they naturally exaggerate the uses and merits not only of the commodity but of a particular make of the commodity. Moreover, the vast majority of advertisements do not confine themselves to pointing out the uses of commodities; they make the appeal not to the reason but to the emotions of the consumer. Suggestion, reiteration, attractive illustration—these are all devices to induce him to buy the article without making comparisons and calculations. They certainly do not assist his judgment as to the relative satisfactions to be obtained from different commodities or as to the relative satisfactions to be obtained from commodities and leisure." D. Braithwaite, "The Economic Effects of Advertisement," *The Economic Journal,* XXXVIII (1928), pp. 19–20.

[16] C. Wilcox, "Brand Names, Quality and Price," *Annals of the American Academy of the Social Sciences,* CLXXIII (May 1934), p. 81.

[17] See Hearing before the Temporary National Economic Committee (May 1939), Part VIII, *Problems of the Consumer,* pp. 3309–3328. According to estimates by G. K. Burgess, former Director of the National Bureau of Standards, there are as many as 10,000 brands of wheat flour, 4,500 brands of canned corn, 1,000 brands of canned peaches, 1,000 brands of canned salmon, 1,000 brands of peas, 500 brands of mustard and 300 brands of pineapple. See S. H. Slichter, *Modern Economic Society* (New York: Henry Holt and Co., 1931), p. 553.

cerned, one thing seems to be certain, namely, that the economic effects of sales promotion are considerably more complex than is usually believed by those who assert that, by enabling the efficient producer to expand the scale of production, advertising and sales promotion have to be credited with a substantial part of the economies which accrue as a result of large-scale production. For in the first place many of these economies are obtainable also without advertising; in fact, it is more reasonable to assume that advertising is the result rather than the cause of large-scale production. Producers first realize the advantages of large-scale production and then, after overexpanding productive capacity, rely upon methods of sales promotion and high-pressure selling to keep overhead costs at a minimum. Second, it cannot be overlooked that less efficient producers also advertise and may thereby take customers away from more efficient producers who are, however, less efficient advertisers. There is even, as Pigou pointed out, "some slight ground for believing that firms of low productive efficiency tend to indulge in advertisement to a greater extent than their productively more efficient rivals." [18] To the extent to which less efficient producers with the aid of advertisements are able to stay in business or perhaps even to enlarge their markets and thus the scale of their production, sales-promotional activities not only fail to produce any of the economies referred to above but represent rather a clear economic loss from the point of view of the economy as a whole. In this connection it is also important to note that sales-promotional efforts of one producer are likely to result in an encroachment upon the markets of other producers, who may be forced to contract their scale of production and consequently be compelled to produce at higher unit costs.

Third, it is evident that the sales-promotional efforts of competing producers and sellers may neutralize one another at least partly, and thus fail to bring about any substantial change in the relative position and the volume of sales of each competitor. For clearly "if each

---

[18] "For, clearly, they have greater inducements to expenditure on devices, such as special packages, designed to obviate comparison of the bulk of commodity offered by them and by other producers at a given price." See A. C. Pigou, *Economics of Welfare*, p. 199.

of two rivals makes equal efforts to attract the favor of the public away from the other, the total result is the same as it would have been if neither had made any effort at all." [19] Obviously, in so far as competing sales-promotional efforts cancel one another, they represent a social loss which is shifted to and borne by the consumer in the form of higher prices.

A fourth factor which adds to the difficulty of appraising accurately the economic effects of advertising is the fact that there is no sure way of determining the actual private returns obtainable from advertising and sales-promotional campaigns. Not only is it impossible for the advertiser to know where and who the consumers are who are just outside his market but, even more important, sales-promotional activities of any individual producer always involve the risk of provoking retaliatory sales-promotional campaigns by other sellers which may either wholly or partially neutralize the effect of the first advertisement. In other instances, advertising by one seller may have the effect of increasing the sales of other competitors and benefit the whole industry. In addition, it is at least conceivable that specialized advertising agents who conduct the bulk of sales-promotional campaigns under modern conditions may mislead their customers in the same manner in which they are sometimes able to mislead consumers. To the extent that this is the case business men may carry "their advertising expenditure past the point at which it ceases to be profitable." [20] These difficulties of ascertaining precisely the actual private returns of advertising lend strong support to the presumption that at least "a considerable proportion of the resources devoted to advertisement is wasted . . . in the sense that it does not lead to a sufficient increase in sales to pay for itself." [21] While any attempt to verify this proposition statistically would encounter insurmountable difficulties inherent in the nature of the case, it is, nevertheless, not without interest to point out that advertising

---

[19] *Ibid.,* p. 198.

[20] A. S. J. Baster, *Advertising Reconsidered* (London: Staples Press, Ltd., 1935), pp. 86–87.

[21] H. Smith, "The Imputation of Advertising Costs," *The Economic Journal,* XLV (1935), p. 690.

outlays and profits are reported to show often no correlation with one another.[22] Although it cannot be said, in the light of the foregoing analysis, that the costs of advertising and sales promotion are a complete economic loss from the point of view of society, there are strong reasons to believe that a substantial proportion of such outlays are unnecessary and wasteful inasmuch as they add to the costs of production without yielding appreciable results either for the individual advertiser or for the consumer.

Closely bound up with the institution of sales promotion, indeed only one aspect of it, is the commercial promotion of fashions and styles. As previously pointed out, fashions have the effect of reducing and destroying the economic usefulness of durable goods at a time when they are still capable of serving their purpose. By thus shortening the cycle of obsolescence for many goods, styles and fashions and their commercial promotion contribute to substantial losses in modern society. This is not refuted by the fact that the development of new styles and fashions for every season plays upon the human desire for variety and apparently meets with the approval of large sections of consumers. For the important thing is not that sales and fashion promotion find some basis in human nature and are able to win the approval of consumers, but rather whether the benefits of these manifestations of monopolistic competition are not entirely out of proportion to the costs involved therein. In other words, what has to be realized is the fact that the operation and growth of advertising and sales promotion is subject to the principle of diminishing returns like any other productive activity. The economies which resulted from the simplification of styles and the reduction of the number of trademarks in wartime indicate that private enterprise has gone far beyond the optimum point in the development of advertising and the promotion of brands and fashions.

3. The High Costs of Distribution

The foregoing analysis does not provide an adequate basis for a quantitative determination of the social costs of distribution. Nor do

---

[22] *Ibid.*, pp. 691–692.

available estimates of the total costs of distribution throw much light on the question whether distribution costs too much. What these data indicate is the fact that the costs of distribution are high and that economies in this area of production would yield substantial benefits. Our analysis of the wastes in retailing and of the economic effects of sales promotion indicates the areas in which possible reductions of costs might be sought.

Starting with an estimate of the relative magnitude of distribution costs, it is of interest to note that it costs considerably more to distribute goods than it does to make them. For 1929, the Twentieth Century Fund estimates that the costs of producing goods amounted to $27 billion and the costs of distributing them reached $39 billion. Of this latter sum, nearly $13 billion was paid for retail distribution and $1 billion for national advertising. From these figures the Fund's study arrived at the well-known conclusion that "59 cents out of the consumer's dollar goes for the services of distribution and only 41 cents for the services of production." [23]

However, more recent estimates by the Federal Trade Commission indicate great variations in the relative importance of distribution costs in different industries. For some products total distribution expenses (advertising, selling, delivery) amount to 30 per cent of total net sales value—a figure which would be considerably below the estimates made by the Twentieth Century Fund. (See Appendix XIII.) Data regarding the growth of distribution in the American economy since 1870 indicate a steady relative increase of the number of persons gainfully employed in distributive organizations, such as wholesale and retail dealers, sales people and clerks in stores, commercial travelers, restaurant and lunchroom keepers and persons employed in transportation. From 1870 to 1930 the percentage of persons employed in retailing, wholesaling and transportation increased from 9.1 to 20.7.[24] At the same time the volume of goods handled per worker in distribution has not increased as fast as that handled in manufacturing. "Workers in distribution . . . handled

[23] *Does Distribution Cost Too Much?*, p. 334.
[24] *Distribution Services and Costs*, p. 20.

only 4 per cent more goods per capita in 1930 than they did in 1870, while the average amount produced by production workers increased by three and a third times." [25] These data indicate that the great advances in the efficiency of manufacturing have not been paralleled in the field of distribution. The question remains, of course, how far the lower efficiency of distribution represents a social cost and how far it reflects the existence of basic obstacles to the application of methods of mass production and mechanization in distribution.

After this short summary of the total costs of distribution, it is not without interest to determine the relative importance of advertising expenses. The annual expenses for advertising vary directly with business conditions. In prosperous years they tend to exceed $4 billion, and have run as high as 3.5 per cent of the total domestic expenditures (personal consumption expenditures plus gross private domestic investment). (See Appendix XIII.)

More significant than these totals are figures relating advertising expenditures to total distribution costs and total net sales. As is to be expected, the relative importance of advertising as a factor of the total distribution costs varies widely from industry to industry. For trademarked or patented consumer's goods, such as electric household materials and flour, advertising costs account for as much as 35 per cent of total distribution costs. (See Appendix XIV.)

Data concerning advertising costs per dollar of sales show similar variations from industry to industry.

Those industries which spent less than a cent per sales dollar were predominantly makers of heavy capital goods, raw or partially finished products for further manufacture, and a few manufacturers of stable consumption goods such as cane sugar, beet sugar, and matches. Those which spent on the average from 1 cent to 3 cents per dollar of sales generally were makers of trademarked consumer goods and industrial machine specialties and those which spent more than 3 cents per sales dollar were largely makers of trademarked consumer goods ranging from clothing and building insulation and wallboard to canned foods, tobaccos, liquors,

[25] *Does Distribution Cost Too Much?*, p. 13.

soaps, cereal preparations and medicines, in which identification and sale by brand name is an important factor in distribution.[26]

Although none of the foregoing figures can be interpreted as measuring the social costs of distribution, they do raise a number of interesting questions.

(1) What price, in terms of higher costs, does the community pay for the "luxury" of 100,000 retail outlets with sales of less than $30 per day?

(2) What are the social costs of an annual rate of business failures of from 9.4 to 35.9 per cent for different retail trade groups?

(3) To what extent are the social costs of retailing characteristic of the entire field of distribution?

(4) Granted that advertising not only manipulates demand but also increases the consumer's knowledge of existing alternatives, the question remains whether the increasing volume of advertising is not mainly of a manipulative kind reflecting steady increase of monopolistic elements (such as product differentiation) in modern industrial society?

(5) How far have the high and increasing costs of advertising and the high costs of distribution in general had the effect of merely offsetting the increased efficiency of manufacturing?

(6) Why should there be such wide variations in the volume of advertising of different products?

(7) Is it socially desirable that the costs of advertising should reach 35 per cent of the cost of distribution and 14 per cent of the net value of sales for particular commodities?

(8) Assuming that the volume of advertising can be pushed beyond the optimum point, is there any guarantee that the competitive process of distribution will not tend to expand the proportion of the national resources devoted to advertising beyond the optimum? More specifically, is the present number of persons employed in sales promotion not a relatively high proportion of the nation's manpower

[26] *Report of the Federal Trade Commission on Distribution Methods and Costs,* Part V, "Advertising as a Factor in Distribution" (Washington: U. S. Government Printing Office, 1944), p. 7.

occupied, in the words of the (London) *Economist,* "in advising the rest of the nation how to spend its money." [27]

The fact that it is difficult to answer these questions is not due so much to the absence of adequate data as to the absence, under conditions of private enterprise, of any framework of reference within which to pass judgment on these matters. Only if we refuse to accept the prevailing preconceptions of the business world which judges worthwhileness exclusively in terms of private costs and returns will it be possible for the social scientist to develop criteria for an objective and social evaluation of the social costs of advertising and distribution.

[27] *The Economist* (November 23, 1946), p. 822.

14

SOCIAL COSTS IN TRANSPORTATION

As POINTED OUT in the preceding chapter, transportation is an integral part of the distributive system. The only reason for devoting a separate chapter to the social costs of transportation is the fact that transportation raises a number of special issues which are more conveniently examined apart from distribution in the narrower sense.

Generally speaking, the social costs of transportation are opportunity costs. As such they belong to the category of those social losses which were the subject of discussion in the last four chapters and which will be traced further in the ensuing chapters dealing with the frustration of science. The social costs of transportation are evidenced in the various forms of wastes and diseconomies which are bound to arise if and whenever the competitive calculus becomes the guiding principle for the construction and operation of transportation facilities.

1. The Factors Which Place Transportation Outside the Competitive Calculus

Fundamentally, there are three factors which place transportation outside the competitive calculus. First, modern transportation techniques call for heavy initial investments of capital. As a result transportation is an industry which operates with a particularly high percentage of fixed costs. This is not merely the result of recent technological conditions but reflects the general fact that transportation is concerned merely with the movement of commodities and not, as is, for example, manufacturing, with their transformation from one form into another. In other words, whereas manufacturing requires an investment of capital in materials this is not the case in transportation. As a result, the proportion of overhead costs in transportation is usually higher than in manufacturing.[1] Now, as long as the density of (i.e., the demand for) transportation between two points is such that one initial investment (that is, one railroad track, one canal, one tunnel) is sufficient to provide the required services it would be wasteful to erect two or more such facilities in order to stimulate competition between independent businesses. For any such duplication of transport facilities would make it impossible for either to operate at full capacity and thus to spread its overhead costs over the greatest possible number of services. The fact that the initial investment required for the construction of most means of transportation is substantial and that the proportion of overhead costs in transportation is unusually high makes duplication of transport facilities particularly wasteful. Even if the density of transportation calls for an expansion of existing facilities, it is usually more economical to enlarge the scale of operation (e.g., by adding another track alongside the old or by increasing the width of the road) and to operate the total equipment as a unit rather than to construct and operate additional facilities under separate management.

Second, it is important to note that the operational efficiency of any single means of transportation "depends also upon the extent of its integration with all other transport facilities. That is to say, each transportation facility must form part of a transportation system in order to yield the greatest possible benefits. Every road has to be properly connected with other roads, every railway, every canal has to be conceived a priori and planned as a part of the total transportation net, and railroads, inland waterways, and highways must be systematically coördinated if they are to yield the highest possible utility. If the establishment of the transport net were left to freely

---

[1] See on this point E. Sax, *Die Verkehrsmittel in Volks- und Staatswirtschaft,* Vol. I, *Allgemeine Verkehrslehre* (Berlin, 1922), p. 61.

formed private enterprises only profitable lines would be constructed which would be highly inadequate as far as the consideration of all collective objectives is concerned." [2] It is easy to see that this need for an integrated transport system is not confined to the national plan; there exists at the same time a genuine need for an international integration and coördination of such national transportation facilities as railroads, canals, shipping and, most important of all, airports and planes.

The third factor which places transportation in a special category and accounts for the fact that the competitive calculus gives rise to important social losses is bound up with the social character of many of the benefits of transportation. In fact, the greater part of the benefits of transportation tend to diffuse themselves to all members of society and remain largely inappropriable by either private producers or consumers. The same railroad, by facilitating the production and exchange of commodities, may enlarge the extent of the market of manufacturers, determine the location of industries, influence land values, and serve important military and cultural purposes. The fact that many of these benefits of transportation accrue to society as a whole makes them a matter of no or only incidental concern for the private operator.

These three factors—the high overhead costs, the fact that all transport facilities in order to yield a maximum of benefits must be planned and operated as integral parts of the national and even international transport system, and the predominantly social character of the benefits of most transport facilities—made it imperative for most countries to abandon the early policy of nonintervention which marked the laissez-faire era of railroad construction during the second half of the nineteenth century. In the United States, where private ownership and competition have always been more developed than in other countries, the recognition of the social character of the benefits of transportation found expression not merely in the fact that construction and operation of some means of transportation (such as roads, highways, bridges, waterways, and harbor facilities)

[2] Translated from Sax, *op. cit.*, p. 139.

with predominantly social returns have become undisputed functions of government but also in substantial public aids granted to virtually all branches of transportation. As a matter of fact, the development of all privately operated land, water and air transportation would have been impossible without active intervention and public aid by government authorities.

In addition to the allocation of public funds for the development of new transport facilities, the public interest in transportation is further evidenced by the far-reaching system of public regulation of privately owned carriers. This system of social control is based upon the recognition of the fact that the competitive process would also lead to a wasteful duplication of services with the subsequent danger of cutthroat competition, financial demoralization of private concerns and the ultimate emergence of monopoly, and would neglect many of the social returns of transportation. Originally intended to prevent monopolistic exploitation of the consumer through excessive and discriminating charges, the system of public regulation of transportation has been gradually expanded to a point where it includes, in addition to the fixing of rates on the basis of the fair-return-on-fair-value principle, the supervision and regulation of the establishment and operation of transport facilities, the maintenance of proper services, and the financial organization of transport concerns, including their accounting and reporting procedures. While the evolution of this mixed system has doubtless prevented the worst social losses which would have resulted from the maintenance of the principle of private enterprise and nonintervention in all areas of transportation, it is itself not beyond criticism. In fact, it is this mixed system of transportation and the peculiar principles which continue to govern the regulation of the private sector which are responsible for important social losses.

2. *Evidence of Social Diseconomies under the Present Mixed System of Transportation in the United States*

The most important limitations of the present system of transportation in the United States are the results of the fact that it prevents the achievement of a sufficient degree of physical and technical integration of existing transport facilities. In the absence of such integration, costs have remained unnecessarily high and certain social returns of transportation have not been realized at all.

Even within the public sector of transportation under government management the emphasis has been much more upon the promotion of new facilities and less upon the effective coördination of new and existing facilities. The Federal Government "operating through separate public agencies each acting as the special advocate of one form of transportation . . . spends an average of more than a billion dollars a year for transportation facilities without comprehensive plans."[3] As one student of public transportation policies points out, "there has been a complete absence of broad plans to include all forms of transportation . . . and nontransportation as well as transportation objectives. Thus the airport plan has no connection with the highway plan and the latter is unrelated to railroad plans, in spite of the fact that tremendous savings and improved services could both be achieved through coördination."[4] As a result, public action in the field of transportation has been marked by "waste of public funds; vague and conflicting objectives; the absence of criteria to guide expenditures; and questionable methods of financing, cost allocation and administration have all furnished evidence of serious shortcomings."[5]

The most noticeable evidence of diseconomies resulting from the absence of an over-all plan in the promotion of transportation facilities and from their insufficient integration is to be found in the existence of costly and unnecessary competition between different transport agencies and, concomitantly, the great duplication of transport facilities. "Each transport agency attempts to share traffic more logically belonging to another. The railroad, struggling desperately to regain its former position, attempts to retain the short-haul and less-than-carload business despite heavy terminal expenses which must often result in handling at a loss. The motor truck invades the long-haul fields by attracting the more lucrative traffic from the rails,

---

[3] *Public Aids to Transportation* (U. S. Office of Federal Coördinator of Transportation, Washington: U. S. Government Printing Office, 1940), Vol. I, p. 9.

[4] *Ibid.*, p. 275.

[5] *Ibid.*, p. 9.

despite the greater economy of the latter. The inland waterway diverts traffic over circuitous routes in order to share in the haul." [6]

In addition to this multiplication of transport services, the lack of integration between existing facilities is further emphasized by by the absence of unified and central terminals. Under present arrangements, freight has to be received at, transferred to, and delivered from widely scattered terminal facilities under diverse ownership. The result is evidenced not only in a considerable loss of time, but also in wasteful transfers and duplication of delivery all of which add to the cost of transportation. "It has been estimated, for example, that approximately two-thirds of the typical completed car movement, involving about 15 days on the average, is spent within terminal areas. The fact that the terminal accounts for one-third of railroad freight operating costs emphasizes further the possibilities of terminal improvement as a means of restoring railroad profitability and reducing costs to travelers and shippers." [7]

According to careful appraisals made by the Federal Coördinator of Transportation, the annual savings likely to result from the unification of freight terminals alone would amount to at least $50,000,-000. Other specific estimates of the potential annual economies which would be obtainable from better coördination of railroad transportation in the United States are as follows: $100,000,000 through the pooling of freight cars; $100,000,000 from the integration of merchandise traffic; and $100,000,000 or more by various changes in passenger traffic.[8] General estimates of the total annual savings anticipated from specific schemes of consolidation or coördination of railroads alone range from a minimum of about $200,000,000 to an outside maximum of $1,000,000,000, with some consensus centering around about half a billion dollars of annual savings.[9]

[6] *Ibid.*, p. 7.

[7] *Ibid.*, p. 3.

[8] These estimates, based upon studies by the Federal Coördinator of Transportation, are quoted from National Resources Planning Board, *Transportation and National Policy* (Washington: U. S. Government Printing Office, 1942), p. 166.

[9] *Ibid.*, p. 162. See also B. N. Behling, *Railroad Coördination and Consolidation, A Review of Estimated Economies* (Interstate Commerce Commission, Statement No. 4023, Washington, 1940).

The relative significance of these estimated savings is indicated by the fact that "each $100,000,000 of economy achieved through railroad unification would be equal to about 3 per cent of the operating expenses of all operating steam railways for the year 1939. Savings of about $500,000,000 would amount to about one-sixth of the operating expenses for that year, and would have reduced the operating ratio from 0.729 to 0.608. Savings of half a billion dollars also would have increased net railway operating income from $638,766,000 to $1,138,-766,000 for 1939, and would have been equal to more than 75 per cent of the fixed charges of the carriers." [10] It must be remembered that these are the anticipated results of railroad consolidation only. Estimates of the total economies obtainable from the coördination and integration of the entire transport system in the United States are not available.

Another limitation of the present mixed system of transportation is that it tends to give rise to unequal competitive conditions and thus contributes to an uneconomic utilization of existing facilities. This will be easily understood in the light of the fact that "under existing conditions air, water and highway facilities are financed in varying degrees through general funds while railroads at present receive no direct support from general taxation." [11] In other words, while some carriers have to cover only part of their costs, the railroads have to charge rates high enough to cover their total costs.[12] As a result of these differences in methods of finance "sufficient volumes of passenger and freight business have been taken from the rails or kept from them, to result in serious financial consequences for rail operation. And it is not merely the traffic lost, but also the necessary lowering of the rates to retain traffic, which has spelled diminishing revenues. Furthermore, in the case of air and water transportation the fact that carriers pay little or nothing for these facilities establishes the conclusion that railroads have been the vic-

[10] National Resources Planning Board, *Transportation and National Policy*, p. 162.
[11] *Ibid.*, p. 258.
[12] The argument that the roads received public support in the past is irrelevant in this connection. For, obviously, profits and business policies are determined by present, or better still by estimates of future, costs and not by costs of the past.

tims of subsidized competition to the extent that traffic moving by
air and water would have moved by rail save for lower rates made
possible through appropriation from general funds." [13] The uneconomic character of such a shift of traffic away from existing railroad
facilities requires no detailed explanation; it is evidenced in the un-
der-utilization of existing transport facilities while at the same time
scarce resources are being used for the construction of new and additional facilities.

The foregoing considerations reveal even more fundamental limitations of the mixed transport system of the United States. As previously pointed out, the present system of public-utility regulations for
the private sector of transportation is based upon the doctrine of fair
return on fair value. This doctrine is itself merely an adaptation of
the principle which regulates private production under competitive
conditions, namely, that the products of every industry must be sold
at prices high enough to cover its costs. In other words, railroad
rates and, indeed, the operation of all public utilities, are regulated
in such a manner that their operating revenues are sufficient to cover
the (total) costs of operation, which include a fair return on private
investments. This principle, which makes railroads the victims of
unequal competition on the part of other subsidized transport agencies, is open to criticism for a number of other reasons.

First of all, as a result of this principle commercial users are
charged the full costs of transport facilities despite the fact that these
facilities yield at the same time substantial social benefits for all members of society. Second, under the influence of the principle of self-
liquidation, private investments and the operation of the railroad
business are likely to neglect to take into consideration the broader
social benefits of transportation. In fact, social benefits and objectives
lie entirely outside the scope of traditional public-utility regulation,

[13] *Transportation and National Policy*, p. 259. "As for motor transportation which
contributed large sums of user revenue for financing highways, it is believed that the
multiple nature of the highway function and the predominance of overhead costs
combine to make it more a matter of conjecture whether vehicles as a class, or
specific types of vehicles, pay a proper share of the highway bill in a particular
State" (*ibid.*, p. 259).

which in its concentration upon the protection of the consumer and private owners "fails to impose definite responsibility for socially desirable action." [14] That is to say, railroads are under no obligation, and, indeed, cannot be expected to construct and operate their equipment with a view to its effects upon national defense, the development of new industries, the stabilization of business and employment either in general or in specific areas, the promotion of social integration, etc.

These shortcomings of the principle of self-liquidation and the resulting failure of the present system of public-utility regulations to provide for an effective maximization of all potential utilities both private and social are, of course, not confined to railroads. They hold true also for other public-utility industries. As Gray pointed out, "public-utility companies are under no legal compulsion to conserve natural resources, to utilize capital efficiently, to employ the best known techniques and forms of organization, to treat labor fairly, to extend service to nonprofitable areas, to improve public health, to strengthen national defense, to promote technical research, to provide service to indigent persons, to institute rate and service policies that will foster cultural and social values, or to develop related benefits such as navigation, flood control, and irrigation. This being the case, private-utility monopolists will have regard for these broad social objectives only when by so doing they can increase or maintain their own profit. Experience has shown that they will not voluntarily strive to attain these ends; moreover, it is clear that public-utility regulation, as at present constituted, cannot compel them against their own interest to do so. Thus, the public-utility concept is functionally impotent in the sense that it is incapable of securing the social objectives that are essential in the modern economy." [15]

[14] H. M. Gray, The Passing of the Public-Utility Concept, *The Journal of Land and Public Utility Economics*, XVI (1940), p. 16.

[15] *Ibid.*, p. 16. In addition to this "obsolescence" of the public-utility concept, Gray emphasizes its recent "perversion" from "a system of social restraint designed primarily, or at least ostensibly, to protect consumers from the aggressions of monopolists" to "a device to protect the property, i.e., the capitalized expectancy of these monopolists from the just demands of society and to obstruct the development of socially superior institutions" (*ibid.*, p. 15). Evidence of such a perversion may be found not

Thus, the major weaknesses of the present mixed system of transportation in the United States may be said to be due to the promotion of transport facilities without sufficient coördination and the absence of an over-all approach to the problem of transportation under which all means of land, water and air transportation are treated as constituent parts of a well-integrated transport system. Instead, different local, State and Federal authorities are responsible for the formulation of transportation policies and different transport agencies seek to compete for traffic which could be carried more economically by others. The consequences of this situation are reflected in a wasteful duplication and uneconomic utilization of transport facilities, with social losses amounting to a substantial proportion of present operating expenses. Finally, the principle of self-liquidation which guides the system of public-utility regulation of railroads was seen to be wholly inadequate and, indeed, incapable of providing for an effective maximization of the social returns of transport facilities.

One positive conclusion emerges from this analysis of social costs in the field of transportation. There is considerable room for real economies in the American transportation industry. The prerequisite for the attainment of these economies would be the physical integration and unification of productive facilities such as railroads, highway traffic, air transport and shipping. In the last analysis, such unification of transport facilities can be attained only under conditions of common ownership, and common ownership means for all practical purposes collective ownership or nationalization of the transport industry.

---

only in various familiar abuses and financial manipulation but also in the attempt by various public-utility industries to protect their own privileged domain against competitors by securing "their inclusion within the restrictive confines of the public-utility status" (*ibid.*, p. 11; see also pp. 11–15).

15

THE FRUSTRATION OF SCIENCE

It may seem incongruous to speak of the frustration of science at a time which has just witnessed the greatest progress in the physical sciences. And yet a moment's reflection will make it clear that the application of the results of atomic research to wartime uses did not take place under conditions characteristic of those under which scientific research is usually conducted in a market economy. It was not private enterprise but a government in wartime that spent two billion dollars for the development of atomic energy. Both the magnitude of the expense and the uncertainty of the result would have prevented private business from engaging in this kind of research. The successful solution of the practical problems raised by nuclear fission is an indication rather of what could be achieved if the traditional methods of competitive research were abandoned.

These considerations raise the question whether the structure, institutions and attitudes characteristic of capitalism tend to encourage or discourage scientific work and the fullest possible utilization of its potential benefits. No elaborate analysis is required to show that science has been the most important factor not only in increasing productive efficiency but also in developing new products and providing an increasing population with a more abundant food supply. In short, science is that agent which, by reducing cost of production, has brought about technological progress. Because the results of scientific research have a direct bearing upon technology and productive efficiency, business has been interested in science and scientific research ever since the discoveries of the seventeenth and eighteenth centuries had laid the foundation for the series of technological innovations usually referred to as the Industrial Revolution. As a matter of fact, during the eighteenth and nineteenth centuries it was primarily the capitalist incentive of private profits and the capacity of science to reduce costs which served to promote scientific advances and determined the place of science in modern civilization. To the extent that scientific research contributes to the solution of business problems, it has become an integral part of the competitive struggle in the market economy and a substantial proportion of all scientific research work is conducted in business research laboratories under private auspices of industrial concerns. Indeed, nothing could be more false than the unqualified thesis that the institutions and attitudes of the market economy tend to be hostile to science. On the whole, capitalism has had an accelerating effect upon the rate of scientific progress.

There are, however, a number of factors which are detrimental to scientific progress and the application of its results in a private-enterprise economy. To trace these factors and thereby to reveal the nature of the social losses which tend to arise in the organization of scientific resources is the primary purpose of the present chapter.

1. Scientific Research and the Competitive Calculus

The fact that the place of science is determined by the contribution it is expected to make to entrepreneurial profits has had farreaching consequences for the conduct and organization of scientific research. It has meant, in the first place, that industrial research is concerned only with a particular type of research problems (namely those capable of adding to private returns), and that it is undertaken only when there is a reasonable probability of profits. As a result, scientific research in the physical and chemical sciences which have the most direct bearing upon production and productive efficiency have experienced a one-sided development, whereas research in other fields which have no direct bearing upon private costs of production have been neglected. For instance, industry does not spend considerable sums on research dealing with the prevention of social costs; scientific inquiries into the requirements of public or even industrial health (i.e., into such problems as optimum temperatures, lighting, air circulation, or prevention of accidents) are not likely to attract much attention.

However, quite apart from this neglect of some fields of research, it is more than doubtful whether the fact that industrial research has come to occupy a place similar to that of other business activities is conducive to the best possible results. To treat scientific research in the same manner as, for instance, advertising and to appraise its economic worthwhileness in terms of the potential surplus of private returns over costs may be sound business practice as far as the individual firm is concerned; but does this mean that the competitive calculus is the best criterion to determine the relative outlays for research and to serve as a basis for its organization? From a broader social point of view the competitive calculus breaks down as a satisfactory criterion for the determination of the relative worthwhileness of research outlays and the organization of science in general. This becomes clear as soon as it is realized not only that scientific research is usually costly but that its results are highly uncertain and can be applied only after considerable delays. The more uncertain and time-consuming the results of research and the greater the probable time lag between investment in research and the application of its results, the more hesitant private enterprise is bound to be to invest its funds in scientific research. And yet, the particular research project may be perfectly justified, i.e., worthwhile in the light of the potential long-run and social benefits expected therefrom.

Because of the neglect of important areas of research despite their social importance, it has never been possible to leave the conduct of research entirely to private enterprise. In addition to private business, it is primarily various government and public agencies and universities and private research institutions which are engaged in various phases of scientific work. Government research is mostly concerned with scientific inquiries of a general nature serving such national and public purposes as national defense, agriculture, public health and public administration. The U. S. Government, for example, maintains both fact-finding agencies and scientific research divisions for the natural sciences, technology, economics and virtually all aspects of the social sciences.[1]

In contrast with industrial and government research, most of the scientific research done in universities and independent research foundations is "pure" research not directed to the immediate solution of practical problems. This type of research, the results of which are even more uncertain and time consuming than the research which contributes to the solution of practical business and government problems, is nevertheless the basis of all applied research inasmuch as it "leads to new knowledge . . . [and] creates the fund from which the practical applications of knowledge must be drawn."[2]

The question is, of course, whether this threefold division of labor constitutes the most efficient organization of science. Before examining this question it is of interest to inquire into the costs and returns of scientific research in present-day society. Such an inquiry into the prewar outlays for research will tend to correct the impression which may have been created by the extraordinary and highly advertised wartime investment of 2 billion dollars in the development of atomic energy. While precise statistical data are not available, it is possible to present a number of significant estimates of both costs and returns of scientific research. Thus "in the decade from 1930 to 1940 expenditures for industrial research increased from $116,000,000 to $240,000,000 and those for scientific research in gov-

[1] The following is a detailed list of subjects covered by federal research before the second World War: Physics, chemistry, metallurgy, engineering for the production of war materials and weapons, radio, telephony, telegraphy, ship construction and propulsion, aeronautics, optics, ballistics, construction of highways, bridges, fortifications and drydocks, geology, geodesy, mineral technology, weather prediction and forecasting, biological problems of agriculture, conservation of resources, flood control, public health and practically every aspect of economics. See National Resources Committee, *Research—a National Resource, Part I, Relation of the Federal Government to Research* (Washington: U. S. Government Printing Office, 1938), p. 9.

[2] V. Bush, *Science the Endless Frontier* (Washington: Government Printing Office, 1945), pp. 13–14.

ernment rose from \$24,000,000 to \$69,000,000. During the same period expenditures for scientific research in colleges and universities increased from \$20,000,000 to \$31,000,000 while those in the endowed research institutes declined from \$5,200,000 to \$4,500,000." [3] These figures are significant not merely because they indicate the relatively small amounts spent for pure research (in universities and endowed research institutes) but also because they show the considerably more rapid increase of investments in applied research (in industry and government) as compared with outlays for pure research. Moreover, the figures indicate that the total annual outlays for research in all three compartments in the United States before the second World War did not exceed 344.5 million dollars. This is considerably less than $\frac{1}{2}$ of 1 per cent of the national income for 1940. Expressed in different terms, the nation as a whole spent more for such purposes as advertising than it invested in scientific research. These comparative figures are mentioned not because it is felt that they demonstrate in themselves the inadequacy of the total outlays for scientific work in the wealthiest country of the world but because they give a better perspective for the argument that prewar outlays for research were totally inadequate for the conduct of the necessary scientific work. In this connection we do not even think so much of the fact that existing facilities are inadequate; that research workers have to work without adequate assistance and apparatus; that salaries are usually not high enough to attract new talents and that there exist other wastes and false economies;[4] we have in mind primarily the fact that there remain large numbers of unsolved problems mostly in certain fields of medical research for the solution of which only negligible sums of money seem to be available.[5]

[3] *Ibid.*, p. 14.

[4] J. D. Bernal, *The Social Function of Science* (London: George Routledge & Sons, Ltd., 1939), pp. 98–107.

[5] It would be interesting, for example, to know how much is spent on research on those diseases which are responsible for 45 per cent of the deaths in the United States, namely, "cardio-vascular disease, including chronic disease of the kidneys, arteriosclerosis, and cerebral hemorrhage" (see V. Bush, *Science the Endless Frontier,* p. 9).

2. Inefficient Organization of Scientific Research: An Obstacle to the Full Realization of the Potentialities of Science

At first sight the threefold division of labor between private firms, public agencies, and universities and research foundations appears to reflect merely the different degrees of appropriability of the results of applied and pure research and as such seems to be a more or less adequate arrangement. In reality, however, the conduct of research in three different compartments conflicts with the intrinsic interdependence which exists between the scientific problems in any given field of knowledge. Moreover, the present "mixed" system of research, like the "mixed" system of transportation discussed in Chapter 14, involves a high degree of uneconomical duplication. There is no guarantee that research into related problems is not conducted in all three compartments at the same time. Indeed, there is an almost complete lack of coördination both within and between compartments concerned with the conduct of scientific research.

As far as industrial research is concerned, considerations of competition and profits make it impossible to establish any coördination between the scientific work of research laboratories of different business units. As a matter of fact, industrial research tends to be shrouded in extreme secrecy; there is but little exchange of information regarding the problems under investigation and the practical results achieved. Consequently, there is no guarantee that unnecessary duplication is avoided and that the same problem is not investigated in a number of laboratories of different competing firms.

What has just been said with reference to the state of industrial research applies with even greater force to the general method of conducting scientific research in three separate compartments. The results of scientific research in one compartment (e.g., industry) may be of the greatest importance for the scientific work under way in the laboratories of public agencies and universities, and vice versa. Similarly, government research in physics, chemistry, aeronautics, telegraphy, construction of highways, etc., is bound to be of interest and practical value to industry. And yet, there exists but little coördination between and hardly any exchange of information about the research conducted by scientists in any of the three compartments. No less significant than this absence of coördination are the lack of coördination and the prevailing secrecy within government agencies on the one hand and within universities on the other. This situation has been described by one of the leading French scientists, Henry Langier, who outlined the condition of research in prewar France in terms which may well apply to other countries also:

> Government agencies traditionally work in extravagant isolation, in systematically watertight compartments. Parallel research work on the same question is frequently carried on in the laboratories of different branches (in itself an excellent idea), but the branches (and this is by no means excellent) ignore each other almost completely. Research workers of the army exhaust themselves on problems already solved by the navy or the air force. Technicians of the army and those of the navy arrive at different solutions of the same problem and proceed to apply their results without ever subjecting them to comparative tests so that both branches might avail themselves of the best apparatus or methods.
>
> Research work in universities is characterized by a fair degree of anarchy resulting from the tradition of total freedom, of unbridled individualism, which prevails in the university laboratories . . . The truth is that scientists all too often incline to total anarchy as a doctrine. The stories of how Archimedes discovered his immortal principle while getting out of his bath, and how Newton discovered the law of gravitation when a falling apple chanced to strike the tip of his nose, have played havoc in the minds of scientists. They have given seductive but fallacious arguments to those who proclaim that discovery is the child of imagination alone, that research rebels against all organization, and that all endeavor to give a rational form to scientific work is a bureaucratic effort serving only to hinder a scientist's freedom of mind and consequently the process of discovery itself. This disastrous doctrine is not yet through with its mischief . . . scientific research in the universities has until now completely escaped all the efficacious complusions of organized freedom.[6]

Even if the foregoing account of the conditions of research in France may not be fully characteristic of conditions in other coun-

---

[6] H. Langier, "How Science Can Win the War," *Free World*, I (1941), No. 1, p. 59.

tries,[7] it throws light on some of the limitations of the organization of scientific research in a capitalist market economy. Extreme secrecy, duplication, lack of coördination, absence of provisions for the exchange of data and results achieved are all inherent in the normal organization of research under present conditions. As a result, hundreds and even thousands of scientists may be engaged in parallel research activities, using the same methods in different laboratories equipped with expensive apparatus and precision instruments. Instead of setting up general plans of research drawn up jointly by different scientists and carried out in such a manner that the various phases of one project are attacked in different laboratories using different methods of approach, scientific research tends to be organized in such a way that highly skilled and scarce scientific resources are used in parallel, secret research conducted in numerous laboratories employing more or less similar methods of approach.

These inefficiencies in the organization of science can have only one effect: a substantial proportion of the money and effort devoted to research is wasted and progress of science is retarded.[8] This is not to suggest that the market economy is inherently incapable of organizing scientific research in a rational manner. In times of emergencies, for example in wartime, it seems to be possible to utilize scientific resources in a more rational way, not only by providing an over-all organization for scientific work but also by determining the relative urgency and importance of different problems to be investigated and by allocating the necessary funds to different research agencies in accordance with the relative importance of their respective work. In the absence of such a program for science and without the creation of a central agency designed to formulate and execute a national science policy, the organization of scientific research is

[7] For the conditions of scientific research in prewar England, see D. Hall, *et al.*, *The Frustration of Science* (London: George Allen and Unwin, Ltd., 1935) and J. D. Bernal, *The Social Function of Science,* chap. 3.

[8] Bernal (*op. cit.*, p. 120) believes that the average loss of efficiency due to lack of organization and duplication is certainly 50 per cent and may actually reach 90 per cent.

bound to remain inefficient and incapable of producing a maximum of returns.

3. The Retardation of Research and the Frustration of Science

From the general inefficiency of the organization of science we now turn to those factors which tend to retard technical progress. There are at least four factors which have to be considered in this connection: (*a*) the inability of small producers to conduct research and apply its results; (*b*) the impact of technical innovations on existing capital investment; (*c*) the effects of depressions upon research; and (*d*) the patent system.

(*a*) *Small Business and Scientific Research.* It is a fact of common knowledge that most industrial research is conducted in the research laboratories of large concerns. In fact, the bulk of industrial research is carried out under the auspices of a few large firms. Why is that so? Is there no need for technological improvements within the small firm? Do the majority of small firms lack the incentive to engage in research that may lead to cost-reducing innovations? Do they hesitate to engage in research work because the innovation may soon be generally applied and thus yield no special returns for the original innovator? The answer is simply that small business cannot afford the costs and uncertainties involved in scientific research and the application of its results. There is considerable room and need for technical improvement in small business. The small producer has the incentive to introduce such improvements; he can add the costs of research to his costs of production and thereby reduce his income tax, and the patent law provides protection against any use of the invention by competitors. If the small concern does not engage in scientific research it is because the costs of research and the risk of its being unsuccessful act as deterrents for all small concerns to undertake any research.

In general, "the position is even worse in agriculture. Here, for research to have any value, it must be undertaken on a very large and expensive scale, and the risks of failure are also considerably greater. Consequently, practically no farmers ever engage in research and only the wealthiest landowners occasionally do so." [9] In the United States, agricultural experiment stations seem to have more or less remedied the situation. In manufacturing nothing has as yet been set up that might serve the purposes of state experiment stations. The result has been not only that the small manufacturer is increasingly and hopelessly outdistanced by his larger competitors but also that important areas of scientific research of considerable usefulness are neglected and retarded.

(b) *The Problem of Obsolescence.* Turning from the neglect of scientific research in small-scale manufacturing to the role of science and technological innovations in large enterprises, one soon discovers another factor which tends to retard scientific progress. Large-scale producers can certainly afford the costs and risks of unsuccessful research. They have all the facilities for protecting the discoveries and innovations of their laboratories by patents and effective patent litigation. But are they likely to have the incentive to apply the results of scientific research? *Prima facie* it may appear that they have the greatest interest in putting into practice all cost-reducing innovations which can be expected to recover the required capital outlays within a relatively short period of time. However, a cost-reducing innovation has the effect of making existing specialized equipment obsolescent, that is to say, its capital value is destroyed. It has been shown that periodic destruction of the value of existing capital equipment by innovations following each other in rapid succession not only is a threat to private investors but is likely to involve substantial social losses. Large-scale producers with a large proportion of fixed investment, and especially monopolists, are likely to avoid these social losses by a more gradual introduction of technical changes. In fact, they could pay up to the capitalized losses involved in the costs of obsolescence for whatever new patented knowledge may affect the value of their fixed equipment. This is the economic basis for the delay in the application of patents which seems to have become a general practice with the growth of big business and mo-

[9] J. D. Bernal, *The Social Function of Science*, p. 137.

nopoly and which, in the United States, has the sanction of the courts.[10] It is true that, to the extent to which these practices lead to a more gradual introduction of technical change making unnecessary the premature scrapping of existing equipment, they need not give rise to socially disadvantageous consequences. And it is, of course, equally true that not every new invention and patent is immediately ready for practical application in production. However, there is considerable danger that the same attitude which induces large concerns to protect existing equipment by delaying the application of patents may be carried to the point where the patent is shelved and where scientific advances and the realization of the broader social returns of science are discouraged altogether. This can be achieved simply by not spending the money on certain lines of research. Evidence of such practices in specific industries could be quoted almost at random.[11]

This tendency of retarding the application of technical knowledge has interesting counterparts in the opposition of labor to the introduction of labor-saving devices in general and in the development of antiscientific attitudes among large masses of people in times of depression. By thrusting the burden of adjustment (i.e., the social costs) caused by technological advances upon the economically weaker groups in society, the *modus operandi* of the capitalist economy tends to generate forces of reaction which have the effect of retarding technical progress altogether. This may be illustrated as much by the early struggle against machines and the prohibition of labor-saving devices as by various more recent laws in favor of inefficient producers both in industry and agriculture. All these measures must be understood as attempts of those left stranded by technical advances under capitalism to set the clock of progress back.[12]

[10] B. J. Stern, "Resistances to the Adoption of Technological Innovations," National Resources Committee, *Technological Trends and National Policy* (Washington: U. S. Government Printing Office, 1937), pp. 39–66.

[11] *Ibid.*, pp. 62–66, and J. D. Bernal, *The Social Function of Science*, pp. 138–147.

[12] For an interesting demonstration that this reaction against technical progress under capitalism is responsible for the growth of antiscientific and anti-intellectual attitudes also and especially among the middle classes, see P. M. S. Blackett, in *The Frustration of Science*, pp. 129–144.

(*c*) *Economic Depressions and Scientific Research.* The effects of depressions upon technological progress become evident as soon as it is recalled that the application of science under capitalism is subject to the competitive calculus in much the same manner in which the conduct of scientific research depends upon private cost and return calculations. That is to say, technological innovations will be applied only if expected returns are adequate to cover the costs of the new process of production. In times of depression, the lack of effective demand tends to make for low prices and low profits. This has the effect of discouraging the application of innovations as long as a further decline in effective demand is to be expected. Similarly, low wage rates during depressions have a retarding influence on the application of science because it is profitable to substitute labor for capital. Apart from these effects, depressions will force business and governments to reduce their appropriations for the conduct of research, with the result that the progress of science is slowed down.

(*d*) *The Patent System.* The last and by far the most important factor which retards the application of science is the patent system. The patent system is a necessary and essential outgrowth of the institution of private property. Without the grant to the inventor of an exclusive privilege of making use of his innovation, every competitor could freely appropriate the fruits of scientific research. The inventor would thus be robbed of his compensation and of any further material incentive for scientific work. This is just as true today under conditions of large-scale industrial research carried out in the laboratories of big corporations as it was in the days of the individual and independent inventor. Without the legal protection of the patent system corporations would be reluctant to devote their funds to scientific research and to apply its results in the productive process. In this sense the original philosophy of the patent system has not lost its validity. It is still true that the grant of exclusive privileges to make use of one's innovations promotes industrial research by adding, as Lincoln put it, "the fuel of interest to the fire of genius." [13]

---

[13] It is, of course, possible to argue that "many innovations would emerge even if they could be accorded no legal protection, for without them, the concern would lose

In fact, I am even inclined to agree—although not without qualification—with Schumpeter's position that new or old concerns or industries which introduce new commodities or processes are true aggressors who, in view of the extreme uncertainty with which the outcome of their innovation is surrounded, require such pieces of armor as patents, secrecy of processes and long-period contracts secured in advance.[14]

The dilemma of the patent system is not that it fails to act as an incentive to research and investment and to the application of science to industry in general, but that its operation tends to "insulate" the invention so as to increase monopolistic elements in modern economic society. It is inherent in the grant of a patent that it blocks the equal access to, and the practical application of, the results of scientific research for all firms. This not only has the effect of putting all other producers in the industry at a competitive disadvantage but it also retards the application of technical innovations in general and ultimately promotes the growth of monopoly. An exclusive privilege of making use of an innovation or improvement puts all competing producers at a competitive disadvantage. Several patents combined provide a convenient and effective means of closing the industry to all newcomers. Not infrequently, the holder of the patents is able to reserve the market for himself and to prevent other producers from competing. Should outsiders, nevertheless, attempt to invade the industry through the use of allied procedures under a separate patent, they face expensive and ruinous litigation for infringement of patent rights. If in the ensuing legal struggle one of the rival companies is not quickly exhausted and leaves the field to the other, both claimants might finally accede to a settlement under

---

its strategic place in industry; they are devices by which a firm keeps ahead—or at least abreast in the competitive struggle." W. Hamilton, *Patents and Free Enterprise,* p. 155. What this hypothetical contention fails to take into account is the fact that without any legal protection business would be much less willing to introduce technical innovations necessitating heavy investments owing to the greater uncertainty which would surround the financial success of the new venture.

[14] J. A. Schumpeter, *Capitalism, Socialism and Democracy,* p. 88. My qualification of this position concerns the fact that the extreme uncertainty which surrounds every investment is not so much in the nature of things as a result of the competitive structure of the economy.

which "each of the contracting parties takes certain processes as his own, acquires the exclusive right to certain wares, or obtains sole control of the market within a defined area." [15] In other cases, where different patents must be used together in a particular productive process, the holders may decide to "pool" their patents or to grant licenses to each other with a view to providing for a uniform policy of production and sale of the article. By thus combining their patent rights with each other manufacturers have been able to "throw a wall about their self-vested interests." [16]

Similar results may be achieved by licensing agreements through which the corporation owning the patent leases the right to use the patented process to other manufacturers. Such licensing agreements may contain restrictive clauses as to sales territory, output and prices. Under such clauses "the sales of each are limited to a certain territory and there is no competition between them . . . Quotas are imposed upon all who produce . . . Plants of licensees are severally limited in their capacities. A system of prices, prescribed by the patentee, becomes a covenant running with the lease. The Government's grant blocks the entrance; whoever would enter the trade must come to terms with the owner." [17]

All this, it might be argued, will not be of long duration, for the expiration of the patent will set an end to any patent pool or licensing agreement based thereon and the invention, by becoming public property, will finally be an addition to the common fund of knowledge for the benefit of all. This argument, however, fails to take into consideration the realities of modern technology and patent procedure. For there are many devices through which the actual life of a patent may be extended beyond its statutory life. First, it is not uncommon to delay the official sanction of the patent by various tactics such as marking the article with the legend "patent applied for." [18] Second, a basic invention may be improved by a hundred devices. Thus "a novel twist may give to an old invention a new lease

[15] W. Hamilton, *Patents and Free Enterprise,* p. 161.
[16] *Ibid.,* p. 161.
[17] *Ibid.,* p. 160.
[18] *Ibid.,* p. 135.

of life; an improvement may freshen a familiar into a novel process." [19] No wonder then that often not one but scores of patents may serve as the basis of many modern manufacturing processes,[20] and that "a series of patents, neatly articulated and accurately timed, may be made to carry on indefinitely." [21] These conditions, together with the fact that the holder of the patent has the exclusive opportunity of further experimenting with the invention, often give him a relatively secure superiority over all potential competitors.

Eventually the corporation may enjoy such security that its grants from the government are no longer needed for active service. The patent to Morse for the telegraph expired before the Civil War; yet Western Union —with Postal as its little sister—carries on. That McCormick once had a patent is now a fact in history; yet almost all reapers are now made by the International Harvester Co. In 1880 a patent was issued to Edison for an electric bulb; the shadow has lengthened into the substance of General Electric. The original patents on shoe machinery had run their course before most persons now living were born; the process is still blanketed by official grants—and over it United is an absolute sovereign. The Bell patents gave to the struggling telephone its start; it matters little today to American Telephone and Telegraph—at least in respect to its ordinary service—whether its devices are patented or not; in either event it would enjoy an exclusive right to their use. An invention may open a new art; the patent upon it may serve for decades to exclude the public.[22]

Today every major firm is surrounded by a wall of patents designed primarily to cut off outsiders from its particular techniques. The real function of the patent is to exploit indefinitely the advantageous position it creates. Patents are thus not only the most important obstacles to the general application of the results of scientific research in industry; they serve at the same time the monopolistic purpose of controlling supply and holding prices at the most profitable levels.

[19] *Ibid.*, p. 140.
[20] "The imperium of the United Shoe Machinery Co. is barricaded by some 6000 patents; Dupont, Hartford-Empire, RCA-Victor have piled patent on patent to secure against invasion the whole range of their activities" (*ibid.*, pp. 46–47).
[21] *Ibid.*, p. 140.
[22] *Ibid.*, pp. 140–141.

In conclusion it may be said that there are several factors in the capitalist market economy which tend to prevent the best possible utilization of scientific resources. These factors, which are the source of substantial social losses, are closely bound up with the fact that the determination of the economic worthwhileness of scientific research in terms of private costs and returns leads to a one-sided emphasis on the development of the physical and chemical sciences, while other areas of research such as the medical, biological and social sciences tend to be neglected. Furthermore, the organization of research was seen to be the cause of considerable inefficiencies. The threefold division of labor between industry, government and universities so far has made coördination between the research work in different laboratories impossible; it involves harmful secrecy and expensive duplication. In other words, a considerable proportion of the money and effort devoted to research is wasted. The application of technical innovations and research is retarded by a number of factors, among which the following are the most important: the inability of small business to invest in costly and uncertain research; the tendency to delay the application of patents in order to protect existing capital equipment from premature obsolescence; recurrent depressions and periods of low wages; and the patent system. As a result of these impediments the competitive market economy fails to develop the full potentialities of science, and industrial practice tends to lag behind scientific knowledge.

Fundamentally "the inefficiency of science simply reflects in an exaggerated form the inefficiency of the economic system under which it has reached its present development." [23] Because so many of the benefits of science are inappropriable social utilities with no market value, scientific resources, both material and intellectual, are wasted. The question is whether the inefficiencies of the organization and utilization of science can be overcome in peacetime or whether this is possible only under the pressures of war and insecurity.

[23] J. D. Bernal, *The Social Function of Science,* p. 121.

NOTE ON OTHER SOCIAL COSTS

The foregoing discussion does not provide a complete account of the social costs of private productive activities in a system of private enterprise. For example, no attempt has been made to trace the social costs which arise in such fields of distribution as banking, insurance, investment, and real estate. The social costs bound up with the artificial maintenance of small-scale production in many fields of economic activity and the social losses caused by the multiplicity of brands and the lack of standardization of commodities have only been touched upon. There is every reason to believe that a more complete study of these and other phases of capitalist production would bring to light considerable additional evidence of social costs. The analysis of these social costs must, however, be reserved to a later study.

The purpose of the present note is merely to direct attention to the existence of two additional sources of social costs which could not be considered in any of the preceding chapters and which, nevertheless, cannot be omitted entirely in a study of this kind. The following observations are highly tentative and should not be construed as an exhaustive discussion of these cases of social costs; they are designed rather to indicate the general direction of further research and analysis.

The first of these additional sources of social costs may be illustrated by the social losses and damages resulting from the competitive utilization of urban land. Under competitive conditions the utilization of urban, like that of agricultural land and, indeed, of any factor of production, is governed by profitableness in terms of entrepreneurial outlays and private returns. In other words, as long as an additional unit of input costs is at least offset by an equal amount of money returns, the private utilizer is likely to intensify the utilization of a given unit of urban land regardless of the consequences which the improvement (i.e., the buildings, the factory, etc.) may have on the property of other persons. The fact that these and similar improvements may have far-reaching harmful effects upon adjoining properties owned by other persons and upon the community as a whole will not and cannot be considered in the competitive calculus determining the intensity of urban land use. It is thus possible, if not inevitable, that private land utilization is carried beyond the point of "optimum utilization" measured in social terms. Such overutilization of urban land may take various forms, such as "robbing the neighbors of their light and air . . . , destroying the beauty of the landscape or the business character of the neighborhood, admitting tenants whose very presence destroys the value of other real estate in the adjoining blocks, etc., etc." [24] Similarly, unregulated competitive utilization of urban land in the past has made for varying building lines and street widths; it tends to result in traffic-congested and unsafe street systems with concomitant street accidents and losses of time, and necessitates the construction of expensive intraurban transit systems. Other evidences of overutilization of urban sites may be found in the existence of slums and poor housing conditions and their manifold consequences. Needless to say, these social costs arising from the overutilization of urban land are the basis for zoning and planning ordinances and may even constitute a *prima facie* case for more drastic measures of public control.

The second case of social costs to be considered here may be regarded merely as a special aspect of land utilization, namely, the losses bound up with the pattern of industrial location which tends to emerge from the competitive process. Today it is generally recognized that the problem of industrial location raises important and complex issues of considerable practical significance. The following discussion is not intended to enter into a complete analysis of these issues. For the sake of argument it will be assumed merely that each industrial concern determines the location of its plant on the basis of comparative costs and returns and that the entrepreneur possesses all the information required to make a deliberate calculation of the

[24] J. M. Clark, "Toward a Concept of Social Value," *Preface to Social Economics,* p. 45.

alternative cost levels at different locations and selects that location at which his private costs (of materials, labor, operation of plant, marketing of products, etc.) are at a minimum. Such a determination of industrial location in terms of private costs and private returns fails to take into account important social costs and potential social benefits of plant location. This will be better understood in the light of the following brief survey of some of the broader aspects of the problem of industrial location. In the first place, it must be realized that the geographical concentration of industry, which seems to result from the selection of plant sites exclusively in terms of private costs and private returns, can easily be carried to a point at which the economies resulting from such specialization, such as lower unit costs of community services or better accessibility, are offset by considerable social disadvantages. Thus, the concentration of industrial production in one or several geographical areas involves not merely transportation costs caused by the necessary transshipment of goods to their markets (in those cases where industrial production tends to be located near the sources of raw materials) but it also tends to give rise to "overrapid depletion of the resources in one region . . . paralleled by inadequate utilization in another." [25] Moreover, under the impact of the establishment of new plants and the development of new industries, the growth of urban communities may proceed in a highly chaotic way, giving rise to overcrowding and unplanned growth of cities. These and similar developments in the past have involved the necessity of expanding urban facilities such as water reservoirs, sewage systems, and schools at costs which fall upon the taxpayer and not upon the owner of the plant. In particular, they have also necessitated the extension of suburban transit facilities which, in turn, force laborers to spend considerable time commuting to and from their homes in great discomfort and at considerable loss of working efficiency. [26]

What is even more important, geographical concentration of in-

[25] National Resources Planning Board, Report for 1942, *National Resources Development* (Washington: U. S. Government Printing Office, 1942), p. 63.

[26] See *Royal Commission on the Distribution of the Industrial Population,* Report, January 1940 (H.M. Stationery Office, London, 1940) (Cmd 6153), p. 97.

dustrial production makes the entire area peculiarly vulnerable to changes in economic conditions. Even a minor decline in demand for the products of its highly specialized industries may expose it to considerable hardship. In addition to the vulnerability to economic changes, geographical concentration of industrial production makes the area and the nation vulnerable to enemy attacks both from the air and by land. Indeed, "the possession of industries which are strategically well placed is worth large numbers of aircraft, warships, tanks and artillery when the balance of military preparedness is weighed up between the nations." [27] The development of atomic weapons has merely further accentuated the need for a pattern of industrial location far different from that which tends to emerge from entrepreneurial calculations in terms of exchange values.

Moreover, the concentration of industrial production in one or two geographical areas may have the further effect of creating and perpetuating inequalities in the economic and cultural development of different areas within the country—a tendency which may be accentuated if vested interests in the industrial regions are able, by means of special price policies and the manipulation of freight rates, to prevent the shift of industrial production to industrially less developed and lower-cost areas.

As an illustration of some of the foregoing observations it is of considerable interest to contrast the pattern of industrial location which tends to emerge from the unregulated competitive process with the policy of industrial location of a planned economy. One of the social objectives of economic planning in the Soviet Union has been the decentralization of industrial production for military reasons and the systematic economic development of backward areas. Ever since the inauguration of the first Five-Year Plan, it has been Russia's policy "to accelerate the development of the poorer and more backward parts of the Union and even to shift the industrial center of gravity toward these raw materials producing regions." [28]

[27] Political and Economic Planning, *Report on the Location of Industry,* a survey of present trends in Great Britain affecting industrial location and regional economic development, with proposals for future policy (London: P.E.P., March 1939), p. 178.

[28] M. Dobb, *Soviet Economy and the War* (London: George Routledge & Son, Ltd., 1942), p. 45.

This process which, according to Dobb, has been particularly marked under the third Five-Year Plan and which involves "a planning of development in the direction of a greater balance in each of the main areas between primary production, finishing plant and metal-using industries," [29] is said to have the net effect of "transport economizing since it brings production nearer to its raw materials and by securing greater specialization and a better balance between the various stages of production in each region saves unnecessary crosshauls of semifinished product." [30] A similar decentralization is underway for consumers' industries "to the extent of making each of the main regions virtually self-supporting . . ." [31]

It is highly significant that the necessity of public control of land use and industrial location in the national interest rather than in accordance with the personal interests of landowners and entrepreneurs is being increasingly recognized in Great Britain, not only for purposes of postwar reconstruction but as a permanent feature of public administration and economic policy.

To conclude: the problem of industrial location must be regarded as another illustration of a potential conflict between the interests of the private producer and those of society. The determination of industrial location in terms of private costs and private returns not only leaves out of account a number of important social costs caused by the entrepreneur's decision but also fails to provide an adequate long-run solution of the problem of industrial location from the point of view of the community. This solution can be found only on the basis of a general appraisal of the *total* costs and benefits of alternative sites of industrial production.

[29] *Ibid.*, p. 51.
[30] *Ibid.*, p. 53.
[31] *Ibid.*, p. 55.

16

SUMMARY AND IMPLICATIONS

DESPITE THE FACT that the preceding chapters do not provide a complete picture of the social costs of private enterprise, it is possible to draw certain general conclusions from the detailed analysis of the various cases of social costs. Before formulating these broader theoretical implications of our study, it may be useful to summarize briefly the major results of our investigation.

1. Summary of Results

Each of the preceding chapters has endeavored to show that private productive activities tend to give rise to a wide variety of social losses not reflected in entrepreneurial outlays. The detailed analysis of these social losses has revealed their heterogeneous origin and character. Thus, whereas some of the social costs of private production could be traced to particular production practices (or neglect of preventive measures) in specific industries, other social losses were seen to arise rather as a result of the workings of the competitive process within the prevailing framework of existing legal and economic institutions.

It was also shown that a considerable proportion of the aforementioned social losses of private production are measurable and can even be expressed in monetary terms. In fact, as has been pointed out repeatedly, a substantial proportion of social losses are reflected in direct monetary expenditures either by private individuals or by public authorities. The fact that these social costs are ultimately reflected in monetary losses and public expenditures emphasizes their "economic" character even in the narrow sense in which the term is used in neoclassical value theory. Other social costs, however, such as the impairment of aesthetic and recreational values and partly also the impairment of human health, are of a less tangible character and can only be estimated in terms other than market values.

Among the social costs of production discussed are the individual and social losses caused by industrial accidents, occupational diseases, woman and child labor; social costs are also reflected in the manifold destructive effects of air and water pollution resulting from inadequate methods of combustion and from the disposal of untreated waste products into streams, rivers and lakes by private firms; moreover, important social costs of production tend to be bound up with the competitive exploitation of both self-renewable and exhaustible natural wealth such as wildlife, petroleum and coal reserves, soil fertility, and forest resources. Social losses also arise in connection with technical changes and the manner and rate of introduction of innovations by private enterprise. We analyzed the general nature of the social costs of economic depressions as well as the social losses resulting from monopoly, which in turn set the stage for the social losses arising in the field of distribution. These losses were seen to be bound up primarily with the wastes and inefficiencies of excessive duplication of retail services and the high costs of sales promotion. As part of the social costs of distribution, the diseconomies of the present transport system were seen to consist in wasteful duplication of facilities and the highly inadequate policy of regulating the transport industry in accordance with the principle of fair return on fair value of investment. In conclusion, an attempt was made to indicate the general nature of the social losses caused by the frustration of science.

What these losses have in common and what makes them truly *social* costs is the fact that they do not enter into the cost calculations of private firms. The are shifted to and are paid for in one form or another by individuals other than the entrepreneur or by the community as a whole or by both. It is true that social legislation and various kinds of governmental regulations, by making individual firms more fully responsible for the social losses caused by their productive activities, doubtless have had the effect of reducing the magnitude of the social costs of production. The need for, and the increasing scope of, such legislation lends additional support to the general thesis that entrepreneurial outlays are not an adequate measure of the true total costs of production.

Our analysis of the manner in which the productive process tends to give rise to social costs provides also an answer to the optimistic view that the interaction and legal adjustment of conflicting interests in modern society offer a sufficient guarantee against the occurrence or at least for the minimization of social losses. Thus, it may be argued that any attempt on the part of individual producers to shift part of the costs of production to the shoulders of other persons is bound to meet with the decided opposition of the latter. Their resistance, or rather the interaction of the conflicting interests, it may be said, tends to produce a more or less equitable adjustment which has the further effect of keeping the magnitude of the social costs at a minimum. Such reasoning, however, fails to consider a number of important facts. In the first place, it overlooks the fact that some of the social costs (e.g., damage to human health) may remain hidden for considerable periods of time during which the persons affected are unaware of the losses they sustain. In other cases, such as the greater frequency and height of floods resulting from soil erosion, the social losses are catastrophic in character and appear to be the result of *force majeur,* although in reality they are caused or at least aggravated by the productive activities of private entrepreneurs. Moreover, some damages, although substantial if viewed in their totality, are distributed over such a great number of persons that each individual sustains only a relatively small loss, which does not seem to warrant defensive action. In still other cases the injured person may simply be unable, financially or otherwise, to take appropriate defensive steps, or he may find it difficult to prove damages.

SUMMARY AND IMPLICATIONS   231

As noted before, this is of considerable importance inasmuch as "judicial precedent requires the demonstration of specific damage rather than general damage and further requires quantitative estimates of the amount of damage experienced by specified individuals." [1] And even if such evidence is available and damage can be proved, effective prevention of damage by means of an injunction can be secured only if it can be shown that practicable means of prevention exist.[2] Another reason why social damages are often caused with impunity by private producers is the fact that individuals to whose shoulders such costs are shifted have not the same economic power, financial resources and general foresight as the highly organized business units responsible for such losses.[3] Furthermore, industries in which the prevention of social losses would be particularly costly might find it more profitable to fight any existing or suggested regulatory legislation than to take remedial action.

Finally, there are those social losses which are intrinsically connected with the operation of the competitive system as a whole—for example, the competitive depletion of energy resources under the "rule of capture" and the tendency to shift the overhead costs of labor to the individual worker in times of depression or after the introduction of technical improvements. Obviously, there is no defense against these social losses except through the abandonment of the customary wage system. In other words, there is no basis for the belief that the interaction and legal adjustment of conflicting interests offer any guarantee that the social costs of production will be kept at a minimum and adequately assessed against entrepreneurial outlays. In the absence of organized group action, social costs tend to become a common phenomenon in the private enterprise economy. Indeed, generally speaking, capitalism must be regarded as an economy of unpaid costs, "unpaid" in so far as a substantial proportion of the actual costs of production remain unaccounted for in entrepreneurial outlays; instead they are shifted to, and ultimately borne by, third persons or by the community as a whole.

[1] See National Resources Committee, *Water Pollution in the United States,* p. 67.
[2] *Ibid.,* p. 68.
[3] S. von Ciriacy-Wantrup, "Land Conservation and Social Planning," p. 111.

Various estimates have been reproduced in the preceding chapters in order to indicate the possible magnitude of specific social costs in monetary terms. No attempt was made, however, to use these estimates as a basis for the calculation of the sum total of the social costs of private enterprise. Several factors militate against such a calculation at the present time. In the first place, none of the estimates advanced, except perhaps those taken from the Smoke Investigation of the Mellon Institute and the studies of the National Resources Committee are based upon any systematic study of the social losses of private production; all present figures are fragmentary in character and should be viewed merely as indicative of possible methods to be used for a more complete determination of the social costs of production. However, no matter how inadequate and fragmentary these monetary estimates of social costs may be at present, they leave no doubt about the fact that the social losses of private production reach substantial proportions. It is reasonable to assume that the social costs of private enterprise are likely to increase in importance and magnitude, the more society becomes aware of and learns to appreciate nonmonetary values. For, as was pointed out in Chapter 2, the final determination of the magnitude of specific social costs for purposes of practical policy remains a matter of collective evaluation and social value.

2. *The Broader Implications of Social Costs*

The broader theoretical implications of the phenomenon of social costs become evident as soon as it is recalled that, with the exception perhaps of Pigou's, they seem to have no room in the conceptual systems of traditional value and price analysis. As was pointed out in the introductory chapter, the theoretical search for levels of equilibrium and for the related processes of adjustment, so characteristic even of modern price theory, proceed from the implicit assumption that entrepreneurial outlays measure the total costs of production. Few of the modern models of cost-price analysis make provision for social costs. Indeed, to judge from most conceptual systems of modern price theory, it appears that social costs are either nonexistent or of no interest or relevance for the analysis of capitalist reality.[4] Fundamentally, therefore, it may be said that the present study has attempted to test the validity of this implicit abstraction of value theory. In the light of the results of our analysis it must be said that the traditional identification of private costs with total costs of production is not only typically incorrect and untenable but also highly misleading in any attempt at obtaining an unbiased and impartial interpretation of the economic process under conditions of private enterprise. As soon as one passes beyond the traditional abstractions of cost-price analysis and begins to consider the omitted truth of social costs, it becomes clear once more that the alleged beneficial orderliness of the competitive process is all but a myth. For, if entrepreneurial costs do not measure the total costs of production, the competitive cost-price calculus is not merely meaningless but nothing more than an institutionalized cover under which it is possible for private enterprise to shift part of the costs to the shoulders of others and to practice a form of large-scale spoliation which transcends everything the early socialists had in mind when they spoke of the exploitation of man by man.

This conclusion would be considerably strengthened if it could be further demonstrated, first, that serious obstacles in modern industrial society stand in the way of rational behavior of both the consumer and the entrepreneur, and second, that market prices and private returns fail to measure the relative importance and magnitude of various social returns which tend to diffuse themselves to all members of society. Such a demonstration, which would have taken us beyond the scope of the present study of social costs, would once and for all invalidate many of the formal and practical conclusions which have been advanced with respect to the competitive calculus and the alleged optimum character of the position of a gen-

---

[4] This is not in contradiction with the fact that various aspects of social costs have found recognition in Pigou's *Economics of Welfare* and in discussions by individual economists. As was pointed out in Chapter 3, the majority of economists look upon social costs as the exception—a minor disturbance—which need not be assimilated into the main body of economic analysis.

eral competitive equilibrium. Indeed, if strictly adhered to, the market test of production in terms of entrepreneurial outlays and private returns would make modern life virtually impossible. For, as Barbara Wootton pointed out, if the criterion of worth-while production is the realization of a surplus of *private* returns over *private* costs measured in terms of exchange values, many goods and services could not be provided "except to consumers who are willing to pay the full costs of them." [5] That is to say, the great majority of people in modern society would have to go without such services. Under no circumstances is it possible to consider the position of general competitive equilibrium as a position of maximum aggregate satisfaction. For if consumers either are not able or are prevented by commercial manipulation of demand from making the best possible use of their income resources; if, furthermore, important social returns are not reflected in private returns and therefore in the economic calculation of the competitive market economy; and if, finally, entrepreneurial outlays fail to measure the true total costs of production, then the competitive equilibrium implies necessarily an arbitrary and highly wasteful utilization of resources. What is maximized is not "aggregate satisfaction" in any comprehensible sense of the term but at best only private exchangeable utilities. And similarly, what is "minimized" is not total unit cost but entrepreneurial outlay; social costs are left entirely out of account in the processes of competitive adjustment. In fact, production may take place at total costs in excess of total gains obtainable therefrom. In other words, competitive equilibrium (and, of course, even less monopolistic equilibrium) neither precludes the use of scarce resources for relatively less important purposes at the expense of more important ends, nor secures a scale of production which can reasonably be called the optimum or least-cost combination.

In the light of these considerations, the familiar conclusions as to the fundamental orderliness and beneficial results of private enterprise do not stand the test of close analysis; they reflect the same

[5] B. Wootton, "Economic Planning," in W. E. Spahr (ed.), *Economic Principles and Problems* (New York: Farrar and Rinehart, Inc., 1940), vol. II, p. 609.

rationalization of a preconceived social and political philosophy which was seen to have shaped and colored the fundamental assumptions and, indeed, the whole development of orthodox and neoclassical price theory. As a result the impressive system of theoretical conclusions of classical and neoclassical economic thought is in need of revision, and serious doubts are cast on the validity and truth of the philosophical foundations from which these conclusions were derived. The possible implications of these results of our analysis for the future of economic science will be better understood if we return once more to the point from which this analysis started and resume the thread of the argument presented in the introductory chapter.

3. The Normative-Apologetic Elements in Traditional Static Equilibrium Analysis

Needless to say, in characterizing the theoretical conclusions of pure economics as normative and apologetic, I do not imply any dishonesty on the part of individual economists. The apologetic and normative character of the theoretical conclusions of equilibrium theory is not necessarily the result of an apologetic attitude, deliberately assumed and maintained in the course of rational deductions. Instead, the apologetic-normative element is inherent in philosophical presuppositions and the resulting imputation of rational order to economic life; it is hidden in the basic assumptions and concepts of economics; it finds its most typical expression in the delimitations of the scope of economic analysis and in the traditional search for levels of equilibrium. Indeed, if anyone were to challenge the economist's impartiality the latter would be likely to protest his scientific objectivity and neutrality by asserting that he is speaking from a purely "economic" point of view. It will not occur to him that it is precisely this purely economic point of view which introduces the normative-apologetic element into his theoretical conclusions and practical judgments. As a matter of fact, it is this attempt to draw and offer theoretical conclusions for the solution of practical problems of economic policy without explicit political premises which accounts for the fact that the conceptual models of modern cost-price analysis perpetuate the old illegitimate union between economic analysis and political economic liberalism. As such, they represent a strange mixture of scientific conclusions and value judgments arrived at by way of rationalization of preconceived sociopolitical ideals, ideologies and metaphysical preconceptions.[6]

This procedure of drawing political conclusions and of dealing with concrete political problems without political premises also accounts for the almost proverbial tension between static-equilibrium theory and economic practice, and tends to make the former increasingly irrelevant for the comprehension and solution of the urgent problems of the present time. In more than one instance, individual economists have been able to use their "pure" economic conclusions openly in the interests of private groups for what looks either like an objective critique or the advocacy, on purely scientific grounds, of various forms of government action.

Although it is probably true that there cannot be economic theory without a grain of social philosophy, since the choice of data in the social sciences is never a matter of pure knowledge but reflects always some prescientific notion,[7] the danger of these propensities of academic economists is too obvious to require elaboration. They may degrade economic science to the level of partisan journalism and in individual instances even justify the appellation of "stooge professors." In any event, in so far as professional economists are not sufficiently conscious of their political premises and biases and offer advice "as if" their conclusions were arrived at on perfectly neutral grounds, they are likely to give rise to a steadily growing distrust of economics by the general public and the statesmen responsible for the formulation of economic policy. To be explicit, these observa-

---

[6] For a more elaborate analysis of the normative-apologetic character of economic science, see G. Myrdal, *Das Politische Element in der Nationalökonomischen Doktrinbildung* (Berlin: Junker and Dunnhaupt, 1932), especially chap. 1. See also B. Wootton, *Lament for Economics* (London: George Allen and Unwin, 1938), pp. 132–182.

[7] Otto von Mehring, "Some Problems of Methodology in Modern Economic Theory," *American Economic Review*, XXXIV (March 1944), p. 94.

tions apply equally well to critics as to partisan advocates of government policy.

In order to substantiate these observations more fully, let us return to our original thesis. As was pointed out in the first chapter, both the origin and the development of economic science can be fully understood only in the light of the philosophical presuppositions of the seventeenth and eighteenth centuries. The essence of these presuppositions was seen to be the unquestioned belief in the existence of a beneficent and rational order of things in social affairs—a belief which can be traced back to the political thinkers of the age, who in this respect shared the preconceptions of the natural sciences. In harmony with their general social philosophy and the prevailing antimercantilistic aspirations of their time, the political economists of the eighteenth century visualized this "natural" order of things in economic life as a system of natural liberty based upon private property and free competition. The Physiocrats and Adam Smith considered it as their task to correlate the detailed phenomena of economic life with one another within a coherent conceptual system in such a manner as to reveal the orderly character of the economic process under conditions of free competition and to prove its beneficial results for society as a whole.

This belief in the existence of a rational order of things in social affairs, to be revealed by systematic research, has shaped the scientific mentality and attitudes of one generation of economists after another. For, fundamentally, it is this belief which accounts for the teleological search for levels of equilibrium and the neglect of the less harmonious aspects of economic life. The search for levels of equilibrium (in terms of exchange values) in turn has shaped to a considerable degree the scope of economic thought. Indeed, it was perhaps inevitable that many economists, in their search for the hidden orderliness in economic life, should have concentrated their attention upon those phenomena which could be shown to further the equilibrating tendencies of competition and to serve the beneficent purpose imputed to the system as a whole. The philosophical presuppositions and the resulting search for levels of equilibrium also accounted for the earlier explicit assumptions such as those of perfect competition and perfect mobility of the factors of production. They are responsible for the original preoccupation with static analysis and the neglect of dynamic changes, as well as for the assumption of rational human conduct. These assumptions of economic theory not only had the legitimate aim of simplifying the complex reality of economic life for purposes of theoretical study but also tended to eliminate the less congenial aspects of reality from the sphere of economic inquiry—those aspects which it would be impossible to construe as contributing to the assumed orderliness of the economic process in the private enterprise economy. This is true not only with respect to such explicit assumptions as those of rational human behavior,[8] perfect mobility of factors of production and free competition (in classical economics); it applies above all to the implicit assumption that the economic can be separated from the so-called noneconomic and that exchange values provide an adequate measure of the former. It is this implicit assumption which explains the acceptance of entrepreneurial outlay as an adequate and significant measure of the true total costs of production and provides the basis for the tacit recognition of market prices and private returns as significant and relevant standards for the measurement of the benefits obtainable from production.

Finally, it is important to note that the tacit presuppositions and the search for the hidden orderliness of the market economy have shaped and are fully reflected in the basic categories of classical and neoclassical economics such as wealth, utility, production, productive labor and, of course, the concept of economy (in the sense of "economizing"). It is not without interest, especially in view of the positive suggestions regarding the scope of economic science to be advanced in the last chapter, to indicate briefly how well these fundamental

---

[8] This assumption has the effect and purpose of making human behavior—an autonomous and, therefore, highly indeterminate and possibly disturbing factor—sufficiently determinate as to make it an integral part of the conceptual system of economic theory. At the same time, the assumption of economic rationality provides an apparently objective basis and justification for the elimination of nonrational behavior as "noneconomic" from the field of economic analysis.

concepts have been adapted to and serve the traditional search for beneficent orderliness in economic life.[9] Indeed, no elaborate analysis is required to show that wealth, for example, is conceived entirely in terms of appropriable, i.e., exchangeable, utilities which can be measured in terms of market prices. To be exact, the modern concept of wealth hinges upon the meaning of utility which points to those qualities of goods and services which can be taken into exclusive possession and as such are subject to measurement in terms of exchange values. Goods and services without these qualities are without utility according to value theory and, consequently, are not considered as wealth. As a matter of fact, utility is not merely a function of physical and economic appropriability and technical exchangeability but is also dependent upon effective demand. In other words, commodities for which there is no demand are said to be without utility, i.e., they are not wealth.

Similarly, production and productive labor are conceived in the same narrow manner as the concept of wealth. In fact, the concept of production has always been dependent upon the meaning of wealth. If earlier economists disagreed about the "productiveness" of certain human activities, their controversy can be understood only in the light of their different interpretations of wealth. Adam Smith regarded the labor of doctors, lawyers and domestic servants as unproductive because he conceived of wealth in an exclusively material sense. Unlike his predecessors, who operated with an even narrower concept of wealth either in terms of gold and silver (Mercantilists) or in terms of the produce of the earth (Physiocrats), Adam Smith considered as wealth all "permanent objects or vendible commodities." This included capital equipment and consumption goods but it excluded services. If today wealth is equivalent to exchangeable utilities in effective demand, production becomes simply the creation of utilities for which there is a demand. "Labor is, in fact, productive when it satisfies a demand—when people are will-

---

[9] The following analysis of some of the basic concepts of economic science is based largely upon L. M. Fraser, *Economic Thought and Language* (London: A. and C. Blake, Ltd., 1937), chap. 11.

ing to pay for it." [10] That is to say, no matter how useful, important or essential goods and services may be, if they are not exchangeable and consequently not measureable in terms of dollars and cents they are not wealth and their creation, for example, under government auspices, is "unproductive" according to the terminology and conceptual system of value theory. Indeed, if strictly interpreted, the definition of wealth and production in terms of exchangeable utilities and with reference to effective demand restricts the validity and meaning of these concepts to a market economy. Labor in an economic system in which the categories of market, exchange and demand do not exist—as, for example, in the manorial economy—would be unproductive in terms of present concepts of production and wealth.

Similarly, the notion of economy or, what amounts to the same thing, the concept of economic optimum are conceived in a manner which makes them applicable only to a market economy; they are identified *per definitionem* with economizing in terms of private costs and returns, i.e., in terms of exchange values. No wonder, therefore, that some economists should have carried this delimitation of concepts and basic categories to its logical conclusion by asserting that the market and the competitive calculus are the prerequisites for the achievement of economy and economic rationality and that all forms of economic organization without free markets are incapable of allocating resources for the attainment of competing ends in a rational manner.

It has to be admitted that with the help of the aforementioned concepts and the explicit and implicit abstractions referred to above, value theory, with the exceptions noted in the case of monopoly theory, did succeed in coördinating a substantial number of detailed economic phenomena into a coherent whole which in effect lends considerable support to the assumed beneficial orderliness of the economic process under conditions of unregulated competition. Given its aims, assumptions, and basic concepts, the theoretical conclusions of modern neoclassical equilibrium economics in support

[10] *Ibid.,* p. 179.

of the system of natural liberty follow tautologically. Value theory was thus bound to become a mere "methodology," a "technique of thinking," to use an expression of Schumpeter's.[11] Once the individual economist has accepted these aims, concepts and assumptions, and as soon as he has mastered the technique of thinking, it is extremely difficult, if not impossible, for him to realize the philosophical presuppositions and hence the limitations of the conceptual system of value theory.[12] Having accustomed himself to the "methodology," he tends to classify all phenomena of economic reality into the traditional scheme of logical categories,[13] and from then on even the most penetrating deductions and the most earnest desire for objectivity cannot produce anything but the normative and apologetic conclusions in support of laissez faire and against any positive regulation and control of the economic process by public authorities. Indeed, it has been argued that only a fallacious interpretation of the basic propositions and conclusions of value theory can justify any other course of public policy than that of noninterference with economic life.[14] In fact, it is this narrow efficiency of the scheme, to borrow a phrase in which A. N. Whitehead refers to physical science, which was the very cause of its supreme methodological success.[15]

In advancing the foregoing observations we do not in the least deny the great positive contributions of classical economics. The classical economists fought against a social philosophy and a system of restrictive regulations which were thoroughly inadequate to make full use of the new technical advances made possible by the inventions and discoveries of the natural sciences during the eighteenth and nineteenth centuries. By introducing into the study of social affairs the rationalistic concepts of natural order and by demonstra-

[11] See J. A. Schumpeter's Introduction to Enrico Barone, *Grundzüge der Theoretischen Nationalökonomie* (Bonn: 1927), p. 7.

[12] G. Myrdal, *Das Politische Element*, p. 34.

[13] *Ibid.*, p. 34.

[14] Cf. G. Sutton, "The Relation between Economic Theory and Economic Policy," *The Economic Journal*, XLVII (1937), 51.

[15] A. N. Whitehead, *Science and the Modern World* (New York: Macmillan, 1925), p. 26.

ting that competition was the "natural law" of such an order, the economists of the eighteenth century "supplied the necessary framework of ideas to meet the need of a new social philosophy adapted to the early days of the industrial revolution." [16] Moreover, in their struggle to break the shackles of mercantilism the classical economists expressed in scientific terms the prevailing aspirations and ideals of economic and political liberty. Thus classical economics served the positive purpose of promoting a development which in its historical setting must be regarded as progressive as far as both the process of production and its scientific interpretation were concerned.[17] Furthermore, by introducing the concept of natural order into the study of economic and social affairs and combining it later with the prevailing utilitarian doctrines, the classical economists protected economic science, as Myrdal[18] pointed out, against the specifically German philosophy of society which in its romantic and organic versions conceived of the state as a metaphysical superorganism to which the individual was subordinated and bound by various kinds of duties.

Today, however, it becomes increasingly evident that neither German state metaphysics nor the preconceptions of a beneficent natural order and harmony of interests in political affairs provide an adequate philosophical foundation for economic science. On the contrary, these philosophical presuppositions of political economy have become the greatest obstacles to the scientific understanding and interpretation of social reality. At the same time, it appears that modern price theory has almost reached the point where not much additional knowledge can be obtained from its present abstractions. Indeed, with the help of mathematical methods modern economists seem to have squeezed out every possible ounce of information from their assumptions and much of what modern firm analysis has achieved appears to be limited to the refinement and elaboration of old solutions and conclusions without throwing much if any new

[16] L. K. Frank, "The Principle of Disorder and Incongruity in Economic Affairs," *Political Science Quarterly*, XLVII (1932), 521.

[17] See G. Myrdal, *Das Politische Element*, p. 85.

[18] *Ibid.*, p. 86.

light upon the problems under discussion. Moreover, a good deal of value and price theory shows a tendency toward a self-sealing system "which has a way of almost automatically discounting evidence which might bear adversely on the doctrine." [19] This exhaustion of the possible content and meaning of its assumptions and its "self-sealing" character seems to make neoclassical equilibrium economics a perfect illustration of A. N. Whitehead's dictum that "systems, scientific and philosophic, come and go. Each method of limited understanding is at length exhausted. In its prime each system is a triumphant success; in its decay it is an obstructive nuisance. The transitions to new fruitfulness of understanding are achieved by recurrence to the utmost depth of intuition for the refreshment of imagination." [20]

[19] J. R. Oppenheimer, "Physics in the Contemporary World," *Technology Review* (February 1948), p. 238.

[20] A. N. Whitehead, *Adventures in Ideas,* pp. 203–204. Copyright 1933 by The Macmillan Company and used with their permission.

17

TOWARD A NEW SCIENCE
OF POLITICAL ECONOMY

BEFORE SETTING FORTH the broader positive implications of our analysis, it is important to emphasize again the limited objective of our study, which was to provide a detailed examination of the social costs of private enterprise. The purpose of the present chapter then is merely to outline, on the basis of the critical conclusions reached in the preceding chapter, some of the steps by which it might be possible to achieve the transition to new fruitfulness of understanding so urgently needed in economics and the social sciences. The reader who expects the chapter to be a point of arrival rather than a point of departure will be disappointed; indeed, he may not even find it very illuminating. The elaboration of a new and coherent system of understanding cannot be the work of one single student but depends upon the collaboration of many minds. In fact, it can emerge only after years of constructive coöperation in the social sciences.

1. Return to Philosophy

The first step toward a reorientation of economic science must be a return to philosophy. Whitehead's statement that "if science is not to degenerate into a medley of *ad hoc* hypotheses, it must become philosophical and must enter upon a thorough criticism of its own foundations" [1] applies with equal force to economics. Indeed, eco-

---

[1] A. N. Whitehead, *Science and the Modern World,* p. 25. Copyright 1925 by The Macmillan Company and used with their permission.

nomic theory has to overcome its philosophical isolation and bring its fundamental presuppositions in line with the present state of philosophical insight. This means more than the abandonment of the belief in a beneficial natural order in social affairs and in the basic rationality of man, long abandoned by modern philosophy and psychology. This new beginning cannot be achieved without the recognition of strong and cumulative tendencies toward disorder and "disequilibrium" under conditions of competition; moreover, through the shift of parts of the costs of production to the shoulders of other persons and the community as a whole, the market economy tends to create serious conflicts of interest in economic life, inasmuch as it sets the condition for an "exploitation" of one group of individuals by another. Instead of denying and partly even concealing the existence of wastes, disharmonies and strong disequilibrating tendencies in economic life and of conflicts of interests, economics will have to make them the object of its analysis in the light of the results of inductive studies.[2] In fact, there is considerable reason to believe that the exploration of disequilibrium and the study of deviations from equilibrium would yield truly significant results in contrast to those obtained by the search for equilibrium of supply and demand in hypothetically static markets.

This is not to suggest that the teleological imputation of beneficent orderliness to the economic process should be replaced merely by an equally teleological imputation of disorder and disequilibrium. Such a procedure is likely to yield the same unrealistic and normative results as the exclusive search for levels of equilibrium did in the past. What we do suggest, however, is that economics devote more attention to the study of the disequilibrating tendencies in socio-economic

[2] It is not without interest to note that the natural sciences, or at least the more philosophically minded scientists, seem to have abandoned the earlier tacit belief in a fundamental order of things in the world of nature. Thus, Whitehead points out that "science can find no individual enjoyment in nature; science can find no aim in nature; science can find no creativity in nature; it finds mere rules of succession" [A. N. Whitehead, *Nature and Life* (Chicago: University of Chicago Press, 1934), p. 30]. Bertrand Russell even thinks that "the universe is all spots and jumps without unity, without continuity, without coherence or orderliness or any of the other properties that governesses love." See "What I Believe," *The Nation* (March 30, 1940), p. 412. See also *A Free Man's Worship* (Portland: T. B. Moscher, 1923).

life and that the discovery of the causes of "disequilibrium" is likely to yield more fruitful conclusions for the formulation of economic policies than the futile search for "natural" and beneficent orderliness in social affairs. Even J. M. Keynes has not abandoned completely this search for levels of equilibrium. His demonstration that there are tendencies in modern economic soc'ety which may produce equilibrium below full employment uses to a large extent traditional tools of analysis and fails to include many of the broader aspects of economic life dealt with in the present study. Even so, Keynes and his followers have made an important beginning, inasmuch as they have destroyed beyond repair the classical belief in economic harmonies between consumption and production.

The suggestion that the basic preconceptions of economic liberalism be abandoned and the philosophical foundation of economics be brought into accord with modern philosophy raises once more the question as to the tasks and purposes of the science. For what are the fundamental aims of economic analysis? In order to answer this question let us state first, even at the risk of being repetitious, what are *not* the aims and objectives of economic science. Obviously, the aim of a science is not to act as a servant to any prevailing form of economic organization; a system of knowledge ought not to be a system of apologetics; nor can it be the purpose of economic science to provide norms or prescriptions for what "ought to be done" except on the basis of clearly postulated political premises and social value judgments. Indeed, a normative system of economics without political premises with every economist offering advice on what ought to be done in the field of economic policy would be the end of economic science.

In fact, the aim of economic science can only be to provide the basis for an impartial and critical comprehension and interpretation of socio-economic reality. Such comprehension requires above all that the basic concepts and categories of economic science be formulated in a manner which transcends the market economy. In short, economic science must overcome "the horizon of contemporary society." [3] While this was perhaps not possible during the nineteenth century, it is possible now after it has become evident that competition and laissez faire are inadequate principles for the organization of economic and social life. More specifically, the task of economic science is to provide theoretical models which can ultimately be used for the explanation of the effects[4] of decisions (plans) both of individuals and of governments under conditions of dynamic change, that is to say, under conditions where simultaneous changes of significant variables over time are fully taken into consideration. In other words, the aim of economic knowledge is to establish theoretical frameworks which show the necessary or possible relations between the many variables of economic reality, thereby enabling individuals and governments to make reasoned choices in full understanding of the probable repercussions of their action. Indeed, the most important task of economic science seems to be the exploration of the repercussions of various measures of public control and economic regulation and thus to provide at least tentative criteria for the formulation of public policy. For there must be no doubt that economic science is above all a science of social economy, i.e., a system of knowledge designed to enable the administrator of public affairs, the statesman, to develop the technique of economic and political administration which modern society requires. What we have in mind is nothing radically new: the recent emergence of a new theory of economic dynamics, and the construction of national budgets designed to reveal the structural relations which connect the various parts of the national accounts, are good examples of the scope and objectives of the system of economic thought advocated here.

If the primary aim of economic science is the comprehension of the repercussions of individual and collective decisions and the establishment of theoretical models in terms of which possible or actual

[3] M. Horkheimer, "The Social Function of Philosophy," *Studies in Philosophy and Social Science,* VIII (1939), p. 329.

[4] "Repercussions" would be a better word; see Ragnar Frisch, "Repercussion Studies at Olso," *American Economic Review,* XXXVIII (June 1948), 367–372.

repercussions can be explained, the concept of social causation assumes once more a role of major importance for the economist. For upon the *concept* of causality depends the *method* used in discovering causal relations. If the causal connection between social phenomena is conceived as a *necessary* relation, as was the case in static-equilibrium analysis in the past, the discovery of the causal connection depends indeed upon deduction and generalizing abstractions. If, however, the causal relation between the variables in the social system is seen not as a *necessary* relation but as one in which anticipations constitute often the most important link, it is essential to conceive of causality largely as an empirical correlation which calls for measurement in terms of coefficients of greater or lower probability, observation, fact finding, case studies and statistical extrapolation. It must be considered as a hopeful sign that a reconsideration of the meaning of causality seems to be under way in both the natural and the social sciences.[5]

2. *The Broadening of the Scope of Economic Investigations*

One of the most important effects of a reconsideration of the philosophical presuppositions of traditional equilibrium economics would be a more general realization of the need for a broadening of the scope of economic analysis. In particular, such a reconsideration would pave the way for the inclusion in economic analysis of everything that appears relevant for the particular problem under consideration. No longer would measurability in terms of exchange values be made the criterion of what belongs to the subject matter of economic science; instead, it would become possible to take seriously J. M. Clark's dictum that "it is unscientific to exclude any evidence relevant to the problem in hand." [6] Indeed, scientific method implies comprehensiveness "even if it involves some sacrifice of other qualities for which science likes to strive." [7] Once this real-

---

[5] See the selected bibliography in R. M. MacIver, *Social Causation* (Boston: Ginn and Co., 1942), pp. 395–400.

[6] J. M. Clark, "The Socializing of Theoretical Economics," in *Preface to Social Economics*, p. 5.

[7] *Ibid.*, p. 5.

ization becomes a general attitude, it will no longer be true to say that economists have succumbed "to an all-too-prevalent methodological fanaticism which prefers the accurate but superficial to the approximate but fundamental, and which makes adaptability to its special technique of investigation, rather than importance, the standard for the selection of problems and the delimitation of the scope of its inquiry." [8]

As a matter of fact, the intrinsic connection and interpenetration of the economic and the "noneconomic" make it quite impossible to define the subject matter of economic science by means of general classifications. In fact, any delimitation of the scope of economic analysis is likely to yield only a distorted picture of the manifold problems with which economic science actually has to deal. It is not surprising, therefore, that most attempts made in the past to define the subject matter of economic science failed to convey an adequate idea of the actual scope of economic analysis. Many of these attempts, especially those based upon earlier concepts of wealth, yielded definitions of economic science which were too narrow, leaving out important economic problems.[9] However, even if a clear-cut delimitation of the scope of economic science were possible such a delimitation would still be unnecessary. For it could not possibly provide any help to the individual scientist in the discovery and deduction of specific conclusions. Indeed, as Myrdal emphasized, just as the chemist cannot draw any scientific conclusions from the definition of chemistry as a science, so the definition of the subject matter of economics cannot be decisive as a scientific argument for or against particular conclusions.[10] It is, therefore, quite true that the only con-

---

[8] J. Viner, "The Utility Concept in Value Theory and its Critics," *Journal of Political Economy*, XXXIII (1925), 659.

[9] For an account of the numerous, now more or less abandoned, definitions of economic science, see A. Ammon, *Objekt und Grundbegriffe der Theoretischen Nationalökonomie* (Leipzig: 1927), ed. 2, and L. Robbins, *An Essay on the Nature and Significance of Economic Science* (London: Macmillan and Co., 1940), chaps. 1 and 2; used with the permission of The Macmillan Company.

[10] G. Myrdal, *Das Politische Element*, p. 236. See also O. Neurath, *Empirische Soziologie, Der Wissenschaftliche Gehalt der Geschichte und Nationalökonomie* (Wien: Julius Springer, 1931), p. 72.

cept with the precise definition of which the economist need not concern himself is that of economic science.[11]

In fact, a delimitation of the scope of economic science in general terms is not only undesirable but may even be harmful. This becomes especially clear in the light of the declared objectives of some of the attempts made in the past to define the subject matter of economic science. Thus it has been pointed out, for example, that the definition of the subject matter of economic science is necessary in order not to leave it to the individual economist to get his own idea thereof.[12] Robbins is even more outspoken in this respect; he proceeds "with an easy conscience" to the description of the general subject matter of economic science in order to prevent "the preoccupation with the irrelevant—the multiplication of activities having little or no connection with the solution of problems strictly germane to his [the economist's] subject." [13] Apart from the somewhat over-confident belief that it is possible to define once and for all the "relevant" and the "irrelevant," irrespective of the particular nature of the problem under discussion, any segregation of the "relevant" from the "irrelevant" is bound to be harmful for three reasons. In the first place, it tends to make economics a closed system of thought by providing a seemingly scientific basis from which it becames possible to brand all arguments directed against specific theoretical conclusions as having been derived from allegedly "irrelevant" data and observations. Second, the specifically Robbinsian definition of the subject matter of economics in terms which do not transcend the capitalist market economy permits the drawing of the "scientific" conclusion that any other form of economic organization is incompatible with the rational utilization of scarce means for the attainment of competing ends. In other words, the definition of economic science in terms of exchange values gives a scientific dignity to what has been called not inappropriately "the undignified farce of sharpshooting at Marxism with toy Austrian popguns from behind a non-

---

[11] G. Myrdal, *Das Politische Element*, p. 236.
[12] A. Ammon, *Objekt und Grundbegriffe*, p. 4.
[13] L. Robbins, *Essay on Economic Science*, p. 3.

existing methodological wall." [14] Third, the endeavor to define the particular subject matter of economics and other sciences has so far led only to the erection and multiplication of artificial boundary lines between the social sciences. This departmentalization of the social sciences as, indeed, of all sciences, tends to obstruct and defeat the search for truth by restricting the scope and horizon of scholarly inquiries. This must be particularly harmful in the social sciences which are concerned with a study of a fundamentally inter-related and integrated social, economic and political reality.

For these reasons the fruitfulness of social and economic research depends upon the progressive elimination of all boundaries which past generations of scholars have found useful for scholastic, peda-gogic and other reasons. [15] The ultimate aim is not merely "collabora-tion" but the closest possible integration and constructive synthesis of the social sciences. Until this aim has been attained individual economists can only endeavor to press beyond the present boundaries of economic science and to explore as fully as possible new develop-ments in psychology, sociology, politics, law, history and ethics with a view to assimilating to their own reasoning whatever results these social sciences may contribute to a better understanding of economic problems.

The only boundary line which must not be abandoned but should even be strengthened is, as Myrdal pointed out, [16] the line between scientific comprehension and dilettantist speculation of a more or less metaphysical and normative character, that is to say between science and pseudo science. To draw this line is, however, the task not so much of economic science as of philosophy. Its solution, more-over, involves issues of intellectual honesty and professional integrity which need not be discussed here.

Nothing that has been said in this section should be construed to mean that I have any quarrel with Robbins' definition of economics as "the science which studies human behavior as a relationship be-

[14] R. W. Souter, "The Nature and Significance of Economic Science in Recent Dis-cussions," *Quarterly Journal of Economics,* XLVII (May 1933), 411.

[15] G. Myrdal, *Das Politische Element,* p. 237.

[16] *Ibid.,* pp. 237–238.

tween ends and scarce means which have alternative uses." [17] On the contrary, I believe that this formulation points to the fundamental economic principle and the common point of view which underlies and unifies all economic analysis. The economic problem arises precisely whenever scarce means with alternative uses have to be adapted to competing ends, i.e., whenever the need for a choice between alternatives arises. Generalizations about human action of this sort are indeed within the province of economic science regardless of whether the alternatives are individual or collective in character. This formulation of the economic principle makes economic science simply the science of human action and both L. Robbins and L. Mises[18] conceive of it expressly in this broad fashion. Whether they would be prepared on this account to include within economic analysis generalizations about social choices and social evaluations of different alternatives, i.e., decisions of governments in matters of economic policy, is another question. There are reasons to doubt this in view of Professors Robbins' and Mises' general social philosophy; in any event, formal value theory has thus far not drawn these logical conclusions from the definition of economics as the science concerned with the problem of choice arising in connection with the allocation of scarce means with alternative uses to competing ends. It has confined its analysis to alternatives measurable in terms of market values. We shall return to this problem in the final section of this chapter.

3. The Reformulation and Enlargement of Basic Concepts

While it is undoubtedly true that there are individual economists who have attempted to reformulate some of the basic categories of economic thought for their specific purposes, these attempts have been confined largely to the field of public finance and business-cycle

---

[17] L. Robbins, *Essay on Economic Science*, p. 16.

[18] Mises calls his treatise on political economy (*Nationalökonomie*) "Theory of Human Action and Economizing" and devotes the first part of the book to an elaborate analysis of human action; see his *Nationalökonomie, Theorie des Handels und Wirtschaftens* (Geneva: Editions Union, 1940).

theory. It may well be that many of these reformulations[19] will ultimately be integrated into a new system of economic analysis. So far, however, this assimilation has not taken place and it is no exaggeration to say that concepts of wealth and production and their definition in terms of exchangeable utilities in effective demand not only have "failed to keep pace with the facts of production"[20] but are among the most important obstacles to an understanding of present-day economic problems. For, indeed, as long as wealth and production are defined with reference to exchangeable utilities in effective demand, the creation of goods and services yielding no exchangeable returns must be considered as "unproductive." The term unproductive, however, in the language of economic science means unremunerative and "not worthwhile."[21] Strictly speaking, the production of goods and services for the gratification of collective needs and social goals such as national defense, most multiple-purpose projects, scientific research and education, in short, the creation of social returns, is "unproductive" according to this definition. No matter how desirable these social purposes may be, from the standpoint of orthodox economic theory any allocation of scarce means to these ends must be considered as "waste." Under these circumstances it is not surprising that pure equilibrium economics throws little light upon the whole problem of public investments and the manner in which to provide for the full utilization of idle resources and manpower under present economic and political conditions.

The primary purpose of a reformulation of the classical and neoclassical concept of wealth and productivity would be to broaden the meaning of these concepts in such a manner as to include the phe-

---

[19] An example of such reformulations of basic concepts is the interesting classification of public expenditures according to their "productiveness" advanced by U. K. Hicks, *The Finance of British Government, 1920–36* (London: Oxford University Press, 1938) and A. H. Hansen, *Fiscal Policy and Business Cycles* (New York: W. W. Norton and Co., 1941), pp. 146–153.

[20] J. M. Clark, "Economics and Modern Psychology," in *Preface to Social Economics,* p. 138.

[21] Here is another instance where apparently neutral definitions and innocent methodological classifications carry normative implications.

nomena of social costs and social returns within the range of economic analysis. Instead of conceiving wealth and production merely in terms of exchangeable utilities, the new concepts of wealth and production will have to be defined in such a manner as to include also nonmarket values. Indeed, wealth consists not merely of goods and services which are traded in markets; it includes all values and utilities irrespective of whether they can be exchanged and evaluated accurately in terms of exchange values. And correspondingly, production refers to the creation of everything that is considered useful and valuable whether exchangeable or not exchangeable, privately appropriable or socially beneficial. Similarly, as has already been pointed out, the principle of economy (that is, "economizing") will have to be conceived in a more inclusive manner than has been the case hitherto. Instead of defining "economizing" merely in terms of exchange values, it is necessary to formulate the principle of economy (and the concept of "economic optimum") in a manner designed to take account of social costs and social returns. In other words, if the concepts of "economy" and "economic optimum" are to have any place in economic discussions they have to be formulated in terms of estimates of total gains and sacrifices (in the sense of displaced opportunities). By thus enlarging the meaning of wealth, production and "economizing" through the inclusion of social costs and social returns, it would be possible to get away from any arbitrary and normative designation as unproductive of activities which create nonexchangeable, social utilities.

Such a broadening of the fundamental concepts of economic science would also open the way for a genuinely economic theory of public revenues and expenditures. Indeed, taxes would be clearly recognized as outlays for production. This is easily understood in the case of taxes levied for the purpose of remedying the losses caused by air and water pollution, erosion, deforestation, unemployment, etc. Public revenues spent for these purposes measure that part of the costs of production which private enterprise is able to shift to society. Exactly the same holds true for other government revenues and expenditures. They represent costs of production in a double sense. In the first place, they are a measure of the cost shifted to society by private enterprise. Second, they are outlays required for the production of such goods and services as private enterprise finds unprofitable to produce. They may be either consumption outlays designed to produce goods and services of immediate utility, or investment outlays for the construction of durable goods such as improved means of transportation or better housing, and medical care yielding social benefits over a period of time. In any event, as far as its economic implications are concerned, taxation has to be looked upon, as Sismondi suggested more than a century ago[22] and as Beveridge pointed out recently, "as a means of reducing private expenditure on consumption and thereby freeing real resources for other uses." [23]

By thus reformulating and enlarging their basic concepts in a manner designed to include social costs and social returns, economists would give recognition to the fact that there exists no fundamental difference between private and social costs of production, and that exchangeable and nonexchangeable utilities are identical in so far as the production of both has to draw upon scarce resources and makes necessary choices, either individual or social, between competing ends. They differ only in so far as their measurability is concerned. It is at this point that we finally come upon the most important category of the new science of economics, namely, that of social value.

4. Social Choices, Social Evaluation and Social Value

If economic science has to concern itself with social costs, as we have tried to demonstrate throughout the present study, and with social returns, it will not be sufficient merely to trace and describe these largely neglected aspects of socio-economic reality in general terms. Nor will it be adequate to present quantitative estimates (in monetary terms) of social costs, as has been done in some of the

[22] J. C. L. Simonde de Sismondi, *Nouveaux Principes d'Économie Politique,* vol. I, pp. 142 ff.

[23] W. H. Beveridge, *Full Employment in a Free Society* (New York: W. W. Norton and Co., 1945), p. 149.

preceding chapters. No matter how important such estimates may be as a first approach to an appraisal of social costs, the final determination of their relative magnitude and significance is likely to be a matter of social evaluation and social value (in the sense of *value to society*).[24] If it is further realized that the magnitude and relative importance of social returns (i.e., the inappropriable benefits obtainable from a wide variety of public investments) cannot be measured in terms of exchange values but require some kind of social estimate, it becames clear that the concept of social value is likely to be one of the most important categories of any system of economic thought willing to explore the nature and repercussions of governmental action and economic policy making.

Formal equilibrium analysis seems to have little to offer toward a solution of this central problem of economic theory. In fact, subjective value theory recognizes only the individual as capable of feeling "pain and pleasure" and hence able to establish preference scales with respect to different commodities and alternative courses of action (choices). This evidently accounts for the fact that "scarcely a breath [of the idea of social value] penetrates to the rarefied atmosphere of technical discussions of the theory of value and distribution."[25] And yet, only "if we can develop a concept of economic value and valuation with reference to society as a whole, independent of market valuations and capable of scientific application to concrete cases, we shall have an intellectual instrument that will pierce the

[24] In using this qualifying term we want to emphasize that our concept of social value has nothing in common with the notion of "social value" developed by J. B. Clark and E. R. A. Seligman, and later by B. M. Anderson. These economists, especially in their earlier writings, endeavored to prove that it is society as such which puts value on commodities and that prices in capitalist exchange economies are genuine social values reflecting the value of commodities to all members of society. The logical and terminological confusion and the strange apologetic purpose of this early American doctrine of social value has been demonstrated especially by J. A. Schumpeter, "On the Concept of Social Value," *Quarterly Journal of Economics,* XXIII (1909), 216–217, 222 ff. See also F. Wieser, *Natural Value* (London: 1893), pp. 52–53; and E. Böhm-Bawerk, "Grundzüge der Theorie des Wirtschaftlichen Güterwertes," *Conrads Jahrbücher,* New Series, vol. XIII (1886), p. 478.

[25] J. M. Clark, "Toward a Concept of Social Value," in *Preface to Social Economics,* p. 53.

insulation [of economic theory] and establish a connection with the ideas that are making things happen." [26]

Despite this neglect of the problem of social value in subjective value theories, social evaluation is not a new problem. On the contrary, it forms the basis of *all* government action and decisions. For "any social policy or decision necessarily rests on a social value judgment, a social concept of social well-being, derived from social thinking." [27] The important question is, of course, how to deal with the problem of social evaluation at the theoretical level. In the first place, what do we know about existing social scales of social preferences? How do governments, on the basis of a given scale of social preferences, determine relative social values and consequently the worthwhileness of different lines of public investments? Can individual preference scales be translated into collective preference scales? Does the process of social evaluation of social costs and social benefits not necessarily imply an evaluation of individual values and preferences? And is there not permanent danger of a conflict between individual and social judgments of well-being inasmuch as citizens will differ on such questions as what value to place on certain social costs and returns, how to distribute the costs involved in preventive measures designed to minimize social costs and, above all, how far to expand the output of social returns accruing to all members of society.

Knowledge about existing scales of social preference may be derived from a variety of sources. Certainly they are reflected in, and can be inferred from, existing public expenditure patterns. The field of public finance and national budgeting provides the most fruitful area of research for the collection of empirical data concerning existing scales of social preferences.

As far as the actual process of decision making and the determination of social values on the basis of a given scale of social preferences is concerned, the fields of public administration and administrative

---

[26] *Ibid.*, p. 54.
[27] F. H. Knight, Foreword to A. L. Macfie, *Economic Efficiency and Social Welfare* (London: Oxford University Press, 1943), p. vi.

behavior in general provide the empirical material in the light of which it may be possible to erect a general theory of social value.[28] Of special interest in this connection is doubtless the manner in which the military and economic high command in a war economy decides the question of how many and what kinds of arms and ammunition are to be produced out of the limited supply of available resources. Although the process of social evaluation may be said to be relatively simple in wartime, owing to the existence of one supreme end from which all other social ends take their respective rank and importance, even the supreme end of winning the war is a complex composite end implying the disposition and allocation of resources among many alternative purposes.

It is true that in many instances it is impossible to assess in advance the social benefits to be expected from a particular course of action. A case in point is the by now famous case of wartime research in the field of nuclear fission, which required a total outlay of 2 billion dollars for results which could be anticipated and estimated only in the vaguest fashion. It is probable that in similar instances social comparisons of outlays and effects can be made only in terms of physical quantities of estimated inputs and outputs of a rather heterogenous character. In other cases, however, it may be possible to use more or less objective standards of adequacy, as, for example, when dealing with medical care, educational facilities, housing and even defense. Here, and in all instances where it is relatively easy to agree on a scale of social priorities, the practical determination of the relative importance of social benefits and their costs may be easily achieved. In all cases it will be possible to arrive at an approximate social estimate of expected social benefits in terms of some kind of social opportunity labor costs similar to the wartime practice of expressing and measuring the ("real") costs of production of a battleship in terms of the number of man-days required for its production (and consequently not available for other purposes). In the last analysis, then, it is only on the basis of a social comparison of

[28] See, for instance, H. A. Simon, *Administrative Behavior* (New York: The Macmillan Co., 1947).

desired effects and available resources (in the light of their alternative uses) that collective estimates of social value and choices can be arrived at in practice.

Viewed in this fashion, the problem of social value represents no basically new theoretical problem. There is no reason, for example, why, for purposes of formal analysis, we cannot speak of "social marginal utility" and "social utility curves" or, if we prefer, introduce collective indifference curves to represent marginal social rates of substitution. Certainly the principle of marginal valuation applies to social valuation and collective choice just as it does to individual valuation and choice. In this sense, at any rate, the theory of social value is not antimarginal.

In contrast, the relationship of individual preferences and social values raises a number of new and more difficult problems. For purposes of formal analysis it may be sufficient to combine individual rates of substitution into total marginal rates of substitution expressing the collective willingness of the group to spend amounts of the general means of exchange for additional social benefits (such as prevention of social costs, education, defense, etc.). This approach, which has recently been suggested by H. R. Bowen, would give us a "curve of total marginal substitution" which may be said to correspond "as closely as possible, under the conditions, to the familiar curve of total demand." [29] The intersection of this collective demand curve with the appropriate (average) cost curve could be regarded as the point up to which output of social benefits could be expanded without creating a conflict between individual and collective choices.[30] However, any attempt to use these tools of formal anal-

[29] H. R. Bowen, *Toward Social Economy* (New York: Rinehart & Co., Inc., 1948), p. 178. For a recent demonstration of the need for a "social utility calculus" in connection with federal budgeting and fiscal policy, see A. Smithies, "Federal Budgeting and Fiscal Policy," in H. Ellis, ed., *Survey of Contemporary Economics* (Philadelphia: The Blakiston Co., 1948), pp. 174–209.

[30] If desirable, this apparatus of formal analysis may be further refined by the introduction of marginal rates of substitution, average cost per person and marginal cost per person so that ideal output of a particular social service might be defined in terms of identity of marginal rates of substitution and marginal cost per person. See Bowen, *Toward Social Economy*, pp. 178–179.

ysis for practical purposes is likely to be blocked by the same difficulties which stand in the way of their being used in the practical problem of profit maximization by individual firms, namely, the difficulty of calculating marginal costs and marginal returns (or marginal rates of substitution in the case under discussion). Consequently it will not be easy to translate individual preference scales into collective preference scales and the danger of a conflict between the two should not be minimized. For all practical purposes it is, therefore, of the greatest importance to develop and adopt more direct methods of discovering scales of individual preferences with respect to social ends and the allocation of resources. Such methods of discovering individual and public preferences will include an extensive use of public-opinion polls and sample inquiries and the use and interpretation of the results of voting as outlined by H. R. Bowen.[31] In fact, "it may be that through properly administered public-opinion polls professionalized public officials can give us all the efficiency now claimed for authoritarian centralized administration, and yet have that administration at all times subject to the dictates of a more delicate barometer of the people's will than is provided by all the technologically obsolete paraphernalia of traditional democratic processes."[32]

However, for both theoretical and practical purposes more is needed than a justification of social preferences and collective decisions in terms of a concept of total welfare as the sum of utilities of all individuals. For even in democratically organized societies the formulation of judgments of social well-being often rests not upon a maximization of individual utilities but rather upon a social evaluation of individual utilities or even of the relative importance which the individual may have for the achievement of a particular social end without or with limited reference to the individual's utility. Moreover, in a democracy the formulation of public policy depends upon the conception which the majority has of common purposes

[31] *Ibid.*, pp. 180–189.
[32] A. Lundberg, *Can Science Save Us* (New York: Longmans, Green and Co., 1947), p. 39.

and common ultimate values, and there are always elements of power exercised by dominating groups which enter into the processes of public decision making. The preferences of minorities and groups without sufficient political influence are, if not neglected completely, taken into account only via the tedious and slow processes of parliamentary compromise. The danger of conflict between individual and social preferences is therefore a real and permanent one for any society. Even "the abolition of all classes" and of dominating groups cannot do away with these conflicts, and no appeal to rationality and public enlightenment can ultimately secure the degree of unanimity in matters of social and economic affairs which would be required in order to establish any true identity between individual and social preferences. Instead of concealing the possibility of conflicts between individual and social values by a concept of total welfare conceived as the sum of utilities of all individuals or by some vague references to "the will of the people" or to "government by and for the people," it is more realistic to recognize the reality of the conflict and accept it, with the Federalists and Karl Marx, as the essential characteristic of the political process. Thus, with the elaboration of a theory of social value, economic science will have to pass even beyond the abstractions and formal solutions of modern welfare economics. Indeed, the ultimate answer to these problems belongs to philosophy and political science; economic science will be quite helpless in dealing with these issues as long as it refuses to abandon its present philosophical isolation.

Thus, only by abandoning the philosophical premises of the seventeenth and eighteenth centuries, by reformulating and enlarging the meaning of its basic concepts of wealth and production, and by supplementing its study of market prices by a study of social value, will economic science finally achieve an impartial and critical comprehension of the economic process, not only in the private enterprise economy but under any form of economic organization. Indeed, by including social costs, social returns and social value within the range of its analysis, economic science would become "political economy" in a deeper and broader sense than even the classical economists conceived of the term. In fact, economic science could then really be said to deal with the problem of social economy and would thus at last prove its status as a system of knowledge concerned with the study of the nature and causes of the wealth of nations.

APPENDICES

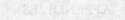

APPENDIX I

Work Injury Frequency Rates and Severity Averages, Major Manufacturing and Nonmanufacturing Groups, 1947[1]

Group	Days Lost per Disabling Injury[2]	Injury Frequency Rates[3]
Manufacturing		
Lumber...................	85	66.0
Furniture.................	64	29.5
Stone, clay, glass...........	65	24.3
Food products.............	65	24.0
Iron and steel..............	91	22.3
Paper products.............	79	22.1
Machinery (except electric)....	56	19.7
Nonferrous metals...........	60	17.1
Transportation equipment.....	83	14.2
Miscellaneous manufacturing..	56	13.5
Textiles...................	65	13.2
Rubber....................	103	13.2
Leather...................	50	13.0
Chemicals.................	96	12.6
Printing and publishing.......	68	9.4
Electrical machinery.........	78	8.8
Apparel...................	33	6.9
All manufacturing...........	73	18.8
Nonmanufacturing		
Construction...............	97.0	40.9
Transportation.............	97.5	27.5
Heat, light, power..........	96.6	18.1
Communication............	98.9	3.0

[1] From *Work Injuries in the United States During 1947*, U. S. Department of Labor, Bulletin 945 (Washington: U. S. Government Printing Office, 1948), pp. 8–10.

[2] Computed by adding the amount of actual time lost because of temporary total disabilities and the standard time charge for deaths and permanent impairments, and dividing the total by the number of injuries.

[3] Average number of disabling industrial injuries for each million employee-hours worked.

APPENDIX II

TOTAL NUMBER OF INDUSTRIAL INJURIES AND INJURY RATES IN THE MINERAL INDUSTRIES IN THE UNITED STATES, 1931–1948[1]

Year	Total Number of Injuries in Mineral Industries		Injury Rates per Million Man-Hours in Mineral Industries		Total Number of Injuries at Coal Mines		Injury Rates per Million Man-Hours in Coal Mines		Injury Rates per Million Tons of Coal	
	Killed	Injured	Killed	Injured	Killed	Injured	Killed	Injured	Killed	Injured
1931	1,707	94,021	1.33	72.99	1,463	80,349	1.82	99.888	3,312	181.888
1932	1,368	66,028	1.42	68.57	1,207	58,972	1.90	92.666	3,357	164.009
1933	1,242	70,158	1.17	66.30	1,064	61,313	1.48	85.258	2,777	160.014
1934	1,429	79,211	1.22	67.83	1,226	68,008	1.59	88.387	2,943	163.270
1935	1,495	80,070	1.23	65.88	1,242	65,575	1.70	89.509	2,925	154.428
1936	1,686	90,608	1.18	63.53	1,342	69,576	1.62	84.193	2,732	141.663
1937	1,759	94,466	1.19	63.73	1,413	68,277	1.74	84.145	2,833	136.884
1938	1,369	69,940	1.20	61.13	1,105	51,314	1.78	82.609	2,793	129.680
1939	1,334	73,253	1.07	58.55	1,078	54,015	1.59	79.645	2,406	120.575
1940	1,716	80,856	1.24	58.37	1,388	59,781	1.85	79.876	2,707	116.576
1941	1,621	87,911	1.05	57.04	1,266	63,465	1.54	77.287	2,222	111.365
1942	1,862	91,675	1.13	55.45	1,471	66,774	1.62	76.411	2,298	108.690
1943	1,799	88,470	1.08	53.01	1,451	64,594	1.40	62.44	2,930	98.92[2]
1944	1,571	83,466	.97	51.57	1,298	63,691	1.20	59.06	2,255	98.99[2]
1945	1,281	75,667	.88	51.71	1,079	59,350	1.10	60.32	2,110	90.44[2]
1946	1,161	74,425	.85	54.58	974	56,800	1.10	64.25	2,190	93.19[2]
1947					1,165				2,315	84.62[2]
1948					1,015				2,000	80.01[2]

[1] Data for the mineral industries 1931–1946 are from U. S. Department of the Interior, Bureau of Mines, *Minerals Yearbook, 1946* (Washington: U. S. Government Printing Office, 1948), p. 78. Data on coal-mine accidents 1931–1942 are from Bureau of Mines, *Coal Mine Accidents in the United States, 1942*, Bulletin No. 462 (Washington: U. S. Government Printing Office, 1944), pp. 102, 106, 115–116. Data for 1942–1948 are from *Minerals Yearbook, 1946*, p. 75 and from Bureau of Mines, *Mineral Industry Surveys* (CMF No. 210), p. 11. Substantial reduction of injury rates per million man-hours in coal mines after 1942 is due to reduction of estimated time required for travel and lunch in bituminous coal mines, which placed manhours worked on a portal-to-portal basis.

. . . . Analysis Branch of the U. S. Bureau of Mines, Nov. 3, 1949.

APPENDIX III

ESTIMATED NUMBER OF WORK INJURIES, BY EXTENT OF
DISABILITY, IN THE UNITED STATES, 1936–1947[1]

Year	All Disabilities	Fatalities and Permanent Total Disabilities	Permanent Partial Disabilities	Temporary Disabilities
1936	1,407,000	16,000	66,000	1,325,000
1937	1,841,000	19,600	122,000	1,700,000
1938	1,375,700	16,400	99,900	1,260,300
1939	1,603,500	16,400	109,400	1,477,700
1940	1,889,700	18,100	89,600	1,782,000
1941	2,180,200	19,200	100,600	2,060,400
1942	2,267,700	19,900	100,800	2,147,000
1943	2,414,000	20,100	108,000	2,285,900
1944	2,230,400	17,600	94,400	2,118,400
1945	2,019,800	17,800	88,100	1,913,900
1946	2,056,100	18,300	92,400	1,945,000
1947	2,059,000	18,800	90,000	1,950,200

[1] Figures do not include work injuries to domestic servants, but do include injuries to employees, and to self-employed and unpaid family workers. Based upon U. S. Department of Labor, Bulletin No. 67 of the Division of Labor Standards (1944), p. 3; and U. S. Bureau of Labor Statistics, Bulletins No. 802 (1944), p. 4, No. 849 (1945), p. 3, No. 889 (1946), p. 2, No. 921 (1947), p. 3, No. 945 (1948), p. 2.

SOCIAL COSTS

APPENDIX IV

Estimated Costs (millions of dollars) of Work Injuries, 1941–1948[1]

Year	Wage Loss[2]	Medical Expense[3]	Overhead Cost[4] of Insurance	Other Indirect[5] Costs	Total
1941.	560	90	190	. . . .	. . . .
1942.	620	100	300	1,300	2,320
1943.	660	110	320	1,300	2,390
1944.	640	100	300	1,300	2,340
1945.	680	100	240	1,300	2,320
1946.	750	130	240	1,300	2,420
1947.	800	140	380	1,300	2,620
1948.	800	130	430	1,300	2,660

[1] From *Accident Facts* (Chicago: National Safety Council), 1942, p. 58; 1943, p. 52; 1944, p. 52; 1945, p. 52; 1946, p. 10; 1947, p. 10; 1948, p. 10; 1949, p. 10.

[2] Includes loss of wages (or the value of service) due to temporary inability to work, reduction in wages when returned to work due to permanent partial disability, and the present value of anticipated future earnings for permanent total disabilities and deaths.

[3] Includes doctors and hospital fees.

[4] Includes all administrative, selling and claim-settlement expenses for insurance companies and self-insurers, but not the money paid in claims. Claim payments are included in the wage-loss and medical-expense totals.

[5] This approximation of losses such as property damage, losses due to interference with production, time lost by workers other than the injured, is based on an all-industry estimate of $325,000,000 for compensation and medical payments, or their equivalent, to which is applied the generally accepted ratio for "direct" and "indirect" costs.

APPENDIX V

RELATIVE LIFE EXPECTANCY OF DIFFERENT SHEET METALS IN
PITTSBURGH AND IN A SMOKE-FREE ATMOSPHERE[1]

Metals	Life expectancy (years)	
	In Pittsburgh	In a Smoke-free City
Galvanized sheet iron.....	3–6	7–14
Galvanized sheet steel.....	3–4	5–10
Tinned sheet iron.........	13–15	18–28
Tinned sheet steel........	6	10
Copper..................	10–20	indefinite
Zinc....................	5	..
Lead...................	10	..

[1] Smoke Investigation, University of Pittsburgh, Department of Industrial Research, Bulletin No. 6, *Papers on the Effect of Smoke on Building Materials* (Pittsburgh, 1913), p. 46.

APPENDIX VI

AMOUNT OF DUST DEPOSITED PER SQUARE MILE IN DIFFERENT
LOCALITIES[1]

City	Investigator	Year	Location	Average Number of Tons of Dust Deposited per Square Mile per Year
Baltimore, Md.	Health Dept.	1928–29	center of city	1,800
Baltimore, Md.	Health Dept.	1928–29	3 miles from center	800
Baltimore, Md.	Health Dept.	1928–29	10 miles from center	340
Cleveland, Ohio	Health Council	1927–29	whole city	780
Grafton, W. Va.	Bureau of Mines	1922	whole town	1,876
Pittsburgh, Pa.	Mellon Institute	1912–13	whole city	1,031
Salt Lake City, Utah	Bureau of Mines	1912–20	whole city	349
Washington, D. C.	Public Health Service	1932–33	7th and B. St.	296[2]

[1] According to "Atmospheric Pollution of American Cities for the Years 1921 to 1933," *Public Health Bulletin No. 224*, U. S. Treasury Department, Public Health Service (Washington: U. S. Government Printing Office, 1936), p. 7.

[2] I. E. Ives and R. R. Sayers, "City Smoke and Its Effects," *Public Health Reports*, vol. 51, No. 1 (Jan. 3, 1936), U. S. Treasury Department, Public Health Service (Washington: U. S. Government Printing Office), p. 18.

APPENDIX VII

ESTIMATES OF SOME ANNUAL COSTS OF AIR POLLUTION
IN PITTSBURGH (1913)[1]

Cost to the Individual:

laundry bills	$1,500,000
dry cleaning	750,000

Cost to the Household:

exterior painting	330,000
sheet metal work	1,008,000
cleaning and renewing of wall paper	550,000
cleaning and renewing of lace curtains	360,000
artificial lighting	84,000

Cost to Wholesale and Retail Stores:

merchandise	1,650,000
extra precautions	450,000
cleaning	750,000
artificial lighting	650,000
department stores	175,000

Cost to Quasi Public Buildings:

office buildings	90,000
hotels	22,000
hospitals	55,000

Cost to the Smoke Makers:

imperfect combustion	1,520,740
Total	**$9,944,740**

[1] Smoke Investigation, University of Pittsburgh, Department of Industrial Research, Bulletin No. 4, *The Economic Cost of the Smoke Nuisance to Pittsburgh* (Pittsburgh, 1913), p. 44.

SOCIAL COSTS

APPENDIX VIII

Relative Importance of Pollution Abatement, Classified According to Drainage Basins.[1]

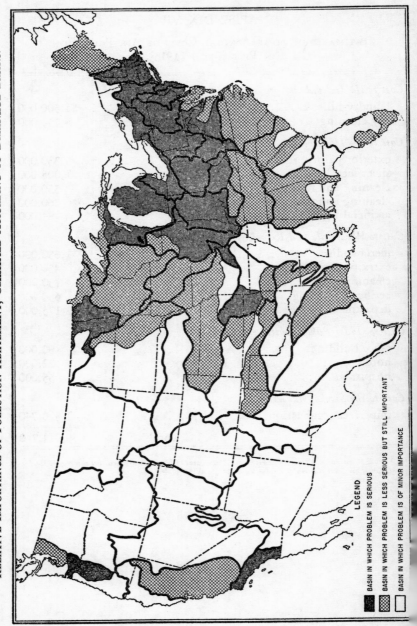

LEGEND

■ BASIN IN WHICH PROBLEM IS SERIOUS

▨ BASIN IN WHICH PROBLEM IS LESS SERIOUS BUT STILL IMPORTANT

□ BASIN IN WHICH PROBLEM IS OF MINOR IMPORTANCE

APPENDIX IX

Approximate Degree of Exhaustion of Economically Available Mineral Resources in the United States, as of 1944[1]

Mineral	Percentage of Original Total Remaining[2]	Years' Supply Remaining[3]
Magnesium.................	100	..
Nitrogen....................	100	..
Bituminous Coal and Lignite..	99	4,300
Salt.......................	99	..
Phosphate rock.............	93	805
Potash....................	92	117
Molybdenum...............	91	422
Iron ore...................	68	111
Natural gas[4]...............	65	48
Anthracite.................	65	195
Sulfur.....................	59	55
Fluorspar..................	56	40
Antimony..................	44	4
Petroleum[4]................	42	18
Copper....................	40	34
Zinc......................	33	19
Tungsten..................	30	4
Manganese.................	30	2
Bauxite[5].................	28	9
Vanadium..................	28	7
Chromium.................	21	..
Chromite..................	..	1

[1] Based upon mineral-reserves estimates prepared by the U. S. Bureau of Mines and the Geological Survey, summarized by Elmer W. Pehrson, "The Mineral Position of the United States and the Outlook for the Future," *Mining and Metallurgy* (April 1945), p. 206.

[2] Original reserves determined by adding the total production through 1943 to estimated reserves of January 1, 1944.

[3] Based on 1935–1939 rate of consumption. Estimates of this kind indicate only order of magnitude of reserves. They do not imply that the remaining reserves can support rates of production large enough to meet the prewar rate of use. In fact, in the case of petroleum any increase in output at this time would be at the expense of efficient recovery. Estimates do not include allowance for future discoveries.

[4] Proved reserves only.

[5] Prewar grade.

APPENDIX IX (Continued)

Mineral	Percentage of Original Total Remaining[2]	Years' Supply Remaining[3]
Gold	20	14
Lead	17	12
Silver	17	11
Mercury	3	3
Cadmium	..	16
Platinum	..	4
Asbestos	..	3
Nickel	..	1
Tin	..	1

APPENDIX X

CHARACTER OF TIMBER CUTTING IN THE UNITED STATES, 1945

Character of Timber Cutting on Commercial Forest Land by Ownership Class, 1948[1]

Ownership class	Commercial forest area (million acres)		Character of cutting[2] (per cent)				
	Total	Oper-ating	High-order	Good	Fair	Poor	De-struc-tive
All lands......	461	403	3	20	25	46	6
Private........	345	302	1	7	28	56	8
Public.........	116	101	8	59	19	13	1
National forest.....	74	65	11	69	19	1	0
Other Federal	15	12	6	37	32	24	1
State and local	27	24	3	44	10	41	2

Character of Timber Cutting on Private Lands by Size of Holding, 1945[3]

Size of holding[4]	Commercial forest area (million acres)		Character of cutting (per cent)				
	Total	Oper-ating	High-order	Good	Fair	Poor	De-struc-tive
Small.........	261	224	0	4	25	63	8
Medium.......	33	29	1	7	31	50	11
Large.........	51	49	5	24	39	28	4

[1] U. S. Department of Agriculture, *Forests and National Prosperity* (Washington: U. S. Government Printing Office, 1948), p. 46.

[2] Percents shown refer to the operating acreage in each class now being managed under cutting practices that rate high-order, good, etc. *High-order cutting* will maintain quality and quantity yields consistent with the full productive capacity of the land and requires cultural practices such as planting, timber-stand-improvement cuttings, thinnings, and control of grazing. *Good cutting* leaves the land in possession of desirable species in condition for vigorous growth in the immediate future. *Fair cutting* will maintain on the land any reasonable stock of growing timber in species that are desirable and marketable. *Poor cutting* leaves the land with a limited means for natural reproduction, often in the form of remnant seed trees. It often causes deterioration of species with consequent reduction in both quality and quantity of forest growth. *Destructive cutting* leaves the land without timber values and without means for natural reproduction.

[3] U. S. Department of Agriculture, *Forests and National Prosperity*, p. 48.

[4] Small = less than 5,000 acres (4,222,000 owners); medium = 5,000 and up to 50,000 acres (3,200 owners); large = 50,000 acres and more (400 owners).

APPENDIX XI

Period	Property Damage[2]
May–June 1903	$ 40,000,000
July 1908	31,139,000
July 1909	5,500,000
March 1912	70,000,000
March–December 1913	171,227,293
June 1915	5,950,000
August 1916	21,700,000
June–September 1921	44,000,000
April–May 1922	16,200,000
October 1923	15,000,000
March–May 1924	7,000,000
Spring–November 1927	333,135,331
June–September 1928	15,935,500
March–October 1929	63,800,000
January–May 1930	10,000,000
Total 1931	2,800,000
September–October 1932	2,500,000
1933	35,322,410
1934	10,351,291
1935	127,144,841
1936	282,546,235
1937	440,739,529
1938	101,099,645
1939	13,833,806
1940	40,466,483
1941	39,524,690
1942	98,506,198
1943	199,733,145
1944	94,000,000
1945	166,000,000
1946	71,000,000

[1] Data from 1903–1932 (with the exception of 1931) are for major floods only and are based upon *Monthly Weather Review* according to H. H. Bennett, *Soil Conservation* (New York: McGraw-Hill Book Co., 1939), p. 609. Data for 1931 and 1933–1946 are total figures from U. S. Weather Bureau, *Monthly Weather Review*, Washington, D. C. See: vol. 62, no. 1, p. 27 and no. 12, p. 466; vol. 63, no. 12, p. 365; vol. 65, no. 1, p. 31; vol. 66, no. 12, p. 426; vol. 68, no. 9, p. 262 and no. 11, p. 329; vol. 69, no. 7, p. 217; vol. 71, no. 11, p. 185; vol. 73, no. 8, p. 137; vol. 76, no. 5, p. 113 and no. 9, p. 208.

[2] Includes losses caused to tangible property, matured crops, prospective crops, livestock and other movable farm property and losses due to suspension of business. No allowance made for price fluctuations and increasing market values in general.

APPENDIX XII

NUMBER OF RETAIL STORES AND SALES BY SIZE GROUPS
FOR 1939, 1935, AND 1929[1]

Size Group	Stores		Sales	
	Number	Per cent	Amount (add 000)	Per cent
$300,000 and over:				
1939	12,630	0.7	$9,855,631	23.4
1935	8,443	.5	6,879,155	20.9
1929	15,029	1.0	12,323,766	25.5
$100,000 to $299,999:				
1939	50,097	2.8	7,955,285	18.9
1935	37,196	2.4	5,828,224	17.7
1929	62,009	4.2	9,786,669	20.2
$50,000 to $99,999:				
1939	93,318	5.3	6,394,703	15.2
1935	72,562	4.6	4,989,553	15.2
1929	127,148	8.6	8,631,797	17.9
$30,000 to $49,999:				
1939	133,221	7.5	5,077,007	12.1
1935	119,705	7.5	4,581,413	14.0
1929	173,269	11.7	6,617,169	13.7
$10,000 to $29,999:				
1939	522,117	29.5	8,938,632	21.3
1935	415,165	26.1	7,114,216	21.6
1929	468,885	31.8	8,349,491	17.3
Less than $10,000:				
1939	958,972	54.2	3,820,532	9.1
1935	935,634	58.9	3,486,428	10.6
1929	630,025	42.7	2,620,760	5.4

[1] U. S. Census of Business, vol. I, *Retail Trade*: 1939, Part I (Washington: U. S. Government Printing Office, 1943), p. 48.

APPENDIX XIII

ADVERTISING EXPENDITURES IN THE UNITED STATES, 1929–1948

Year	Estimated Advertising Outlays[1] (billions of dollars)	Private Domestic Expenditures[2] (billions of (dollars)	Advertising Outlays as Per cent of Private Domestic Expenditures
1929............	2.6	94.6	2.8
1930............	2.6	81.0	3.2
1931............	2.3	66.5	3.5
1932............	1.6	50.1	3.2
1933............	1.3	47.7	2.7
1934............	1.6	54.7	2.9
1935............	1.7	62.4	2.7
1936............	1.9	70.8	2.7
1937............	2.1	78.6	2.7
1938............	1.9	70.8	2.7
1939............	2.0	77.4	2.6
1940............	2.1	86.0	2.4
1941............	2.2	100.6	2.2
1942............	2.2	102.0	2.2
1943............	2.5	108.0	2.3
1944............	2.7	119.3	2.3
1945............	2.9	133.8	2.2
1946............	3.4	177.2	1.9
1947............	4.3	198.0	2.2
1948............	4.8	223.8	2.2

[1] Based on expenditures for advertising in magazines and radio broadcasting, newspapers, outdoor advertising, television, and business papers; volume figures converted to expenditure figures by McCann-Erickson, Inc., Research Department, courtesy Dr. Hans Zeisel, published in part in issues of *Printers' Ink;* 1935–1948 figures in *Printers' Ink,* June 17, 1949.

[2] Personal consumption expenditures plus gross private domestic investment from *Survey of Current Business,* July 1949, p. 10.

APPENDIX XIV

ADVERTISING COSTS PER DOLLAR OF NET SALES, DISTRIBUTION EXPENSE
PER DOLLAR OF NET SALES, AND PERCENTAGE OF ADVERTISING
TO TOTAL DISTRIBUTION COSTS FOR SPECIFIED COMMODITIES,
1939[1]

Industry	Advertising Costs per Dollar of Net Sales (cents)	Total Distribution Expense per Dollar of Net Sales (cents)	Ratio of Advertising to Total Distribution Costs (percent)
Foods:			
Cereals..............	8.01	30.85	25.98
Coffee..............	5.26	20.66	25.44
Biscuits and crackers..	4.74	29.72	15.96
Flour...............	4.54	13.17	34.49
Canned fruits and vege-			
tables.............	1.97	10.64	18.53
Meats..............	.46	5.57	8.32
Sugar..............	.20	3.87	5.28
Clothing and household goods:			
Electric household ap-			
pliances...........	5.67	15.84	35.82
Men's shirts and collars	2.82	12.29	22.94
Men's and boys' outer			
wear..............	2.06	11.27	18.31
Women's hosiery.....	2.18	10.69	20.35
Carpets and rugs......	2.24	11.42	19.64
Women's dresses......	.85	12.02	7.08
Other lines:			
Rubber tires and tubes.	4.26	22.22	19.17
Paints and varnishes...	3.01	23.31	12.92
Cement.............	1.97	16.28	12.11
Petroleum products...	1.75	21.80	8.03
Lumber.............	.40	11.40	3.51

[1] From *Report of the Federal Trade Commission on Distribution Methods and Costs.* Part V. Advertising as a Factor in Distribution (Washington: U. S. Government Printing Office, 1944), p. 8.

INDEX

Abramson, V., 126

Accident Facts, see National Safety Council

Advertising, *see* Distribution; Monopoly

Agriculture, social costs of, 34–36, 127–134; destruction of natural balance, 128–130; effect of taxes, 131; effect of tenancy, 131; evidence and estimates, 139–142; flow resources, 127; losses obscured by increasing returns, 130; water resources, diminution of ground-water stores, 129–130, 134; *see also* Air pollution; Deforestation; Erosion

Air pollution, 34, 67–79, 229; corrosion, 70, 269; cost of artificial lighting, 76, 271; destruction of property values, 69–71, 271; dust, 76–77, 270; effect on building materials, 69–70, 269; Engels, F., 34; evidence and estimates, 76–78, 269, 271; fogs, 72, 73, 76; human health, 34, 71–74; in Donora, Pa., 74; loss of light, 72, 73; monetary losses, 76–78, 271; plant and animal life, 74–76; real estate values, 76; soil fertility, 74–75; weather, 72

Air Pollution in Donora, Pa., 74

Ammon, A., 249, 250

Anderson, B. M., 256

Andrews, E. F., 63

Andrews, J. B., 55, 63

Animal resources, depletion and destruction of, 94–105; calculation of social losses, 97; competitive exploitation, 94–97; disregard of capital losses, 95–97; distortion of market value, 95; effect of conservation, 100; "efficient" hunting methods, 100, 102; evidence and estimates, 97–105; inadequate cost accounting, 95–97; money losses, 103–104; salmon fisheries, 97–98; seals, 99–100; shad fisheries, 97–98; time preference, 94–95, 104; Veblen, 101; whaling, 100–101

Annual Report of the Assistant Attorney-General, 179

Arnold, T. W., 179

Ashworth, J. R., 77

Atomic Energy, 85, 106–108

Baines, Sir Frank, 78

Baster, A. S. J., 191

Bauer, O., 164, 166

Behling, B. N., 202

Bennett, H. H., 137, 140–142, 276

Bernal, J. D., 211, 214, 216, 217, 222

Beveridge, W. H., 255

Blackett, P. M. S., 217

Boer, A. E., 184

Böhm-Bawerk, E., 4, 6, 256

Bonar, J., 3

Bonger, W. A., 169

Borden, N. H., 188

Bowen, H. R., 259, 260

Braithwaite, D., 189

Bunce, A. C., 97

Burnes, A. R., 109, 110

Bush, V., 210, 211

Cairnes, J. E., 147

Cantillon, R., 3